Empirical Studies in the Psychology and Sociology of Aging

abstracted by
Irene M. Hulicka
STATE UNIVERSITY OF NEW YORK COLLEGE AT BUFFALO

under the general editorship of
B. R. Bugelski

THOMAS Y. CROWELL COMPANY New York
Established 1834

Library of Congress Cataloging in Publication Data

Hulicka, Irene M
  Empirical studies in the psychology and sociology of aging.

  Includes bibliographical references and index.
  1. Aging—Psychological aspects.   I. Title.
BF724.55.A35H84   1977   155.67   77-1842
ISBN 0-690-0150-0

Thomas Y. Crowell Company, Inc.
666 Fifth Avenue
New York, New York 10019

Cover design by Melissa M. Goldsmith

Manufactured in the United States of America

CONTENTS

Contents

CHAPTER IV *Learning*   37

✓ CHAPTER V *Memory*   67

Contents

CHAPTER XI *Work, Retirement, Health and Widowhood* 219

CHAPTER XII *Institutional Living* 249

Contents

PREFACE

The impetus to prepare this book came from Dr. B. R. Bugelski, Distinguished Professor of Psychology, State University of New York at Buffalo. He had found, as many others probably have, that in a one-semester course, it is not possible to review thoroughly in class all of the research reports that are worthy of the students' attention. Nor is it realistic to expect that all members of a large class can obtain in the library and study with comprehension more than one hundred complex research articles during a single semester. His solution with respect to his undergraduate course on the Psychology of Learning was to provide the students with abstracts of many of the most relevant articles. The solution proved so satisfactory in terms of amount of material covered and comprehended by students and their appreciation for accessibility of research literature that Professor Bugelski decided to share the abstracts with other professors and students by publishing them in a book entitled *Empirical Studies in the Psychology of Learning*, T.Y. Crowell, 1975. I have followed his lead by preparing this book of abstracts of empirical studies in the psychology and sociology of aging.

I have been teaching a sophomore-level class on the Psychology of Aging, which typically enrolls forty or more students with a wide variety of academic majors and diverse personal and career reasons for enrolling in the course. Although some of these students will take subsequently more advanced courses on the Psychology of Aging offered by our department, many of them will, for one reason or another, be able to take only the one course on aging. Most either enter the course with or soon develop a keen desire to learn as much as they can about aging and older people in general, or about some more narrowly defined aspect of aging. In spite of the fact that I usually assign a fairly substantial reading list, including three or four books and twenty or thirty journal articles, students bombard me with requests for additional reference material, either in conjunction with term papers or projects or simply because they want to know more about specific topics. Also, I very frequently receive requests for references on aging from students who are not enrolled in my classes and from nonstudents. Often, I have a twinge of guilt when I refer a student to or require him or her to read a journal article that was written for experts in the field. Although I have found that the student can pull out the relevant information from sophisticated journal articles, the ratio of information acquired to time and effort expended does not reflect the best use of student's limited time. Consequently, I was much taken by Professor Bugelski's idea of abstracting articles for use by students and by other people who are interested in acquiring research-based information, but who do not need to know the exact details of the statistical analyses used in each research project.

This is not to say that I do not believe students should receive a thorough training in research methodology and statistical analyses and that they should be able to read and comprehend complex scientific articles. My students would probably be all too ready to agree that in my courses they are expected to think and act like scientists. I find, however, that the use of the abstracted articles enhances, rather than detracts from, their scientific training. Because of the brevity and comprehensibility of the abstracts, students can, of course, read many more abstracts than original articles, thus acquiring a broader base of information. Most students become so interested in the topics introduced in some of the abstracts, they subsequently read the original articles and then proceed to related articles. They report that they find the original articles much easier to understand after having read the abstracts and claim that they actually read more original articles than they would if the abstracts were not available.

In selecting the articles to abstract for this collection, I was guided by a number of factors. The study of aging and age changes and differences in behavior and attributes is not and should not be limited by narrow disciplinary boundaries. Therefore, I tried to include a fairly representative selection of articles to introduce the student to the variety of psychological and social problems relevant to the study of aging. Of course, it was impossible to include articles on every topic that engages the attention of social gerontologists, and some topics are of such great importance or interest that it seemed appropriate to include several abstracts on the same topic.

Frankly, I attempted, and I am not sure with what success, to achieve a balance between what I think students ought to study and what I think they want to study. Other guiding factors in the selection process were to look for papers that opened or might encourage new areas of research and my wish to present more than one side of an issue. Some articles were chosen because of the importance of the problem investigated, the excellence of the research design, and the impact of the findings either on theoretical and scientific work or on social policy. Some of the articles were included because of topical interest or because of their potential to encourage new areas of research rather than because of methodological excellence. Many valuable papers had to be omitted because they could not be abstracted without undue violence to the subject matter or because the theoretical issues could not be reduced intelligibly. A few of the abstracts are atypically long, simply because some articles could not be condensed as readily as others. Where important researches have been overlooked, I can only regret my lack of insight and hope that copies of reprints will be directed to me for a revised and enlarged edition.

Perhaps there may have been a bias operating, both in my selection of articles and in some of the research which has been conducted recently. Until about twenty years ago, much of the research on aging seemed to have been designed primarily to demonstrate the existence of age differences, with relatively little attention paid to delineating the reasons for differences between age groups. This practice fitted with the popular stereotype that observed differences between older persons and younger persons were simply due to the aging process. Gradually, it has become apparent that it is not appropriate to blame or otherwise attribute to the aging process *all* the differences that exist between younger and older people. Researchers, quite appropriately, have been attempting to identify the factors, other than age *per se*, that contribute to observed differences between age groups. This emphasis has become sufficiently strong, so that on reading the gerontological literature one almost gets the impression that scientists are attempting to demonstrate that *none* of the differences between younger and older people should be attributed to age *per se*, and perhaps because I have so often heard statements such as "Well, it's just that he is getting old. What can you expect?" that I may have had a tendency to favor for inclusion those articles that either demonstrate relatively small age differences or accounted for differences between age groups in terms of factors other than age *per se*. For my own biases, I apologize.

In offering this collection to persons interested in the study of aging, I am keenly aware of my debt to those psychologists, sociologists, physicians, social workers and others who prepared the original papers. There is little in this collection that is original on my part, and I greatly appreciate the willingness of those authors who kindly gave me permission to abstract their work. Some authors very kindly suggested clarifying changes and directed my attention to articles that I had not included. I must, of course, take full responsibility for whatever errors and distortions I was unable to perceive. I am very grateful to the Editors and/or Publishers of the *Journal of Gerontology*, the *Gerontologist*, *The International Journal of Human Development and Aging*, *Omega*, the *Canadian Journal of Psychology*, *The Journal of the American Geriatrics Society*, *Geriatrics*, *Human Development*, *The New England Journal of Medicine*, *The Journal of Genetic Psychology*, *The American Journal of Psychiatry*, *The Journal of Vocational Behavior*, *Experimental Aging Research*, Columbia University Press, and D. Van Nostrand Co., and to the American Psychological Association for permission to abstract articles which appeared originally in their publications.

In the preparation of this volume, I had the highly competent assistance of Ms. Judy Stolzman, whose generous help was invaluable. Two students, Lori Geismar and Betty Davis, very efficiently handled many of the details with respect to requesting authorizations and collating materials, and, as always, my colleagues were helpful.

INTRODUCTION

An attempt was made to organize the papers summarized in this volume in a reasonably logical topical order. The initial paper on demography is followed by papers on intellectual functioning, perception, learning, memory problem-solving, and creativity. The papers on cognitive functioning are followed by a series of papers on self-perceived and attributed age differences; life satisfaction and adjustment to aging; personality; environmental effects on behavior; work, retirement, health and widowhood; institutional living; and perceptions of time passage and death. Occasionally an abstract that does not exactly fit within the general topical category is included in that category because it adds a new dimension to a problem introduced in a preceding abstract. Many of the abstracts are relevant to two or more of the topical categories. The subject index provided at the end of the book should be helpful to the person who is interested in summarizing material from these abstracts pertaining to specific topics.

In the table of contents at the beginning of the book the authors are listed with abbreviated titles of their research articles. At the beginning of each abstract the exact title of the original article and its bibliographic citation is provided. Accordingly, the index of authors at the end of the volume does not include bibliographic citations. In all cases, where determinable, the abstract lists the author's degree; the inclusion of the degree gives at least some slight indication of the disciplinary affiliation of persons engaged in research on aging; of course, the Ph.D. provides no indication of whether the author is a psychologist, sociologist, political scientist or a member of some other discipline.

Although it is anticipated that this volume will be of considerable value to persons engaged in the study of the psychological and social aspects of aging, it is not intended to serve as a substitute for integrating and synthesizing books and articles on aging. It is recognized that with the increased demand for courses on aging and the limited number of persons who have gerontological expertise, many faculty members who perceive themselves as ill-equipped to offer courses on aging find themselves pressed into service to do so. Moreover, many people who work with the aged or for other reasons are interested in aging are engaging in independent study of gerontological topics. For such people, a few suggestions about relevant books and journals might be helpful. In offering suggestions with respect to useful journals and books no attempt will be made to be inclusive. Rather, a few fairly representative publications will be listed so that the student of aging may have some limited assistance in selecting appropriate reading materials.

Two highly recommended journals are the *Journal of Gerontology* and the *Gerontologist*. As their titles indicate, these journals are devoted exclusively to articles on aging. The *Journal of Gerontology* publishes primarily basic research articles; in addition to articles on psychological processes and social gerontology, each issue of this journal carries a number of articles on the biological and medical aspects of aging. The *Gerontologist*, which is designed for the professional who wants to be informed about developments in the aging field, publishes articles on a variety of topics, including demography, ecology, institutionalization, social policy, nutrition, cross-cultural comparisons, and problems of the aged. It will be noted that a very high proportion of the articles selected for inclusion in this volume were originally published in either the *Journal of Gerontology* or the *Gerontologist*. The *International Journal of Human Development and Aging*, the *Journal of the American Geriatrics Society*, *Geriatrics*, and two new journals, *Experimental Aging Research* and *Educational Gerontology: An International Quarterly*, publish articles very germane to the study of aging. All of the journals from which articles have been abstracted for this volume, as well as a number of other journals, have at least an occasional article on aging. Most of these journals are ordinarily available in university libraries.

Until a few years ago, it would have taken little time to list and describe briefly all of the books that would be recommended to the person initiating a study of aging. However, now a number of good books are available, including some that provide a fairly comprehensive overview of age-related topics and others that deal fairly intensively with one or a limited number of topics. Works that provide broad or fairly broad topical coverage include the following: Atchley, R. *Social Forces in Later Life*. Belmont, Cal.: Wadsworth, 1972; Bengston, V. L. *The Social Psychology of Aging*. New York: Bobbs-Merrill, 1973; Botwinick, J. *Cognitive Processes in Old Age*. New York: Springer, 1967; Botwinick, J. *Aging and Behavior*. New York: Springer, 1973; Butler, R. N. and Lewis, M. I. *Aging and Mental Health*. St. Louis: C. V. Mosby, 1973; Eisdorfer, C. and Lawton, M. P., eds. *The Psychology of Adult Development and Aging*. Washington, D.C., American Psychological Association, 1973; Huyck, M. H. *Growing Older*. Englewood Cliffs, N. J.: Prentice-Hall, 1974; Kalish, R. A. *Late Adulthood: Perspectives on Human Development*. Monterey, Calif.: Brooks/Cole, 1975; Kimmel, D. C. *Adulthood and Aging*. New York: John Wiley and Sons, 1973; Palmore, E., ed., *Normal Aging*. Durham: Duke University Press, 1970; Palmore, E., ed., *Normal Aging II*. Durham: Duke University Press, 1974; Scott, F. G. and Brewer, R. M., eds., *Perspectives in Aging*. Corvaliss: Oregon State University, 1971 (2 volumes); and Woodruff, D. S. and Birren, J. E., eds., *Aging: Scientific Perspectives and Social Issues*. 1975.

Each of the above books, of course, lists many references which could assist the student in his selection of reference material for more specialized topics. A few examples of books available on fairly narrow topics within the field of aging are as follows: Britton, J. H. and Britton, J. O. *Personality Changes in Aging*. New York: Springer, 1972; Botwinick, J. and Storandt, M. *Memory, Related Functions and Age*. Springfield, Ill.: Charles C. Thomas, 1974; Davis, R. H. and Smith W. K., eds., *Drugs and the Elderly*, Los Angeles: Ethel Percy Andrus Gerontology Center, 1973; Davis, R. H., Audet, M., and Baird, L. *Housing for the Elderly*, Los Angeles: Ethel Percy Andrus Gerontology Center, 1973; Davis, R. H. and Neiswender, M. eds., *Dealing with Death*. Los Angeles: Ethel Percy Andrus Gerontology Center, 1973; Jarvik, L. S., Eisdorfer, C., and Blum, J. E., *Intellectual Functioning in Adults*. New York: Springer, 1973; and Pastalan, L. A. and Carson, D. H., eds., *Spatial Behavior of Older People*. Ann Arbor: Univeristy of Michigan, 1970. Books of readings of potential value to the student who is initiating a study of aging include: Atchley, R. C. and Seltzer, M. M., eds., *The Sociology of Aging: Selected Readings*. Belmont, Cal.: Wadsworth, 1976; Brantl, V. M. and Brown, M. R., eds., *Readings in Gerontology*. St. Louis: C. V. Mosby, 1973; Charles, D. C. and Looft, W. R., eds., *Readings in Psychological Development Through Life*. New York; Holt, Rinehart and Winston, 1973; Chown, S. *Human Aging*. Baltimore: Penguin, 1972; Davis, R. H. and Neiswender, M., eds., *The Psychological Needs of the Elderly: Selected Papers*. Los Angeles: The Ethel Percy Andrus Gerontology Center, 1973; and Davis, H. R. and Neiswender, M., eds., *Aging: Prospects and Issues*, 1973. A brochure prepared by the Ethel Percy Andrus Gerontology Center, entitled *About Aging: A Catalog of Films* provides a comprehensive list of films and their sources.

It is hoped that the present volume, *Empirical Studies in the Psychology and Sociology of Aging*, in conjunction with other literature, will be helpful to persons who are interested in studying the process of aging and the behavior of older people. The study of aging might be more interesting, challenging, and valuable, if, in the course of using these materials, the student notes not only what we know or think we know about aging and the behavior of aging people but, in addition, considers carefully what we do not know. The interested and perceptive student should be able to identify dozens of unanswered questions. Perhaps the student may contribute to information about aging by designing and conducting research in an attempt to answer one or more of the questions he raises. Several of the abstracts presented in this volume report research conducted when the investigator was an undergraduate or first-year graduate student.

CHAPTER I

Demography

Abstract 1

Demography of the Aged

NEAL E. CUTLER, Ph.D. and ROBERT A. HAROOTYAN, Ph.D.

"Demography of the Aged" in D.S. Woodruff and J.E. Birren, eds., *Aging: Scientific Perspectives and Social Issues.* New York: D. Van Nostrand Co., 1975, 31-69.[1]

This selection, a chapter from a major book on aging, was designed to present basic demographic information about the aged in the United States. Additional information, discussion of trends, and identification of data sources is available in the original chapter.

Table 1 presents historical trends in life expectancy. Whereas the life expectancy at birth increased by 23.6 years from 1900 to 1970, the corresponding increase at age 65 has been only 3.3 years, an indication that medical advances and other life-saving improvements have had their major impact on younger people (primarily infants and young children) rather than older people.

Table 2 presents life expectancy figures for several countries. In the United States, life expectancy at birth of 67 years for males and 75 years for

Table 1
Average Life Expectancy at Birth and at Age 65
in the United States, for Various Years

Age	1900	1939	1949	1955	1959	1970
At birth	47.3	63.7	68.0	69.6	69.9	70.9
At age 65	11.9	12.8	12.8	14.2	14.4	15.2

Table 2
Life Expectancy at Birth and Percentage of Population
Age 65 and Over for Various Countries

Country	Year	Life Expectancy at Birth		% of Population aged 65 and over
		Male	Female	
U.S.A.	1970	67.0	75.0	9.9
Canada	1971	68.8	75.2	8.1
Mexico	1970	61.0	63.7	3.7
Japan	1970	69.1	74.3	3.1
USSR	1970	65.0	74.0	11.8
Denmark	1969	70.8	75.7	12.1
United Kingdom	1971	68.8	75.1	13.1
Kenya	1969	46.9	51.2	3.6
Austria	1970	66.6	73.7	14.2

females is fairly comparable to that of other highly developed countries. In less developed countries, such as Mexico and Kenya, life expectancy is much lower. The percentage of the population age 65 and over varies widely from country to country; for example, in Austria 14.2 percent of the population is at least 65 years old, whereas in Mexico and the United States, 3.7 percent and 9.9 percent, respectively, of the population is 65 years or older.

The absolute numbers of persons age 65 and older in the United States has increased from 3,099,000 in 1900 to 20,177,000 in 1970, while the elderly component of the total population has increased from 4.1 percent to 9.9 percent. It is predicted that by 2020 there will be more than 40 million persons in the United States age 65 and older. The proportion that the elderly will constitute of the total population by that time will depend on birth rate trends. If the current low birth rate (an average of 2.1 births per woman on completion of childbearing years) continues, older people will constitute more than 13 percent of the total population. However, if the birth rate were to increase substantially (e.g., from 2.1 to 3.1 per woman during her childbearing years), the proportion of the elderly within the total population would decline somewhat from the current level.

Demographic changes have significance for the economic arrangements of society as, for example, by affecting the relationship between the "dependent" population and the supportive or working population. The dependent population is typically composed of the young and the old. The usual definitions of "old" and "working" populations are 65 years and older, and 18 to 64 years, respectively. This does not mean to imply that every person over 65 and under 18 years is a dependent and that every person between 18 and 64 is in fact working. However, the calculation of a simple "old-age dependency ratio" by calculating the ratio of persons age 65 and older to persons age 18 to 64 permits examination of trends. In the United States the old-age dependency ratio has been increasing steadily, as follows: 1930 — .097; 1940 — .118; 1950 — .133; 1960 — .167; 1970 — .177. If the low birth rate continues, by 2020 the old-age dependency ratio will be .213. One major economic situation that is currently being influenced by changes in the old-age dependency ratio is the Social Security system. Although retired recipients of Social Security benefits have contributed to the pension system, benefits are greater than contributed shares. In such a

Table 3
Sex Ratios by Age and Race in the United States for
Various Years: (males per hundred females)

	1900	1930	1960	1970
All races				
All ages	104.4	102.5	97.8	95.8
Under 15	102.1	102.8	103.4	103.8
15-24	98.3	98.1	101.4	102.3
25-44	109.1	101.7	96.9	96.9
45-54	113.9	109.4	97.2	93.2
55-64	106.5	108.3	93.7	89.8
65 and over	102.0	100.4	82.6	72.1
White				
Under 15	102.4	103.2	104.0	104.5
65 and over	101.9	100.1	82.1	71.6
Negro and other races[1]				
Under 15	100.0	99.0	100.0	100.0
65 and over	102.9	105.7	90.1	79.8

1. "Negro and Other Races" classification is affected by incorrect inclusion of some persons of Spanish surname.

case, the younger working population must contribute payments to support the recipients of the benefits. As the ratio of the dependent population to the working population increases, there are fewer working people to contribute to the support of more dependent people.

Table 3 presents the sex ratio by age and race in the United States for various years. In 1900 males outnumbered females in all but one of the age groups (15 to 24). By 1960 females outnumbered males in all age categories over the age 24, with the male-female discrepancy increasing with increased age. By 1970 the proportion of males to females from age 24 and older had decreased still further. For example, in 1900 in the over 65 age group there were 102 males per 100 females; by 1970 the ratio had dropped to 72:100. The change in the male-female ratio has been somewhat less drastic for blacks than for whites. Although war deaths have contributed to the proportionately low number of surviving men in the older age groups, the sharp decline in the sex ratio has been largely due to the increase in male deaths caused by degenerative diseases. As Table 4 indicates, the male death rate for cancer, heart disease and most other causes is higher than for females.

Table 4
Sex Ratio by Cause of Death in the United States: 1969
(male to female ratio)

Cause of death	Ratio (male to female)
All causes	1.350
Diseases of the heart	1.396
Cerebrovascular disease (stroke)	0.876
Malignant neoplasms (cancer)	1.259
Influenza and pneumonia	1.302
Bronchitis, emphysema, and asthma	3.984
Arteriosclerosis	0.807
Accidents (all types)	2.377

Of the total older population in 1970, almost three-quarters (14.6 million) lived in urban areas, and of these urban elderly, the majority (6.8 million) lived in central cities. The fact that older people are disproportionately concentrated in central cities makes urban problems of congestion, transportation, living costs, crime and housing of paramount concern to those interested in the health and well-being of older persons. The four states with the largest numbers of older residents are New York (1.96 million), California (1.80 million), Pennsylvania (1.27 million), and Illinois (1.09 million). Although the migration rates for older people are relatively small in comparison to the rest of the population, old-age residential migration has brought increasing numbers of older people disproportionately to the southern and western states.

Table 5
Median Total Money Income in 1971 for Groups Within the Total Population and the Population Aged 65 and Over

	Total Population	Population aged 65 and over
Families		
male head, wife present	$10,999	$5,394
male head, other marital status	8.722	6,879
female head	5,144	5,476
Total for families	10,930	5,450
Unrelated individuals	3,316	2,199
Total	10,285	5,453

Table 5 presents information on the total monetary incomes in 1971 for the total population and the over age 65 population in the United States. The median annual income of families in which the head-of-household was 65 or older was approximately *half* the median income for all families in that year ($5,453 versus $10,285). For all types of families among the older population, one fifth (19.9 percent) had annual incomes of less than $3,000 in 1971, as compared with 8.3 percent for the total population. Of all persons age 65 and older, 21.6 percent (4.3 million) fell below the official low-income level in 1971 ($2,424), in comparison to 12.5 percent of all persons under the age of 65. Despite contemporary increases in benefits from Social Security, private pension plans, and Medicare, the economic situation of older people is a major social problem. The combination of relatively fixed incomes and substantial annual inflation has made the economic plight of the older person particularly precarious.

Table 6 summarizes marital status and living arrangements of older people by sex. The fact that more females than males are widowed and live alone is, of course, accounted for by the higher death rates for older men. A fairly large proportion of the older people, 36.2 percent of the females and 14.7 percent of the males, live alone (an increase since 1960). Despite popular assumptions, a relatively small proportion of the older population is institutionalized; in 1971, 3.6 percent of the older men and 4.6 percent of the older women resided in institutions.

Table 6
Percent Distribution of the Population Age 65 and Over by Marital Status and by Living Arrangement, by Sex: 1971

	Male	Female
Marital status		
Single	7.1	7.3
Married, spouse present	70.1	34.5
Married, spouse absent	2.9	1.7
Widowed	17.1	54.2
Divorced	2.7	2.3
Total	99.9	100.0
Living arrangement		
In families	79.7	57.5
Head of family	72.7	8.7
Wife	N/A	33.8
Other relative	7.0	15.0
Living alone	14.7	36.2
Living with unrelated individuals	1.9	1.6
In an institution	3.6	4.6
Total	99.9	99.9

CHAPTER II

Intellectual Functioning

Abstract 2

A Forty-Two Year Longitudinal Study

W. A. Owens, Ph.D.

"Age and Mental Abilities: A Second Adult Follow-Up."
Journal of Educational Psychology, 1966, *57*, 311-325.

Men who were originally tested on the Army Alpha test of mental abilities at age 19 were retested on the same instrument at ages 50 and 61. This paper reports the findings for age 61 and examines the extent and nature of changes in test scores over time.

Method

The Ss were 96 males, of mean age 61 in 1961, who had originally been tested at Iowa State University as entering freshmen with a mean age of 19 years. In 1950, 127 of the original sample were retested. Of the 31 individuals tested in 1950 and not retested in 1961, 13 were deceased, five were disabled, five could not be located and eight refused to participate. The majority of Ss had majored in agriculture or engineering and were in the upper-end of the occupational-intelligence hierarchy.

The Army Alpha (Form 6) was readministered to all 96 respondents, either by the investigator or by examiners who lived in the vicinity of the respondents. All scores were converted to standard scores derived from a standardization group of 1,000 cases which had an arbitrarily assigned mean of 5 and a standard deviation of 1. Shifts in mean scores were thus reported in units of the norm standard deviation. Statistical analysis involved examination of difference scores to determine whether mean difference scores departed significantly from that of a distribution with a mean of zero.

Results

The major finding was that the Army Alpha scores of these 96 Ss remained remarkably constant over the period from 1950 to 1961. On the eight subtests none of the difference scores approached significance; on five subtests there was a slight negative change and on three there was a slight positive change. When the subtests were combined to form the verbal component, the numerical component and the reasoning component, the decrement on the numerical component was significant ($p < 0.01$).

Figure 1 presents graphically the test performance trends for component and total Army Alpha scores for the three times of testing.

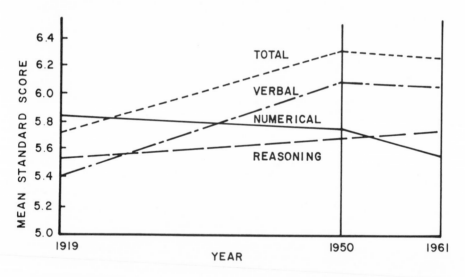

It will be noted that both total score and verbal score increased significantly between age 19 and age 50 and remained relatively constant from age 50 to age 61. The reasoning score showed a very slight but nonsignificant increment at the second and third times of testing, while the numerical score showed decrements between age 19 and age 50 and again at age 61. Because a true function cannot be determined from three point estimates, it seemed most parsimonious to connect these points with straight lines. However, the argument from the data is clear: accelerating declines in these abilities begun 30 to 40 years previously should be more apparent in the last decade than these declines are. The implications are that any declines that have begun have done so more recently. A possible exception is the case of the numerical component. The sample was heavily loaded with engineers who may have reached a peak of quantitiative sophistication at college graduation; many of them subsequently moved into less technical work, presumably thereby lessening their need for and ability to maintain quantitative knowledge and skilles.

An attempt was made to estimate the "true" or intrinsic changes in the individual, separate and apart from the cultural changes. To achieve this, the scores of the 1919 freshmen were compared to those of a comparable group of freshmen in 1961. This comparison suggested that a cultural change had resulted in an overall increment to the reasoning score, primarily on the Analogy Test portion of that score; in 1919 the Analogies Test was probably quite unfamiliar to freshmen, as were all group tests of intelligence. In 1961 it was not unfamiliar to either 19-year-olds or 60-year-olds. Thus what appeared to be a small gain in reasoning for the 61-year-olds may be better accounted for in terms of an increased level of sophistication with this type of test, in the midst of which the senior S really lost ground in the relative sense.

Based on the assumption of the onset of some differential organic changes, it had been hypothesized that slight but significant increases in the magnitudes of both individual differences and trait differences from 1950 to 1961 should be revealed. Comparisons of the relevant variances for 1950 and 1961 provided no support for the hypothesis.

The decade from age 50 through age 60 was one of relative constancy in mental ability test performance for the present Ss.

Abstract 3

A Thirty-Five Year Longitudinal Study

JEANNE G. GILBERT, Ph.D.

"Thirty-Five Year Follow-up Study of Intellectual Functioning," *Journal of Gerontology*, 1973, 28, 68-72.

The purpose of this study was to compare the present mental efficiency of persons in later life with the mental efficiency they showed 35 to 40 years earlier, when they were in their 20's or early 30's.

Method

The subjects were 14 persons who had been members of a control group in a study conducted during the mid to late 1930s, at which time the Babcock-Levy Test of Mental Efficiency had been administered. At initial testing, the Ss had been in their 20's or early 30's. When the same test was readministered, the participants ranged in age from 60 to 74, with a mean age of 65 years. There were five males and nine females in the subject sample. All were of relatively high socio-economic status and none were institutionalized. Only two women denied being in reasonably good health. Subjects were of definitely superior intelligence; the initial average vocabulary score was 18.7 (range 16-22) and on retest was 19.7 (range 18-21).

The Babcock Test of Mental Efficiency uses the score on the Standford-Binet (1937) vocabulary test as the mental level of the S, and a series of 29 short tests combined into six groups (as indicated in Table 1), which are then averaged to produce a mental efficiency score. Speed enters into the scores of most of the groups of tests. The discrepancy between the mental level and the mental efficiency score (ideally 0) gives the Efficiency Index. A plus Efficiency Index indicates efficient mental functioning, a minus Efficiency Index inefficient functioning.

Table 1
Average Early and Late Efficiency Scores and Efficiency Indices at Two Different Times

Subtest Category	Efficiency Scores			Efficiency Indices		
	1930's	1970's	p	1930's	1970's	p
Vocabulary	18.71	19.71	n.s.			
Easy - Old Material	18.24	17.39	n.s.	+1.08	−0.21	<.02
Repetitions	16.97	15.95	n.s.	−0.20	−1.94	<.01
Initial Learning	17.21	13.18	<.01	+0.16	−4.50	<.001
Retention	18.84	13.22	<.01	+1.34	−4.95	<.001
Motor Reactions	20.05	16.10	<.01	+2.39	−2.17	<.001
Easy Continuous	17.68	14.78	<.01	+0.29	−3.49	<.001
Total Score	18.19	15.15	<.01	+1.00	−2.82	<.001

Results

The mean Efficiency Scores and Efficiency Indices obtained in the 1930s and the 1970s are presented in Table 1. The vocabulary score showed a slight but insignificant increase. Efficiency scores showed an overall decline which was significant for total score and four of the six subtest scores.

Perhaps a more accurate way of showing the actual decline in efficiency is to compare the efficiency indices of each individual obtained in the 1970s with the indices he obtained in the 1930s when, supposedly, he was at his peak of intellectual functioning. This comparison is presented in the right half of the table. These data provide evidence for significant declines on all subtests. In other words, although some subjects maintained a fairly good level of efficiency, especially in certain areas, they were generally functioning at a level lower than that of 35 years previously.

Abstract **4**

A Cross-Sequential Study of Cognitive Behavior

K. WARNER SCHAIE, Ph.D. and CHARLES R. STROTHER, Ph.D.

"A Cross-Sequential Study of Age Changes in Cognitive Behavior," *Psychological Bulletin,* 1968, 70, 671-680.

In studies of age changes, cross-sectional and longitudinal studies ordinarily yield contradictory results. Most cross-sectional studies of cognitive behavior report peak performance in the early 20's or 30's, with steep decrement gradients thereafter. Most longitudinal studies report either a slight decrement, no decrement or slight increments at least into the mid-fifties. In cross-sectional studies, differences between age group can be a function of actual age differences, differences between cohorts (generations), or both age and cohort differences. In longitudinal studies, differences can be due to age changes, or to environmental effects over time, or to both age changes and time differences. Thus the cross-sectional method confounds age differences with cohort differences, and the longitudinal method confounds age changes and time differences.

The confounding could be avoided by a design allowing for the joint analysis of age, cohort and time differences. Ideally, this would require the longitudinal study of successive cohorts over the entire age range of interest, an undertaking ordinarily not feasible for the study of human behavior. However, the cross-sequential method, which involves the sequential analysis of data from two or more cross-sectional studies, permits a relatively short-term investigation of the problem.

The cross-sequential method is designed to obtain two or more measures from each of the cohorts included in the initial cross-sectional study, so that age changes occurring within generations can be contrasted with age differences between generations measured at a given point in time. This can be accomplished by testing random splits of the original sample at successive points in time or, as was done in the present study, by obtaining repeated measurements on all retrievable members of the original sample.

The cross-sequential design permits: (a) evaluation of cross-sectional age gradients at two or more points in time; (b) the construction of a composite longitudinal age gradient, each section of which represents the age change for a given cohort over a constant time interval. Because the effect of environmental change will be constant for all age groups, differences in measured change ought to be due to the effect of maturational variance.

This research involved the application of the cross-sequential method to examine age changes in cognitive behavior. Because developmental studies have been criticized because of widely different initial characteristics of the various age groups, a representative sample was selected carefully. Nevertheless, successive generations in a dynamic society must have different characteristics. The explicit purpose of the cross-sequential design is to differentiate components of developmental change which are indeed a function of differences in initial level between generations from those which are attributable to maturational change.

Method

A stratified random sample of 500 Ss was drawn from members of a prepaid medical plan. Quotas of 25 men and 25 women were obtained for each five-year age interval from 20 to 70 years. Seven years later 302 individuals from the original sample were retested with the same instruments. Comparisons indicated that attrition had occurred on a fairly random basis.

The Primary Mental Abilities Test (PMA) (Thurstone and Thurstone, 1949), the Test of Behavioral Rigidity (TBR)(Schaie, 1955, 1960) and a socioeconomic status questionnaire were administered. The PMA yielded scores for Verbal Meaning (VM), Space (S), Reasoning (R), Number (N) and Word Fluency (WF), a general index of intellectual ability $(V + S + 2R + 2N + W)$ and an index of educational aptitude $(2V + R)$. The TBR yielded scores on the variables of Motor-Cognitive Rigidity, Personality-Perceptual Rigidity, Psychomotor Speed and Social Responsibility. All scores were transformed into t scores with means of 50 and standard deviations of 10.

Results

Cohort differences (usually called cross-sectional differences) were very significant (p<0.001) for all variables except for Social Responsibility (p<.05). Quite different findings occurred for the analysis of the longitudinal time differences. If the hypothesis of intellectual deficit with age is justified, then a decrement should occur at every adult age level and for every cohort over the seven-year interval. Such overall time differences were found to be significant only for two variables, which are primarily measures of response speed and fluency (Verbal Meaning and Psychomotor Speed), and for the intellectual ability index of which Verbal Meaning is a component. It must be concluded, therefore, that the cross-sectional differences in all other variables represent differences between generations rather than age changes. Some significant interactions between time and cohort levels were calculated, implying that there are positive age changes for some cohorts and negative for others.

The techniques for constructing appropriate gradients to permit comparisons between cross-sectional and longitudinal findings were as follows: Cross-sectional estimates were obtained by averaging the two mean scores available for each cohort. Longitudinal estimates were obtained by calculating average age changes over a five-year interval for each interval in the range covered; each estimate was based on two cohorts. For example, the longitudinal age change from 25 to 30 was computed by subtracting the mean scores obtained in 1963 from the mean scores obtained in 1956 for groups aged 25 and 30 in 1956 and multiplying by 5/7 to adjust for the disparate time span.

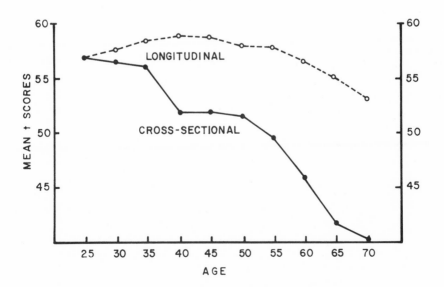

If the cross-sectional age differences for a given variable are a function solely of maturational change, then the two gradients should coincide. If the cross-sectional differences include the effects of differential environmental opportunities and/or genetic changes, one would expect discrepancies between the two gradients. Whenever cohort differences are positive (i.e., improvement in environmental conditions) the cross-sectional gradient will drop below the longitudinal, because the performance of the older cohort will be below that of a younger one even if there is no maturational change. Conversely, the longitudinal gradient will fall below the cross-sectional for those variables where there is a decrement in ability over generations.

The cross-sectional gradient and longitudinal gradient based on the cross-sequential data for Reasoning (Figure 1) are very different. According to the cross-sectional data, Reasoning peaks at 25 then declines fairly consistently with a steep decline from age 35 to 40 and from 50 onwards. The cross-sequential data show continuing increments until age 35, a plateau until approximately 45, and no substantial decrement until 60. These data suggest that age decrement on Reasoning within generations is quite mild and probably not seriously disabling within the age range studied; differences among generations are much in excess of differences within a given generation.

Because of space limitations, the graphs for the other variables will not be reproduced. The graph for Reasoning is fairly representative of the graphs for Verbal Meaning, Space, educational aptitude, and Personality-Perceptual-Rigidity, in that for these variables the cross-sectional data reflect lower scores for successive cohorts after early adulthood, whereas the cross-sequential data either remain fairly constant or peak at a later age and show relatively small decrements in late adulthood. The graph for Motor-Cognitive Rigidity (a measure of flexibility) also resembled that for Reasoning except that the cross-sequential data showed increments to age 60 and a plateau thereafter. For Word Fluency and Psychomotor Speed, both the cross-sectional and cross-sequential gradients declined progressively, with the cross-sequential gradient showing the steeper decline. For Intellectual Ability and Social Responsibility the two gradients were generally very similar throughout the age range. However, for Intellectual Ability both gradients declined progressively, whereas for Social Responsibility, both gradients increased up to age 55 and declined thereafter.

The most important conclusion from this study is that much of the variance attributed to age differences in past cross-sectional studies must properly be assigned to differences in ability between successive generations. Age changes over time within the individual appear to be much smaller than differences between cohorts, and textbook age gradients may represent no more than the effects of increased environmental opportunity and/or genetic improvement. The findings on longitudinal age changes suggest further that levels of functioning attained at maturity may be retained until late in life except where decrement in response strength and latency interferes.

Abstract 5

Growth and Decline of Intellectual Characteristics

DEAN TREMBLY, Ed.D. and JOHNSON O'CONNOR, M.A.

"Growth and Decline of Natural and Acquired Intellectual Characteristics," *Journal of Gerontolgy*, 1966, *21*, 9-12.

This paper examines age of maturity and age of decline of specific aptitudes.

Method

SUBJECTS: The test scores of a sample of 33,283 male Ss, age six to over 60, were derived from the files of a nationwide research and testing organization. Most of the persons in the sample had submitted to testing in the hope of gaining a better understanding of their knowledge and aptitudes. The uniform selection factor was the payment of a fee for the tests. The sample included a broad range of socio-economic and educational levels.

Tests: Five tests were administered: (1) English vocabulary, consisting of 150 five-choice items; (2) an 88-item tonal memory test, in which a tune with three to eight notes was played and then repeated with a one-note change; the S was required to identify which note had been changed; (3) a ten-item design memory test in which the S attempted to reproduce a straight line design which he had studied for 12 secs.; (4) an eight-item, six-digit number memory task with the numbers presented visually; (5) a 90-item inductive reasoning test with each item containing six pictures. The S was required to identify three of the pictures which had some common relationship. Only the number memory and inductive reasoning tests were administered individually.

Results and Conclusions

Scores on the vocabulary test, a measure of acquired knowledge, rose rapidly during the early years (age six through the 20's) then more slowly, but never reached a plateau and never declined. In contrast, scores on the aptitude tests rose rapidly during the early years, reached a plateau and then declined. Tonal memory matured at age ten and began to decline at 45, with a plateau of 35 years. Design memory matured at 14 and began to decline at 32, with a plateau of 18 years. Number memory matured at 18 and began to decline at 27, with a plateau of nine years. Inductive reasoning was the latest aptitude to mature and the earliest to decline, with a peak rather than a plateau between ages 21 and 23.

These data suggest that the earliest maturing traits may be the latest to decline, whereas the latest maturing traits may be the first to decline. It may be speculated that in the phylogenetic development of the human race, some of the specialized abilities appeared before others; for example, perceptual powers were undoubtedly attained long before the powers of reasoning, and the gift of song before the concept and memory of numbers. Perhaps the more complex and later-appearing intellectual processes are controlled by the newer parts of the brain, which in turn might mature more slowly and deteriorate more rapidly than the older parts of the brain.

Abstract 6

Age, Education and Psychometric Performance

SAMUEL GRANICK, Ph.D. and ALFRED FRIEDMAN, Ph.D.

"The Effect of Education on the Decline of Psychometric Test Performance with Advanced Age," *Journal of Gerontology*, 1967, 22, 191-195.

The general decline of psychometric test performance associated with advancing age has been well documented. However, a number of sociocultural variables related to mental test performance are also different for different age groups. One such variable is education. This study tested the following hypotheses: in a broad spectrum of psychometric tests relating to such areas as cognition, attention, perception, visual motor coordination, and sensory acuity, the negative correlation of education with age is a very significant factor in the functional decline associated with advancing age. Control of this factor, therefore, will reduce and in some cases eliminate much of this apparent functional decline.

Method

SUBJECTS: Seventy-seven Ss with a mean age of 59.1 years were recruited from community sources. None had a history of hospitalization for mental illness nor significant symptoms of depression. The age range of the 36 males was 47 to 74 years, of the 41 females, 47 to 79 years. Twenty-one of the Ss, of whom 15 were in the older half of the sample, were foreign born, but all had lived in the United States for at least 30 years. Education was measured on the basis of number of years of formal schooling or special training reported by the S. Care was taken to equate foreign with U.S. education and adjustment was made for significant cultural experiences which could be regarded as informal but systematic education. The educational range for the group was four to 18 years (M = 8.51, SD = 3.0). The correlation between age and education was -.42.

PROCEDURE: A battery of 33 psychometric tests was administered individually to all Ss. Included were 11 verbal tests (e.g., WAIS information and similarities, easy and hard associates, Stroop test); eight perceptual-cognitive tests (e.g., WAIS picture completion, tachistoscopic object recognition, ambiguous figure, auditory vigilance); and 14 perceptual, motor, and sensory tests (e.g., WAIS digit symbol substitution, area tapping, reaction time, far and near visual acuity).

Results and Discussion

Of the 33 test scores, 27 declined significantly with age. When education was partialed out, only 19 scores showed a significant negative correlation with age. Of these 19, 13 were essentially measures of biological efficiency, and the other six tapped such mental factors as perceptual flexibility, sustained attention and abstract thinking. Generally, tests in which speed of functioning was a critical factor showed a significant decline with age, regardless of the type or area of functioning. Tests that involved learning, rhythm discrimination, memory (immediate and remote), visual motor coordination in the reproduction of geometrical figures, and depth perception did not seem to show significant decrements with age. The strongest correlation with age after education was partialed out was for the Ambiguous Figure test ($r = -.75$). Excluding the Ambiguous Figure test, significant correlations with age when the effect of education was controlled ranged from -.26 to -.49.

The results point in the direction of biological factors accounting for some aspects of the decline in functioning with age. Tests involving psychomotor performance and sensory efficiency are clearly performed poorly by the aged and would almost certainly be associated with biological decline. Psychological factors seemed to be particularly important in such areas as accumulated intellectucal attainments, changes of motivation and interests, recent experiences and consolidation of habits. Complex factors such as perceptual flexibility and abstract orientation would seem to be of both a biological and psychological nature. These findings suggest that a single factor is not likely to account for the kinds of psychometric test performances manifested by the aged. The results support the hypothesis that the negative correlation of education with age is a very significant factor in the functional decline attributed to advanced aging. This suggests that the decline in functioning with age is less extensive and slower in developing than is often reported.

Abstract 7

Intellectual Functioning in the Aged

JEROME FISHER, Ph.D. and ROBERT C. PIERCE, M.A.

"Dimensions of Intellectual Functioning in the Aged," *Journal of Gerontology*, 1967, 22, 166-171.

The measuring instruments ordinarily used to assess the intellectual functioning of elderly people were developed for use with a much younger population. It seems questionable to attribute the same meanings to the scores of older and younger people. To do so is to implicitly carry forward a criterion of "something like scholastic success." This study attempted to identify dimensions of behavior that are conceptually appropriate and empirically relevant to the assessment of intellectual functioning in the aged.

Method

SUBJECTS: The subjects for the major portion of the study were 534 patients, 60 years and older, who were admitted consecutively to the psychiatric wards of a large general hospital. Mean age was 74 years, and 47 percent were males, 53 percent females. The sample was reassessed approximately fourteen months (FU-1) and 23 months later (FU-2). Of the original 534 patients, 33 percent (175) were not tested initially because of physical condition, death, rapid discharge or scheduling errors; 40 percent (211) were tested at FU-1 and 28 percent (149) at FU-2; 21 percent (113) were tested on all three occasions; by FU-2, 44 percent (236) of the original sample had died. A stratified sample of 600 persons aged 60 and over from the community was established for comparison purposes.

Assessments: The 24 variables assessed were selected because they are conventionally obtainable either from psychological test scores or from a psychiatrist's mental status examination. Formal tests included the Information, Comprehension, Arithmetic and Digit Span subtests of the WAIS and the Kent E-G-Y test. Psychologists also rated Ss on 11 four-point rating scales designed to assess affect, attention, cooperation, consciousness, idea association, memory orientation, perception, rapport, testability and thought quality. Ratings by social interviewers were used to assess further the presence of psychological disturbances of cognition, perception and mood; individuals were asked if they felt confused, "blue," upset, etc., and their "yes" or "no" replies constituted a simple two-point rating scale. The psychiatrist rated the patient independently on "Psychological Status" and on "Personality and Behavior" for the latter, using a rating of one for no inappropriate behavior and a well-integrated personality and a rating of four for deterioration, regression or disruptive behavior. The 24 behavioral ratings and scores were subjected to a cluster analysis.

Table 1
The Four Derived Clusters and Their Identifying Variables

Intellectual Functioning (59%)		*Social Accessibility* (37%)
Information		Rapport
Comprehension	WAIS	Cooperation
Arithmetic		Affect
Digit Span		Personality
Cognitive Accessibility (57%)		*Dysphoria/Depresssion* (20%)
Orientation		Delusions
Consciousness		Blue/Depressed
Attention		Upset easily
Testability		
Idea Association		

Results

The four dimensions and the variables composing them which emerged from the cluster analysis of the baseline data for the hospitalized group are listed in Table 1 (the percentages indicate the percentage of common variance accounted for by the cluster; the total is greater than 100 percent because of overlap in variance). Because "Dysphoria/Depression" had low factor loadings and involved yes/no ratings by patients, it was set aside as a salient dimension. Intellectual Functioning, Cognitive Accessibility and Socail Accessibility could be considered salient dimensions if stability across and within samples could be demonstrated.

Cluster analysis was applied to the patient data for FU-1 and FU-2 and the community sample data for FU-1. For all analyses, the same three salient clusters emerged with highly similar cluster membership and factor loadings.

These common findings suggest that the three dimensions, Intellectual Functioning, Social Accessibility and Cognitive Accessibility and their measures generate sufficient and appropriate amounts of generality to make the assessment of individual differences among the psychiatrically ill and the community elderly psychometrically feasible. The results underscore the discriminatory power of Cognitive Accessibility and Social Accessibility as empirically relevant dimensions in assessing the intellectual functioning of the aged. (Presumably low Cognitive or Social Accessibility would function as depressants on estimates of intellectual functioning.)

Abstract **8**

Cautiousness in Intellectual Performance

WILLIAM R. BIRKHILL, Ph.D. and K. WARNER SCHAIE, Ph. D.

"The Effect of Differential Reinforcement of Cautiousness in Intellectual Performance among the Elderly," *Journal of Gerontology*, 1975, *30*, 578-583.

Performance of the elderly on conventional measures of intellectual ability may be significantly attenuated by their reluctance to respond to test items about which they are uncertain, i.e., by their cautiousness. The purpose of this study was to examine the performance of elderly people on a standard intelligence test under two levels of risk (high and low) for the situation in which the omission of a response is neither rewarded nor penalized (omission optional), in contrast to the situation in which failure to take risk is disadvantageous (omission discouraged).

Method

SUBJECTS: Eighty-eight persons, including 56 females and 32 males, who were residents of congregate living facilities for the elderly, volunteered to serve as subjects. The mean age of the sample was 73 years (range — 62 to 86 years) and mean years of education was 12.6.

Test Materials: The Primary Mental Abilities Test (PMA) Form AM was used as a measure of intellectual performance. It consisted of five subtests presented in the following sequence: Verbal Meaning, Space, Number, Reasoning, and Word Fluency.

PROCEDURE: Ss were randomly assigned to four experimental groups, each composed of 14 females and eight males. All Ss were tested under standard instructions for the PMA, except that each experimental condition received a different instructional set with respect to the consequences (reinforcement contingencies) of risk-taking behavior in the test situation.

The four experimental conditions were: (1) *omissions optional – low risk (OL)*. This involved a three-cent gain for each correct answer and a .5 cent loss for each wrong answer. Ss were told that it was to their advantage to try to answer all items; (2) *omissions optional – high risk (OH)*. This involved a three-cent gain for a correct answer, a three-cent loss for an incorrect answer and a one-cent loss for no answer. Ss were told that if they were unsure of the answer, it was advantageous to leave it blank; (3) *omissions discouraged – low risk (DL)*. This involved a three-cent gain for a correct answer, a .5 cent loss for an incorrect answer, and a three-cent loss for no answer. Ss were told that it was to their advantage to guess; (4) *omissions discouraged – high risk (DH*. This involved a three-cent gain for a correct answer, a three-cent loss for a wrong answer, and a four-cent loss for a blank. Ss were told that it was to their advantage to guess.

All Ss were given 30 cents at the beginning of testing and were told that they could not lose any of their own money. All Ss received a minimum of 21 cents at tne end of testing. A group testing situation was used, ordinarily with four Ss per group. All Ss completed a seven-item version of the Spielberger State Anxiety Scale.

Results and Discussion

Table 1 summarizes the mean performance on PMA subtests by experimental conditions. The results suggest that the standard test situation appears to

Table 1
Mean Performance on PMA Subtests by Experimental Condition

| | Experimental Condition | | | | |
Subtest	OL	OH	DL	DH	Standard* Condition
Verbal Meaning	28.6	20.1	24.8	25.8	22.2
Space	14.3	9.1	11.6	13.2	8.8
Reasoning	9.1	5.6	6.4	7.7	5.9
Number	26.7	19.8	20.6	22.9	17.3
Word Fluency	34.1	27.3	35.1	32.4	29.6

*Data from another study with 87 Ss with mean age of 74 years.

be most closely analogous to the omission optional — high risk (OH) experimental condition. In general, performance was better under the omissions optional — low risk (OL), omissions discouraged — low risk (DL) and omissions discouraged — high risk (DH) conditions in comparison to the omission optional — high risk (OH) and standard conditions. The hypothesis that the OL group would achieve significantly higher performance on the PMA factors than the OH group was supported for the verbal meaning, space, and reasoning subtests and the trend was also in the expected direction for number and word fluency. The hypothesis that no significant difference would be found between the DL and DH groups was supported for all PMA subtests. Confirmation of these two hypotheses supports past research findings concerning cautiousness among the elderly, in that these elderly Ss showed less reluctance to respond to low-risk situations only when failure to register a response was not penalized.

Subjects in the high-risk conditions (OH and DH) scored consistently better when omissions were discouraged (DH) than when omissions were optional (OH). Under the low-risk conditions (OL and DL) there was a trend for higher scores under the omissions optional (OL) condition. Mean anxiety scores were significantly higher for Ss, for whom omission was discouraged. These results suggested that cautiousness operates least under conditions of low anxiety combined with low risk, but can also be minimized under conditions of high anxiety given that the risk is also high.

The results of this study suggest that the performance of the elderly on the PMA, a test of intellectual ability, can be enhanced markedly by the programming of reinforcement conditions. Thus, further support is provided for the view that ability-extraneous factors may be crucial mediators of intellectual performance of elderly people.

Abstract **9**

Developmental Assessment of Intelligence

CAROL A. FURRY, M.A. and PAUL B. BALTES, Ph.D.

"The Effect of Age Difference in Ability: Extraneous Performance Variables on the Assessment of Intelligence in Children, Adults and the Elderly," *Journal of Gerontology*, 1973, *28*, 73-80.

A major problem plaguing age-comparative research involves the question of measurement equivalence. Although it has been demonstrated that ability-extraneous but performance-related variables such as performance sets, testing conditions, and instructional variables may affect scores on learning tests, and that the effects of such performance variables may be different at different ages, no evidence has been accumulated on the question whether performance variables exhibit substantial age differences in the context of intelligence measurements. This study investigated the possibility that various age groups, particularly the elderly, may be affected differentially by performance-related factors which would jeopardize the interpretation of age differences in intelligence tests as being indicative of true differences in task-specific abilities. The performance-related effects investigated were subtest position and pretest fatigue.

Method

SUBJECTS: A total of 240 male and female subjects, including 80 aged 11-14 (mean age 12.5), 80 aged 30-50 (mean age 38) and 80 aged 51-80 (mean age 64). Comparison with census data indicated that the samples were generally representative except that educational level was somewhat higher than for the general population.

Materials: The Primary Mental Abilities Test (Thurstone and Thurstone, Form AM, 1949) which consists of five subtests presented in the following order: VM - Verbal Meaning (4 min.), S - Space (5 min.), R - Reasoning (6 min.), N - Number (6 min.), and WF - Word Fluency (5 min.). In addition a fatiguing treatment, a modified version of the Finding As Test, was administered to half the Ss.

PROCEDURE AND DESIGN: A 2 (sex) × 3 (age) × 2 (fatigue) × 5 (position) design was used with four Ss per cell. Ss were assigned randomly to the conditions of position and pretest fatigue. The position treatment involved variations in the order and number of PMA subtests as follows: I - VM, S, R,

N, WF; II - S, R, N, WF; III - R, N, WF; IV - N, WF; V - WF. The pretest fatigue condition was defined by the inclusion of the 20-minute letter cancellation task prior to the five PMA conditions.

Subjects were tested in groups of four to eight. Testing times ranged from ten minutes (position condition V, no fatigue) to two hours (position condition I, fatigue).

Results

Contrary to expectations, varying positions of subtests did not, by themselves, produce marked age differences in performance. Manipulation of preexperimental fatigue resulted in age by pretest fatigue interactions for three (WF, R, VM) of the five PMA subtests. For Verbal Meaning and Reasoning, the major result is that preexperimental fatiguing magnifies cross-sectional differences among adolescents, adults and elderly Ss. For Word Fluency, age by fatigue relations are complicated by position effects with the adolescents and elderly showing opposite fatigue-position effects; the adolescents performed best under fatigue in the later positions, whereas the fatigue-later positions combination produced the weakest performance in elderly Ss.

These data support the hypothesis that part of the often-observed age differences in components of intelligence is not indicative of a loss in task-specific abilities, and that differential age functions may, in part, reflect the operation of nonintellective factors such as pretest experience. Questions may be raised about the validity of conclusions involving differential age functions for various components of intelligence. Various methodological controls may be necessary to separate performance from ability-related components in developmental research.

CHAPTER III

Perceptual Functioning

Abstract 10

Reorganization of Perceptions with Age

JACK BOTWINICK, Ph.D., JOSEPH S. ROBBIN, M.A.
and JOSEPH F. BRINLEY, M.A.

"Reorganization of Perceptions with Age," *Journal of Gerontology*, 1959, *14*, 85-88.

This study addressed the relationship between age and modifiability of activity. Specifically, it compared two age groups with respect to type of percept that is organized and with respect to ability to alter or reorganize this percept.

Method

SUBJECTS: Seventy-four male volunteers, 37 within the age range 65 to 81 years (mean age = 71) and 37 within the age range 19 to 34 years (mean age = 25) were the subjects. All were community residents except three older persons, who lived in a home for the aged. Mean years of formal education were 11 years and 14 years for the older and younger groups respectively.

Materials: Use was made of three figures, frequently described as the "wife," the "mother-in-law" and the "ambiguous" pictures. Although the three figures varied only in small details, the "wife" could be readily perceived as a rather stylish young woman, the "mother-in-law" picture was a rather severe older woman, and the "ambiguous" picture permitted the perception of either the "wife" or the "mother-in-law."

PROCEDURE: Initially, the "ambiguous" figure was shown to each S, and he was asked what he saw. If either the young or the older woman was reported within 90 secs., he was informed that another picture could be seen and was asked what it was. If the S did not perceive the second figure within 90 secs., either the unambiguous "mother-in-law" or "wife" picture, whichever was appropriate, was shown for 90 secs. If the figure was not peceived, the features were identified. The "ambiguous" figure was then presented again for 90 secs., and the S was asked what he saw.

Table 1
Percept Reorganizaion by Young and Elderly Men

	Young Men	Elderly Men
Number reporting as first percept:		
wife	28	33
mother-in-law	8	2
neither	1	2
Reorganization of percept with only verbal suggestion		
number reorganizing	7	1
number not reorganizing	29	34
Reorganization of percept after seeing alternative unambiguous figure:		
number reorganizing	24	8
number not reorganizing	5	26

Results

The elderly Ss were subdivided into those with 12 or more and those with 11 or less years of education. Because level of education did not have a significant effect on perceptual performance, the results of the categorization by education level will not be reported in this summary.

The results are summarized in Table 1. The two age groups did not differ with respect to number forming an initial percept, although proportionately more of the younger than the older men perceived the "mother-in-law" initially. The data show clearly that the older group had greater difficulty than did the younger group in reorganizing or altering the initial percept.

Abstract 11

Developmental Changes in Perception

PETER E. COMALLI, JR., Ph.D.

"Cognitive Functioning in a Group of 80- 90-Year-Old Men," *Journal of Gerontology*, 1965, 20, 14-17.

In an earlier study the performance of persons ranging in age from six to 80 years was compared on four perceptual tasks. It was found that the performance of an aged group (65-80) was more similar to the performance of children than to adults of middle age. These findings were interpreted as consistent with a developmental theory of regression, i.e., whereas developmental progression proceeds in terms of increase in differentiation and hierarchic integration, in regression the shift is reversed from a state of greater to one of lesser differentiation and hierarchic integration.

This study was designed to extend the empirical findings by examining the performance of an 80-to 90-year-old group in comparison to the available data on persons aged six to 80, and to test the hypothesis that the 80-to 90-year-old group would manifest greater "regression" than a 65-to 80-year-old group.

Method

SUBJECTS: The "new" subjects for this study were 20 male Spanish Ameri-

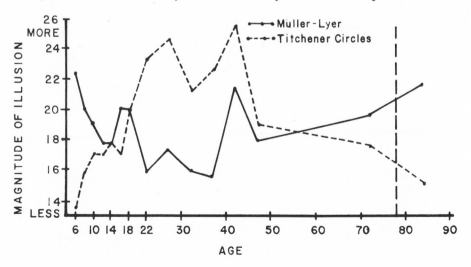

can War veterans between the ages of 80 and 90 (mean age = 83.2 years) and 15 males between the ages of 65 and 80 (mean age = 71.6 years). All were relatively healthy, ambulatory and living in the community.

PROCEDURE: All Ss were tested on the Perception of Verticality, Müller-Lyer Illusion, Titchener Circles Illusion and Stroop Color-Word tests under conditions identical to those used in the earlier study with persons aged six to 80 years.

Results

Figure 1 summarizes mean performance by age on the Müller-Lyer Illusion and the Titchener Circles Illusion. On both of these tests, as on the other two, there was a clear trend for the performance of the very old Ss to become increasingly like that of young children and increasingly different from that of young and middle-aged adults. The 80- to 90-year-old group demonstrated significantly greater regression than the 65- to 80-year-old group on the Stroop Color-Word Test, and on the other three tests performed less well, but not significantly so, than the 65- to 80-year-old group. In the overall developmental picture from six to 90 years of age, the performance of the 80- to 90-year-old group in this study confirms the previous finding that the perceptual performance of the aged is more similar to that of children than to adults of middle age.

Abstract **12**

Perceptual Functioning of Institutionalized and Noninstutionalized Aged

PETER E. COMALLI, JR., Ph.D., DONALD M. KRUS, Ph.D. and SEYMOUR WAPNER, Ph.D.

"Cognitive Functioning of Two Groups of Aged: One Institutionalized, the Other Living in the Community," *Journal of Gerontology*, 1965, *20*, 9-13.

Earlier studies have shown that some aspects of the perceptual-cognitive functioning of elderly people are more similar to that of children than to middle-aged adults. Within a comparative-developmental framework, these observations have been interpreted as reflecting "regression." The present study examined further the value of the concept of regression in aging by contrasting groups of older people, similar for chronological age, but different in terms of whether they were or were not institutionalized. It aimed to determine whether cognitive functioning of an aged institutionalized group manifested greater regression than that of a noninstitutionalized group.

Method

SUBJECTS: Fifteen institutionalized subjects between the ages of 67 and 81 were contrasted with 15 noninstitutionalized subjects between the ages of 65 and 80 years. All were ambulatory and in relatively good physical health. The groups were similar with respect to educational level and prior occupation. The institutionalized subjects had been referred for custodial care.
PROCEDURE: All Ss were tested on the Perception of Verticality, Müller-Lyer Illusion, Titchener Circle Illusion and the Stroop Color-Word tests.

Results

The institutionalized group performed reliably less well on the Stroop Color-Word Test. On the other tests differences between groups were not significant, but all differences were in the predicted direction, i.e., the performance of institutionalized group was more like that of children than was the performance of the noninstitutionalized group. It was concluded that the institutionalized group showed greater regression than the community group.

Abstract 13

Ignoring Irrelevant Information

P. M. A. RABBITT, Ph.D.

"Age Decrements in the Ability to Ignore Irrelevant Information," *Journal of Gerontology*, 1965, 20, 233-238.

This experiment examined the prediction that the difficulty of discriminating between relevant and irrelevant information increases with age.

Method

SUBJECTS: The young group consisted of three men and eight women aged 17 to 24 years (mean age 19.0). The older group consisted of two men and nine women aged 65 to 74 years (mean age 67.4). The young Ss were undergraduate students; most of the old Ss were university graduates and all had held very senior positions.

Materials: Eight packs of 48 cards, 2¼ x 3½ in., four for each of two experimental conditions.

Condition I: Half the cards were marked with the letter A and half with the letter B, with the letter stencilled in one of nine possible locations. The Ss were required to sort the packs into two piles by separating the A cards from the B cards. The four packs differed with respect to the inclusion of irrelevant information as follows: Pack 1: No irrelevant information; Pack 2: one other letter (from C to Z) appeared on the card; Pack 3: four irrelevant letters were added; Pack 4: eight irrelevant letters were added.

Condition II: Each card had one of eight relevant letters (A, B, C, D, E, F, G or H) in contrast to one of two relevant letters (A or B) in Condition 1. Variations among the four packs were the same as Condition 1, i.e., no one, four or eight irrelevant letters added.

PROCEDURE: Order of conditions was counterbalanced with one day intervening between conditions. Ss were instructed to deal the cards as fast and accurately as possible into the number of piles appropriate for the condition (two for Condition I, eight for Condition II). Packs in each condition were presented in random order until each had been sorted ten times. Sorting times and errors were recorded.

Results

Few errors were made and differences between age groups and conditions for errors were not significant.

Sorting time varied significantly (p <0.001) as a function of age, conditions and packs. The older Ss sorted the cards more slowly than the young, both groups took longer to sort the cards into eight piles than two piles, and sorting was slowed for both groups by the addition of irrelevant symbols to the display. The increase in relevant symbols from two to eight resulted in equivalent increases in sorting time for old and young people. However, the sorting times of the old Ss increased more sharply than those of the young with increases in the number of irrelevant letters on the card (p<0.01 for interaction of packs × age).

These findings demonstrate that the speed with which Ss ignore irrelevant symbols on a visual display varies with the number of relevant items for which they are set to search. The amount of irrelevant information in which the relevant information is embedded is also a factor. The old Ss took longer to discriminate between relevant and irrelevant stimuli and differences between age groups increased sharply as a function of increases in the number of irrelevant stimuli. It may be that differences in techniques of perceptual information processing make it more difficult for older people to ignore irrelevant visual information.

Abstract 14

Set in Relation to Age

JACK BOTWINICK, Ph.D., JOSEPH F. BRINLEY, M.A. and JAMES E. BIRREN, Ph.D.

"Set in Relation to Age," *Journal of Gerontology*, 1957, 12, 300-305.

This experiment studied set as a function of age by comparing two age groups with respect to the relationship between reaction time and an irregularly presented series of preparatory intervals.

Method

SUBJECTS: Subjects were 27 males aged 61 to 83 years (mean age = 68.0) and 27 males aged 20 to 36 years (mean age = 27.0). Most of the subjects were employees of the Public Health Service, but nine of the older group were retired, and of these four resided in a home for the aged. Four of the younger group were research volunteers.

PROCEDURE: Each S was given practice trials. The experiment consisted of two series of 25 measurements each, with the two series separated by 100 reaction-time measurements relevant to another research project. The preparatory intervals used were of 1.0, 1.5, 2.0, 2.5, 3.0, 4.0, 5.0 and 6.0 sec. duration. Each series contained four of the 2.0 sec. intervals and three each of the other seven intervals. A fixed quasi-random order of intervals was used, with the order reversed in series 1 and 2.

The S was instructed to press a response key when given a verbal instruction "ready" and simultaneously presented with a warning signal, a glow of a neon bulb presented for 0.50 sec. He was instructed to release the response key as soon as possible after hearing a tone stimulus. The stimulus was presented by earphones for 0.20 sec. duration. Reaction time, i.e., time from onset of the stimulus to release of the response key, was read to the nearest .01 sec.

Table 1
Simple Auditory Reaction Time* as a Function of
Preparatory Interval for Young and Elderly Subjects

	Preparatory Interval in Seconds							
	1.0	1.5	2.0	2.5	3.0	4.0	5.0	6.0
Young	220	201	186	182	177	176	176	179
Elderly	311	263	246	240	225	213	222	223
Elderly - Young	91	62	60	58	48	37	46	44

*Mean of the individual median measurements, in msec.

Results

The median reaction times were computed for each S for each preparatory interval of both series 1 and 2. Because the results for the two series did not differ significantly, data from the two series were combined. The group means of individual median reaction times for series 1 and 2 are presented for each preparatory interval in Table 1. The differences between the eight preparatory intervals were statistically significant ($p < .01$) for the combined groups and for each age group alone. There was also a significant age difference ($p < .01$) for speed of response. Of greater interest was the finding that decrease in reaction time as a function of increase in length of the preparatory interval was significantly different between age groups ($p < .01$). The largest age difference occurred with the shortest (1.0 sec.) preparatory interval. Age differences with the longer intervals were less and, at least up to intervals of 4.0 sec. duration, appeared to be functionally related to the length of the preparatory interval. The data indicated clearly that the older group, compared to the younger one, was at a disadvantage with the shortest preparatory interval.

Two alternative hypotheses were offered to account for the disproportionately high age differences at the shortest preparatory interval. One hypothesis is that with age there is an increase in the amount of time required to organize a response or to develop optimum expectancy. The other hypothesis is that the larger age differences with the shorter intervals are explainable by the time required to recover from, or to reorganize as a result of, overestimation caused by the presence of longer intervals in the series. A reanalysis of the data provided tentative support for the second hypothesis.

Abstract **15**

Hearing Loss in Older Patients

T. NEWELL DECKER, M.Ed.

"A Survey of Hearing Loss in an Older Age Population," *Gerontologist*, 1974, *14*, 402-403.

This study addressed the problem of unidentified hearing loss in older patients.

Method

Patients admitted for evaluation and treatment to the rehabilitation medicine department of a large hospital were evaluated for hearing loss as part of the overall evaluation program. Persons who could not understand or respond to instructions were regarded as untestable. The age range of the 120 patients who were tested was six to 92 years, with 84 in the 60 to 80 range.

Results

Only 20 of the persons seen had normal hearing, 14 could not respond to pure tone stimuli for one reason or another, and 85 had hearing that was defective to some measurable degree. For 35 of the patients the hearing loss was severe, though they may have been helped by amplification, speech reading training, or suggestions on how to maneuver the communication system. Another 44 patients could clearly have benefited from hearing aid amplification or auditory training. Of the 79 people who could have bene-fited from a hearing aid, only 13 wore one, and of these, 5 were fitted with aids which were inappropriate for the degree of loss present or with aids which were in disrepair. Thirteen patients had conductive hearing losses which required treatment and would have gone unattended had the routine hearing test not been administered.

In this study, more than 70 percent of the patients over 50 years of age had hearing losses sufficient to prevent them from interacting in a satisfactory manner with those around them. Patients in their sixties and seventies alone accounted for more than 40 percent of the hearing losses which were identified.

Abstract **16**

Hearing Loss and Cognition*

SAMUEL GRANICK, Ph.D., MORTON H. KLEBAN, Ph.D. and ALFRED WEISS, M.D.

"Relationships Between Hearing Loss and Cognition in Normally Hearing Aged Persons," *Journal of Gerontology*, 1976, *31*, 434-444.

This study examined the possibility that there may be significant relation-ships between auditory acuity in aged persons whose hearing is within normal limits for their age and various aspects of their cognitive function-ing.

Method

SUBJECTS: The first group of subjects consisted of 47 men who had been specially selected for their good health and freedom from significant physiological and psychological pathology. Data from this sample were collected during their participation in an extensive biological and behavioral study at the Clinical Center of National Institutes of Health. This group had a mean age of 75.9 years. The second group consisted of 38 women, most of whom had some serious medical problems but who were ambulatory and able to cooperate with the hearing, and other biological and psychological testing quite well. Their mean age was 75.9.

Procedure: Hearing acuity was measured for each ear in terms of decibel loss at frequency levels ranging from 125 to 8,000 cps. Psychological tests included most of the subtests of the Wechsler Adult Intelligence Scale and the Raven Progressive Matrices. The female Ss were also tested on the Ammons Picture Vocabulary Test.

Results

Both samples of subjects had a good deal of reduced auditory acuity at the upper frequency levels, particularly at 4,000 cps and above. For the lower frequencies, however, particularly those within the usual speaking range of the human voice (500 to 2,000 cps), the losses were much lower, indicating that the Ss were not hard of hearing.

Even within the limited age range of the samples, age correlated negatively with hearing acuity and with several of the measures of cognitive functioning. When the effects of age were controlled statistically, there was clear evidence that hearing losses were associated with relatively reduced intellectual functioning for both samples of subjects.

For both samples, the strength and extent of the relationship between auditory acuity and cognition was much greater for the verbal type intellectual measures than for the nonverbal or performance type tests. The two WAIS subtests, Vocabulary and Information, which are generally associated with retained cognitive effectiveness by the aged, were among the tasks showing the most serious decline in relation to hearing loss. The results generally indicated that those subjects who retained their hearing best were also those who tended to function best intellectually.

These findings have important implications with respect to the interpretation of intellectual test results with aged subjects. How hearing acuity interacts with learning, especially of verbal materials, also deserves serious attention. Moreover, how other sense modalities, such as vision and proprioception, are involved in cognitive test results, particularly those involving spatial perception and visual motor coordination, should be examined.

CHAPTER IV

Learning

Abstract 17

Age and Health Effects on Learning

Irene M. Hulicka, Ph. D.

"Short-Term Learning and Memory Efficiency as a Function of Age and Health," *Journal of the American Geriatrics Society*, 1967, *15*, 285-294.

In many of the early studies demonstrating that cognitive efficiency declines with age, elderly subjects were unselected with respect to health, were hospitalized, or were residents in homes for the aged, whereas young subjects, recruited primarily from educational institutions, were presumably generally healthy. Consequently, much of the decrement in performance attributed to the process of aging might have been due to the poorer health status of the older subjects. This study tested the general hypothesis that if the decrement attributable differences between age groups for health are taken into account, the decrement in scores on learning and memory tasks that can be attributed to the aging process will be minimal.

Method

SUBJECTS: The nonhealthy subjects were 120 hospitalized male veterans, 20 of whom fit in each of the following age categories: 17-29, 30-39, 40-49,

50-59, 60-69 and 70-85. Participation was voluntary. Patients from psychiatric wards and those with diagnosed brain damage and severely impaired speech, hearing or vision were excluded, as were those with a score of less than 5 on the WAIS vocabulary scale. Health status was estimated from the number of diagnoses listed in the most recent medical summary and the number of months of hospitalization during the preceding five years.

The healthy Ss included 20 persons in each of the following age categories: 17-29, 50-59, 60-69. They included hospital attendants, college students, hospital volunteers, and members of community organizations. All nonpatient Ss professed to be in good health; the few reported hospital admissions during the preceding five years were for nonchronic conditions. The nonpatient groups contained an approximately equal number of males and females; absence of sex differences for experimental task scores ($F<1.00$) allowed for combination of data from the two sexes.

Learning-Memory Tasks: To avoid noninterest and fatigue effects, particularly among the hospitalized and older Ss, an attempt was made to select brief tasks which would be fairly interesting to members of all age groups. Four tasks were administered in sequential order: (1) Task 1 — Recognition of faces. Pictures of ten young women were shown for 5 sec. each. The S then had to select from ten sets of three pictures the faces that had been presented previously. (2) Task 2 — Memory for names and faces. Pictures of eight men, each paired with a common first name, were presented for eight sec. each. The pictures were then shown in random order and the S was asked to provide the name. (3) Task 3 — Logical memory. The S was shown pictures of three men, one at a time, while the experimenter read a brief paragraph about the man (e.g., name, occupation, hobbies, family). Subsequently, the pictures were presented in random order, and the S was asked to report as much as he could remember from the paragraph. (4) Task 4 — Paired associates. Eight names paired with nouns were presented on a memory drum for four trials.

Results

When hospitalized Ss were considered separately, and health status was ignored, there was a significant age-related drop in scores for three out of the four tasks (all but Task 4). However, when the variance associated with health status was partialled out through analysis of co-variance, differences between age groups were not significant for any of the tasks. Simple correlations revealed a significant negative relationship between age and task score for all four tasks. However, second-order partial correlations, which held constant the effects of health status, again indicated no relationship between age and score on any of the tasks. Thus, for the hospitalized Ss, what initially appeared to be a large age-determined deficit in learning-memory scores could be accounted for chiefly by the poorer health status of the older patients.

When the nonpatient age groups were considered separately, there was a significant age-related drop in score for Task 3 only. Also when like-aged patients and nonpatients were compared, the nonpatients performed significantly better on all tasks except Task 3.

To demonstrate the possibility of erroneous conclusions if comparisons are made between age groups that are not comparable for health status, the 17-29 year group of patients was compared to the 60-69 year group of nonpatients. Although the young Ss earned significantly higher scores on Task 3, the elderly Ss earned significantly higher scores on Tasks 2 and 4 and performed as well as the young Ss on Task 1. Obviously, this comparison does not justify the conclusion that scores on some learning-memory tasks increase as a function of age. Yet, in many studies that have demonstrated a decline in cognitive efficiency as a function of increased age, the young Ss have undoubtedly been much healthier than the elderly Ss.

Abstract 18

Paced and Self-Paced Learning with Age

ROBERT E. CANESTRARI, JR., Ph.D.

"Paced and Self-Paced Learning in Young and Elderly Adults," *Journal of Gerontology*, 1963, *18*, 165-168.

There is evidence to indicate that there is a marked performance deficit with age in paired-associate learning and, further, that the older person is greatly handicapped when he is required to perform psychomotor tasks under paced conditions. This study was designed to investigate the effects of paced and self-paced schedules on the rate of learning paired-associates by young and old adults.

Method

SUBJECTS: The older group consisted of 30 males between 60 and 69 years of age (mean age = 65.4); the 30 males in the younger group ranged in age from 17 to 35 years (mean age = 23.9). Subjects were recruited from persons seeking work at a local employment agency and were paid for participation. The groups were comparable for education, socio-economic status and vocabulary score was the WAIS.

Materials: Three paired-associate lists of equivalent difficulty were presented on a memory drum.

PROCEDURE: There were two paced conditions (1.5-sec. and 3-sec.) and one self-paced condition. In the paced conditions the S was given the usual instructions for paired-associate learning and told to respond with the response word before the pair came into view. For the self-paced task, the S was told how to operate the apparatus so he could proceed at his own pace. A counterbalancing design (Graeco-Latin) was used so that all three lists and all conditions of pacing were presented to all Ss. The measure of learning was the total number of errors, identified as errors of omission and commission, made in reaching the criterion of one perfect recitation.

Table 1
Mean Errors and Mean Time Per Self-Paced Trial

Measure	Group	1.5 Sec.	3 Sec.	Self-Paced
Total Errors	Young	12.23	7.90	6.27
	Old	50.90	25.90	15.30
Omission Errors	Young	10.73	6.10	4.77
	Old	46.57	21.47	9.90
Commission Errors	Young	1.60	1.80	1.50
	Old	4.23	4.60	5.40
Time in Seconds per	Young	—	—	43.14
Trial	Old	—	—	53.08

Results

Table 1 summarizes mean errors and mean time per self-paced trial for the two age groups. These results indicate that the younger Ss performed better than the older Ss under all conditions, but that the difference between age groups was greatly reduced in the self-paced condition in comparison to the paced conditions. For both age groups the worst performance was under the 1.5-sec. paced schedule, and the best performance was under the self-paced schedule. The older Ss performed better under the self-paced schedule than the 3-sec. paced schedule, but the change from a 3-sec. paced schedule to a self-paced schedule had no appreciable effect on the performance of the young Ss. Errors of omission decreased under self-paced conditions, but errors of commission remained at the same level under all conditions of pacing. The older subjects used significantly more time under the self-paced condition than the young Ss did; both groups used the extra time primarily to make the response to the stimulus word rather than to study the pair. These results suggest that some of the observed performance deficit of the older person is due to the paced character of the task rather than a true learning disability.

Abstract **19**

Paced and Self-Paced Learning Schedules

IRENE M. HULICKA, Ph.D., HARVEY STERNS, Ph.D.
and JOEL L. GROSSMAN, Ph.D.

"Age-Group Comparisons of Paired-Associate Learning as a Function of Paced and Self-Paced Association and Response Times," *Journal of Gerontology*, 1967, 22, 274-280.

Several studies have demonstrated that the age-related deficits for scores on learning, retention, and other tasks can be reduced by manipulating conditions under which the task is presented. Generally, these studies have involved either manipulation of temporal schedules or instructions concerning strategies for coping with the task. This study examined the effects of paced and self-paced association (study) and response schedules on the paired-associated learning scores of young and elderly adults who had been advised to use mediating connections between the pairs. It was predicted that the older Ss would use more time to select an association or to attempt to learn the pair, as well as to make their responses, and hence, that the older Ss would show the least deficit under a totally self-paced schedule. Age differences in the use of associative links were also examined.

Method

SUBJECTS: Forty-eight elderly (mean age = 70.2) and 48 young (mean age = 15.5) people with 16 males and 32 females were in each age group. Participants were recruited from the community and were paid for participation.

Materials and Design: The learning tasks were four paired-associate lists, equated for difficulty,consisting of 20 pairs of nouns per list for the young Ss and 10 pairs each for the older Ss (a total of 80 pairs for each young S and 40 pairs for each older S). For each list the first ten pairs for the young Ss comprised the entire list for the old Ss.

There were four experimental conditions: LL — limited association time (3 sec.) and limited response time (3 sec.); LU — limited association time (3 sec.) and unlimited response time; UL — unlimited association time and limited response time (3 sec.); and UU — unlimited association and response time. All Ss were tested under all experimental conditions; order of conditions was completely counterbalanced. Association and response latencies were recorded.

PROCEDURE: Each S was tested individually. After practice trials were given to ensure that the S understood standard paired-associate instructions and his tasks in relation to the recording device, he was advised that it would be easier to learn the words of the pair if an image or phrase were selected to link them together, and examples were given. Also, after each set of experimental instructions a sample list was administered to ensure that the S understood the temporal schedule for that specific condition.

Each list was read only once, either with a three-second interval between pairs, or at a self-paced rate, depending on the experimental condition. Fifteen seconds after the single learning trial, a single recall trial was administered, in which the S was instructed to respond with the second word of the pair when the first word was given. Immediately after the recall trial, instructions for the next experimental condition were given, the sample list was administered, followed by the single learning and single recall trial. This procedure was repeated for all four conditions.

Following the final recall trial, the S was questioned about techniques he had used in his attempt to learn each of 16 preselected pairs, four from each list. Responses were taped, and subsequently three judges assigned the learning method to one of six categories, depending on whether the S's report indicated that he had used: (1) visual imagery; (2) verbal connection; (3) rote memorization; (4) a miscellaneous idiosyncratic technique; (5) had found the pair too odd to form a connection; (6) had not had time to form a connection.

Results

The young Ss earned higher recall scores than the older Ss under all conditions. Neither age group showed improvement from the LL condition (totally paced) to the LU condition (self-paced response time); both age groups showed significant improvement from the LL condition (totally paced) to the UL condition (self-paced association time). Both age groups performed best under the totally self-paced (UU) condition. Thus, for both age groups the self-paced association schedule resulted in improved performance, regardless of the nature of the response schedule, whereas the self-paced response schedule improved performance only if the association schedule had also been self-paced. Contrary to expectations, the older Ss showed equivalent rather than more improvement than the young Ss, from the totally paced to the totally unpaced condition, perhaps because the older Ss, also contrary to expectation, did not use more association time than the young Ss under the self-paced association schedules.

The older Ss reported the use of mediators less frequently than the young Ss (for 72 percent versus 86 percent of the pairs), used verbal mediators for more pairs (38 percent versus 20 percent), used visual mediators for fewer pairs (34 percent versus 66 percent), and reported that more pairs were too odd to form a connection than the young did (21 percent versus 4 percent). Both age groups recalled significantly more items from pairs for which they reported the use of mediators.

Abstract **20**

Age and Intervals in Paired-Associate Learning

ROLF H. MONGE, Ph.D. and DAVID F. HULTSCH, Ph. D.

"Paired-Associate Learning as a Function of Adult Age and the Length of Anticipation and Inspection Intervals," *Journal of Gerontology*, 1971, 26, 157-162.

A number of studies have demonstrated that in comparison to young Ss, older Ss show disproportionately poorer performance on learning tasks at fast paces, and that the discrepancy between the performance of older and young Ss can be reduced, but not eliminated, by slowing the pace. Explanations for improvement in performance of older Ss at slower paces have tended to concentrate on the length of time available for the S to orally produce the response term, and thus interest has centered on the anticipation (response) interval. However, the effects of pace upon performance at different ages require examination of the effects of the inspection (study) interval and the possible interactive effects of the anticipation and inspection intervals. This study investigated the effects on the performance of adult males of different ages of variations in the anticipation and inspection intervals.

Method

Design: A 2 x 3 x 3 factorial analysis of variance model with two age levels (20-39 and 40-66 years), three anticipation intervals (2.2, 4.4, and 6.6 sec.), and three inspection intervals (2.2, 4.4, and 6.6 sec).

SUBJECTS: Seventy-two white community-living males from each of the two age intervals (mean ages 28.3 and 49.4 years), who were paid for participation. Within each age interval, Ss were assigned at random to one of the nine combinations of anticipation and inspection intervals. Analyses of variance revealed no significant effects for score on a vocabulary test or for occupational level, but the younger Ss had significantly more formal education than the older Ss.

Materials: A three-item practice list and a ten-item experimental list (Ticket-Angry, Factory-Ready, Market-Unusual, Attention-Normal, Kitchen-Certain, Insurance-Pleasant, Diamond-Simple, Stranger-Favorite, Habit-Delicate, and Lawyer-Empty) typed in four random orders for presentation on a memory drum.

PROCEDURE: Standard paired-associate instructions were given before and after four trials on the practice list. Training on the experimental list continued to a criterion of one errorless recitation.

Table 1
Mean Number of Trials to Criterion

Anticipation Interval (Sec.)		Inspection Interval (Sec.)					
		2.2		4.4		6.6	
	Age	*20-39*	*40-66*	*20-39*	*40-66*	*20-39*	*40-66*
2.2	M	10.0	24.9	9.0	24.5	6.0	19.8
	SD	5.5	17.2	10.7	20.3	2.9	13.3
4.4	M	11.0	12.6	7.0	10.4	7.9	7.2
	SD	11.8	7.4	4.9	12.3	4.8	4.6
6.6	M	6.8	11.4	5.0	6.2	5.0	5.4
	SD	4.0	4.4	3.9	5.3	2.4	3.3

Results

Table 1 presents trials to criterion on the experimental list as a function of age, anticipation interval and inspection interval.

Analysis of variance indicated that Age, Inspection Interval, Anticipation Interval and Age X Anticipation Interval were significant at $p < 0.01$. The younger Ss performed better than the older Ss, and performance was better at both ages with longer inspection intervals and with longer anticipation intervals. The significant Age X Anticipation interaction effect indicated that the older Ss benefited proportionately more than the younger did from longer anticipation intervals; both age groups benefited to approximately the same extent from the longer inspection intervals.

The anticipation interval accounted for 11.04 percent of the variance among groups, the inspection interval 5.40 percent, age 6.94 percent and Age X Anticipation interaction 4.02 percent. Thus, age, singly and in combination, accounted for only 10.96 percent of the variance.

Abstract 21

The Use of Mediators

IRENE M. HULICKA, Ph.D. and JOEL L. GROSSMAN, Ph.D.

"Age-Group Comparisons for the Use of Mediators in Paired-Associate Learning," *Journal of Gerontology*, 1967, 22, 46-51.

Many studies have demonstrated that the learning of paired-associates by young adults can be facilitated by experimentally built-in or by subject-selected mediators. In this study it was predicted that unless specifically instructed to do so, older Ss would use mediational techniques less frequently than young Ss, and that instructions to use mediational techniques would result in proportionately more improvement in learning scores for older than for young Ss.

Method

SUBJECTS: The subjects were 72 elderly people (mean age 74.1) recruited from Senior Citizens Centers and homes for the aged and 72 young people (mean age 16.1) recruited from the community. All Ss were paid a nominal fee.

Design: Eighteen old and 18 young Ss were assigned to each of four experimental conditions which varied in terms of instructions for paired-associate learning. Ss in the No Special Instruction condition (NI) were given standard paired-associate instructions. Ss in the other conditions were given standard instructions plus instructions designed to increase the use of mediational techniques. Ss in the Self-Image Instruction condition (SI) were told to attempt to form an image which included both items of the pair. Ss in the Experimenter Image Instruction condition (EI) were given a word or phrase which linked the words of the pair and advised to imagine the scene suggested by the phrase. Ss in the Verbal Instruction condition (VI) were given the connecting word or phrase used in the EI condition and were advised to use the phrase to help remember the pair.

Materials: There were three lists, each composed of 20 pairs of concrete nouns. For the young Ss the complete 20 pair lists were used, but the old Ss were presented only the first 10 pairs from each list. Differential list lengths were used to avoid a ceiling effect with young Ss and the discouragement or resentment of the elderly Ss. The lists were equated for difficulty. Examples of the pairs and connecting phrases are: bear-stool (bear on stool); army-bank (army attacks bank).

PROCEDURE: After administration of the vocabulary subtest of the WAIS and a learning and recall trial on a 10 pair trial list, Ss were assigned to one of the four experimental conditions so that the four groups within each age range were matched for vocabulary score and number correct on the trial list. Instructions appropriate to the experimental condition were then given, and a practice list was administered to ensure that instructions were comprehended. Each of the three lists was presented once, at the rate of one pair every ten secs. For the NI and SI groups each pair was read twice, because Ss in the EI and VI groups heard the pair once alone and once in the connecting phrase. A single learning trial for one list was followed immediately by a single recall trial, with a maximum of eight secs. for the response. Two minutes after the completion of the recall test for one list, the next list was presented. After the recall trial for the third list, each S was asked about techniques he had used in his attempt to learn each of 15 preselected pairs.

Results

Table 1 summarizes number and percentage of items recalled correctly on trial and experimental lists. In comparison to the NI condition, the young Ss

Table 1
Mean Performance on Recall of Trial and Experimental Lists

	Group	Recall (Mean no. Correct)		Recall (Mean % Correct)		% Improve. from NI Condition
		Trial List	Experimental Lists	Trial List	Experimental Lists	
Old	NI	2.8	10.4	28	35	—
	SI	2.8	15.8	28	53	18
	EI	3.0	13.6	30	45	10
	VI	2.8	14.0	28	47	12
	Mean	2.85	13.5	28.5	45	13.3
Young	NI	7.2	41.7	72	70	—
	SI	7.2	48.4	72	81	11
	EI	7.2	46.9	72	78	8
	VI	7.1	42.8	71	71	1
	Mean	7.18	45.0	71.8	75	6.7

earned significantly higher recall scores under the SI and EI but not the VI condition, whereas the older Ss earned significantly higher recall scores under the SI and VI conditions, and higher, though not significantly so, scores under the EI condition. The young Ss outperformed the old Ss under all conditions, but the old Ss showed greater proportionate improvement than the young in each of the SI, EI and VI conditions in comparison to the NI condition (average 13.3 percent vs. 6.7 percent). Both age groups performed best under the SI condition.

Without instructions to use mediators, the old Ss reported the use of mediators only half as often as the young Ss did (for 36 percent vs. 68 percent of the pairs). When instructed to use mediators, the old and young Ss reported their use for 69 percent and 84 percent of the pairs, respectively. Both age groups performed better on those pairs for which use of mediation was reported. The old Ss averaged 65 percent correct recall on pairs for which mediation was reported in contrast to 13 percent for nonmediated pairs; for the young Ss the corresponding figures were 83 percent and 63 percent. The old Ss reported the use of visual imagery mediators less frequently than the young (for 34 percent vs. 77 percent of the pairs) but reported the use of verbal mediators more frequently than the young (for 26 percent vs. 6 percent of the pairs).

Abstract **22**

Item Concreteness and Age in Paired-Associate Learning

EDWARD J. ROWE, M.A. and MORRIS M. SCHNORE, Ph.D.

"Item Concreteness and Reported Strategies in Paired-Associate Learning as a Function of Age," *Journal of Gerontology*, 1971, *26*, 470-475.

Paivio and his associates have shown that young people use imaginal mediation to a greater extent when one or both members of a pair of words are highly concrete than when both members of the pair are abstract, and that high-imagery word pairs are learned more readily than low-imagery word pairs. The present study examined whether concreteness facilitates the learning of older people and also assessed the spontaneous use of mediators by Ss of different ages for both abstract and concrete pairs of words.

Method

SUBJECTS: Forty-eight females, of whom 16 were young (mean age = 18.4 years), 16 were middle-aged (mean age = 50.4 years) and 16 were old (mean age = 72.8 years) participated. None were institutionalized. Ss were paid for participation.

Materials: The lists to be learned consisted of six pairs of concrete and six pairs of abstract nouns. The abstract nouns had low ratings for concreteness and imagery on the Paivio, Yuille and Madigan norms, while the concrete nouns had high ratings for concreteness and imagery. All were high frequency words and of medium values with respect to meaningfulness. To control for pair difficulty, two different combinations were used for each of the abstract and concrete nouns, and for half the Ss receiving each set, the words of each pair were reversed (i.e., the stimulus item became the response item and vice versa).

PROCEDURE: Each S was tested individually. The words were typed on 4" x 6" index cards, with two words per card for study trials and only the stimulus word on the card for test trials. Study and test trials alternated until two successive errorless test trials or eight test trials, whichever came first. A self-paced schedule was used for both study and test trials; e.g., in study trials, S read each pair aloud, then turned card face down when ready for next pair.

Following the paired-associate task, the S was asked to indicate the method that had been used to connect each pair of words together for recall, using as method categories repetition, verbal mediation, imagery, no method or other method.

Results

A general decline in performance with increasing age was observed for both types of items, but all age groups performed better on the concrete than on the abstract pairs. All age groups used verbal mediation more frequently than imagery for abstract pairs and imagery more frequently than verbal mediation for concrete pairs. Both the young and the middle-aged groups reported the use of mediational strategies more frequently than the old group did. Moreover, the young group reported the use of mediational strategies more frequently for abstract than for concrete pairs, whereas the old reported the use of mediational strategies more frequently for concrete than for abstract pairs. Because the differential between age groups for learning score was greater for abstract than for concrete pairs, it may be that the use of predominantly concrete words in verbal learning and memory studies involving age comparisons serves to underestimate any age effect.

Abstract **23**

Age and Stimulus Meaningfulness

ILENE WITTELS, Ph.D.

"Age and Stimulus Meaningfulness in Paired-Associate Learning," *Journal of Gerontology*, 1972, 27, 372-375.

The "meaningfulness" of words is often determined by measuring the percentage of subjects responding to a stimulus word. The Ss used for assessing meaningfulness in most studies, usually young adults, are not representative of the general population. At least part of the poorer performance on paired-associate tasks of older Ss in comparison to younger Ss may be due to the difference in association values in the words for the old and young. This study tested the hypothesis that by using verbal stimuli approximately equal in "meaningfulness" for both young and old Ss, the typical decline seen in later life in learning paired-associates would be lessened or nonexistent.

Method

SUBJECTS: The 102 Ss were American-born white women in two age groups, 18 to 24 (mean age = 19.7) and 60 to 82 (mean age = 70.9). The younger group was composed of undergraduate students, the older of retired teachers, all of whom had bachelors or masters degrees. All were in apparent good general health and without significant visual or hearing impairments. The two age groups performed similarly on the vocabulary test of the WAIS. Within each age group the Ss were randomly assigned to one of three experimental conditions: *Personal, Generational, and Cross-Generational.*

Materials: The 15 stimulus words for the paired-associate learning were anger, bath, carpet, cottage, eagle, hammer, loud, mutton, needle, rough, stem, swift, thief, and thirsty. Examination of various norms suggested that the stimulus list had little or no inter-item association value.

PROCEDURE: Each S was asked for ten associations to each of the 15 stimulus words. For the *Personal* condition, the paired-associate learning task was made up of the 15 stimulus words paired with the S's own fifth association response to that word. In the *Generational* condition, each S learned a Personal list developed from the responses of one S in her own age group. In the *Cross-Generational* condition each S learned a Personal list of one S in the other age group.

In the paired-associate learning test, the list was presented in four different orders and was administered until the S had three perfect trials, or for a maximum of 15 trials. On the first trial the paired-associate card was shown for four sec. On subsequent trials, the stimulus card was presented until the S responded, for a maximum of four sec.; then the stimulus-response card was shown for one sec.

Results

The two measures of performance were total number of errors and number of trials to criterion, with a maximum of 15 trials. Neither trials nor errors varied as a function of condition. Both trials and errors varied significantly ($p < 0.001$) as a function of age. The young Ss made fewer mean errors (2.94) than the older Ss (10.65) and took fewer mean trials (5.41) than the old (7.90). The hypothesis was not confirmed. Either meaningfulness is not an important variable in comparisons of old and young adults for paired-associate learning, or the techniques used in this study did not achieve the intended equation and variation for meaningfulness.

Abstract **24**

Learning to Learn

DAVID F. HULTSCH, Ph.D.

"Learning to Learn in Adulthood," *Journal of Gerontology*, 1974, *29*, 302-308.

Traditionally, decrements in performance on cognitive tasks with increasing age have been interpreted as the result of universal, intrinsic, biologically-based aging processes. Recently, various investigators have suggested that cognitive decrements during adulthood are a function of nonuniversal, extrinsic and experientially-based antecedents. This study investigated adult age differences in memory performance and memory organization within the framework of a learning-to-learn paradigm. If part of the older individual's cognitive difficulty stems from deterioration of higher order learning skills due to lack of practice, then practice on successive tasks should reduce age differences in performance as the skills needed for effective learning are reacquired.

Three questions were addressed, as follows: (a) Does learning to learn occur at all age levels? (b) Does degree of learning to learn vary as a function of age level? (c) What is the nature of higher order skills involved in learning to learn at the various age levels?

Method

SUBJECTS: The 114 white female Ss were paid volunteers recruited from the community and the university. There were 42 Ss aged 18-27 (mean = 19.62 years) and 18 Ss in each of the following age ranges: 40-49 (mean = 45.50 years), 50-59 (mean = 54-60 years), 60-69 (mean = 65.17 years), and 70-85 (mean = 74.22 years). Apart from the younger group, which earned lower vocabulary scores and had fewer years of education, and the 40- and old groups, which had more years of eduction than the others, the groups were fairly comparable for vocabulary scores and years of education.

Design: A minimum learning-to-learn paradigm consisting of two successive lists was used. The overall design consisted of a 5 (age levels) × 2 (lists) × 5 (blocks of two trials) model with repeated measures on the last two factors.

Lists: The three 30-word lists of nouns were equated with reference to frequency-of-occurrence and imagery categories. The three possible combinations of two lists were used equally often within each age range, and the order of individual lists within combinations was completely counter-balanced.

PROCEDURE: All Ss were tested individually. Practice on each of the lists consisted of ten study-test cycles. For each cycle the study phase consisted of one presentation of the 30 words, each word appearing for 1.5 sec.; the test phase consisted of written recall and was terminated after a pause of 1.5 min. during which no words were recalled. Order of presentation was constant for the study trials, and Ss were permitted to recall the words in any order. There was a four-min. interval between the two lists.

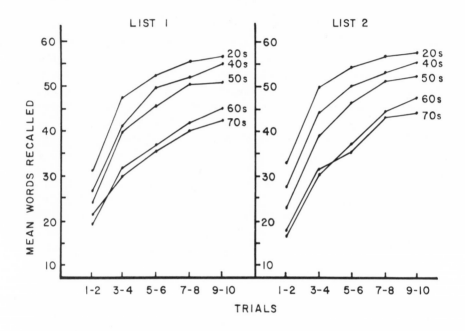

Results and Discussion

The mean number of words correctly recalled as a function of age levels, lists and trials is shown in Figure 1. Differences between age groups were significant ($p < 0.001$), with the greatest difference occuring between the 50-and 60-year-old groups. List II performance was superior to List I performance at all age levels ($p < 0.001$). Thus, even with a minimum amount of practice, learning to learn was observed across the age range. However, the degree of learning to learn varied as a function of age and stage of learning ($p < 0.001$). Contrary to intuitive expectations, the older Ss did not show greater improvement from list I to list II than the younger Ss. Indeed, for the oldest group, list II scores were significantly lower than list I for the initial learning trials. The reverse was true late in the learning process. In contrast, for the youngest group. list II scores were significantly higher than list I scores at all points in the learning process. The other age levels showed a transition from one pattern to the other. These data suggest that despite the selection of materials to minimize sources of specific inter-list negative transfer, the older Ss experienced negative transfer in the early stages of list II learning. Other research has indicated that older people are more susceptible to interference than young people are. However, by the later stages of learning, learning-to-learn effects became apparent to the degree that list II scores were superior to list I scores for all age groups.

Also computed were two measures of organization designed to assess how Ss organized the material in relation to the structure of the input (input-output organization) and the structure of their output on the preceding trial (output-output organization). The first measure reflects degree of concordance between order of presentation and order of recall, the second, degree of concordance between order of recall on successive trials. For both organization measures, there was a decline in score as a function of increased age ($p<0.001$). Also, for both measures, increases in number of words recalled from list I to list II were paralleled by increases in organization. Ss at all ages showed higher organization scores on list II than on list I at all points in the learning process. These data also suggest that the older Ss' decrease in performance from list I to list II in the initial stages of learning was a function of interference rather than the unavailability of high order skills involved in learning to learn.

Because these results demonstrate that older adults exhibit significant learning-to-learn effects even under conditions of limited practice, it would be relevant to investigate the limits of improvement under conditions of extensive practice, and the extent to which these effects transfer to different types of problems, and to specify further the nature of the organizational processes involved in learning to learn.

Abstract **25**

Practice and Age Differences in Reaction Time

F. Hywel Murrell, M.A.

"The Effect of Extensive Practice on Age Differences in Reaction Time," *Journal of Gerontology*, 1970, *25*, 268-274.

Many experiments have demonstrated the inferiority of older persons to younger persons on various performance tasks. The reported differences may, however, represent not only initial differences in the ability being tested but also differences in capacity to meet an unfamiliar situation. This study was conducted to examine the effect of extensive practice on age differences in reaction time.

Method

SUBJECTS: Three females, aged 57, 18 and 17 years, all of whom were naïve with respect to the experimental task, served as subjects.

Apparatus: The display consisted of a vertical semi-circle of eight lights, with a corresponding horizontal semi-circle of brass discs on the response panel, at the center of which was a start disc. The S held a stylus on the start disc. When a stimulus light came on, the S was required to move the stylus as quickly as possible to the corresponding response disc. The interval between the onset of the light and the stylus leaving the start disc was recorded to the nearest ten msec. Discs could be covered to allow for any number of choices from one to eight. A buzzer gave a fore-period of one sec.

PROCEDURE: The experiment was planned to measure the effect on RIT (Response Initiation Time) of spaced practice over a total of 20,000 responses under one-choice, two-choice and eight-choice conditions. However, the 57-year-old S died after she had made 16,250 responses and the other Ss had made 12,500 and 13,500 responses respectively. Data collection was terminated at that time. Generally, daily sittings were held with either 100 to 150 RIT measurements per day. However, there was no testing on weekends, nor when Ss were on vacation or were sick; gaps in testing of one and two months occurred.

Results

The younger Ss showed improvement almost from the beginning but the older S remained essentially at the initial level for the first 300 responses, prior to demonstrating improvement. Initially, the older S's responses were significantly slower than those of the two young Ss. In the one-choice condition, the initial differences disappeared after 500 responses, and thereafter there were no systematic differences between Ss. In the two-choice condition, the 57-year-old S was slower than one of the young Ss until 5,000 responses had been made, and slower than the other until 10,250 responses had been made, but subsequently was faster than either of them. In the eight-choice situation, the 57-year-old S was slower than the two younger Ss until 8,000 and 10,250 responses had been made, and thereafter was faster than either of them. Thus, age differences were related to amount of practice and complexity of the task (number of choices). When the Ss were well practiced, breaks of up to two months resulted in little loss of speed.

When the subjects were naïve, age differences were substantial. However, the differences were largely eliminated, and even partially reversed by practice in this experiment. Thus, experiments conducted without extensive practice may yield results that are inapplicable to experienced individuals.

Abstract 26

Practice of Speeded Responses

JACK BOTWINICK, Ph.D. and LARRY W. THOMPSON, Ph.D.

"Practice of Speeded Response in Relation to Age, Sex and Set," *Journal of Gerontology*, 1967, 22, 72-76.

The study of speed of response has been prominent in the effort to understand the aging process. However, little attention has been devoted to problems of measurement of speed of response in relation to age. Understanding of the significance of rate of responding is perhaps impossible without knowledge about problems of measurement of the behavior in question. In this study speed of response, measured as simple auditory reaction time (RT), was examined as it changed with practice, and these changes were examined as a function of age and sex in the context of anticipatory RT set.

Method

SUBJECTS: The Ss were 58 men and 54 women, of whom 52 were elderly (67 to 92 years) and 60 were young (18 to 35 years). All had at least 12 years of education and none was institutionalized.

PROCEDURE: All Ss were seen individually. Ss within both age categories were assigned to one of three conditions which varied with respect to preparatory interval (PI). One group experienced a regular 0.5 sec. PI, a second group a regular 15.0 sec. PI, and a third group experienced an irregular series comprising PIs of 0.5, 3.0, 6.0, and 15.0 sec. A regular PI is an interval of time that is constant between a warning signal and stimulus; an irregular series involves PIs that are varied from trial to trial. Both warning signals and the stimulus to which the S was to respond were tones. RT was measured as the time from onset of the stimulus until the S raised his finger to terminate the stimulus. There were 21 trials in each of the regular PI conditions and 85 trials in the irregular PI condition. Median RT for each block of five or six trials was computed for each S.

Results

The results indicated that RT varies with practice, and this variation is a function of preparatory set as defined by the PI duration and the context of the PI. Moreover, the age and sex of the S modify these relationships. Although overall the old were slower than the young, the elderly men and women tended to be excessively slow on the first five trials of the 0.5 sec. regular PI. This observation introduces the need to re-evaluate studies of set in relation to age when the focus is on short duration PIs and especially if a short series of trials was given, or the trials early in the series were weighted heavily.

The sex of Ss had differential effects in practice of RT. With the regular 15.0 sec. PI, younger women tended to become slower with the last block of trials. It was in the irregular seris of PIs that sex effects were most apparent, particularly with respect to the 0.5 sec. interval. Both young and elderly women improved with practice in a way that men did not, indicating that women were not as adequate as men in responding quickly to a short, uncertain time-interval without some experience. Men required little warm-up.

Analysis of the RT data of the irregular series without regard to PI indicated that in general young men and young women did not differ with respect to practice, but elderly men and women did. Therefore, the aging patterns of practice effects were different for men and women.

No explanation is offered for these interactions. However, it seems clear that if measurement of speed of response is to be meaningful in its applicability, the role of practice, age of S, sex of S and condition of preparatory set must be specified as part of the operations of measurement.

Abstract **27**

Learning by Mature and Aged Rats

CHARLES L. GOODRICH, Ph.D.

"Learning by Mature, Young and Aged Wistar Albino Rats
as a Function of Test Complexity," *Journal of Gerontology,*
1972, 27, 353-357.

Most research studies have failed to obtain age differences in learning for
young and old rats. Studies that have not obtained consistent age differences have generally used relatively simple tasks of low complexity; in
studies that obtained age differences, the tasks have been more complex.
The purpose of this research was to compare tests that vary in complexity, in
order to determine a test appropriate for the study of age differences in
learning ability. The tests used were a straight runway, and one-choice,
four-choice, and 14-choice-point mazes.

Experiment I (Straight Runway)

SUBJECTS: Eighteen Wistar female albino rats, nine aged eight months and
nine aged 27 months. Young and aged rats were maintained at 80% and
75% respectively for predeprivation weight.

Apparatus: A straight runway, 30 inches long, excluding start and goal
chambers.

PROCEDURE: Ss were adapted to the reward solution (condensed milk-10
gm sucrose/100 ml) in the home cage for four days prior to testing. Fifteen
seconds after release in the start box the panel was raised to allow access to
the runway. Time to reach the reward in the goal box was recorded. After
completion of drinking (10 to 15 seconds), the S was removed. Each S was
given four trials per day on four consecutive days, with one hour between
trials.

Results

Time scores were quickly reduced between and within days, but age differences were not significant.

Experiment II (One-Unit T-Maze)

SUBJECTS: Ss were 32 Wistar male albino rats, 16 aged eight months and 16 aged 27 months. Maintenance and test experience were the same as in Experiment I.

Apparatus: A 1-unit T-Maze. The reward solution was placed at the end of one of the goal chambers on each trial.

PROCEDURE: The same as in Experiment I, except that five consecutive trials (a series) were given during each of four days of training. On the initial trial both goal chambers contained the reward solution. The initial choice chamber was correct on all subsequent trials.

Results

Young and aged rats did not differ significantly in percentage of correct responses, time to reach the reward, or alternation behavior.

Experiment III (Four-Choice Problems)

SUBJECTS: Forty Wistar albino rats, eight and 27 months old, with 20 rats at each age (ten male and ten female). Maintenance and test experience were the same as in Experiment I.

Apparatus: Four maze problems were devised by means of barriers and blocks within a 25-inch square open field. The length from start to goal was 60 inches for all problems and each problem had four choice points.

PROCEDURE: The same adaptation procedure was used as in Experiment I. The Ss were tested on four consecutive days, with a different problem randomly assigned each day. For each problem there were four repeated tests (a series) with one hour between each test. Scores were obtained for time to reach the goal and number of errors (a wrong turn or reversal of direction in relation to goal) per trial.

Results

Age differences were not statistically significant for time scores during the four trials of the first series, but differences between age groups increased on the initial trial of series 2, 3 and 4 with group differences statistically significant on Trial 1 of Series 4 ($p<0.01$). During the later trials age differences were small and not statistically significant. The mature-young rats made significantly fewer errors than the aged rats ($p<0.01$); the major differences in error scores were obtained on Trial 1 of the last three test series.

Experiment IV (14-Choice T-Maze)

SUBJECTS: Thirty-two Wistar male albinos, six and 26 months old, with 16 in each age group.

Apparatus: A 14-unit T-maze.

PROCEDURE: Initial adaptation was similar to that in Experiment I and also included being adapted to run the length of a 48-inch-long straight runway to obtain reward. The rats were tested for one trial per day for 20 days in the 14-unit maze. Time to traverse the maze and errors were recorded. Errors were plotted for each S as a function of choice point and trial. Six consecutive errors at a specific choice point was the criterion for a perservative response.

Results

On the initial trials the two age groups did not differ significantly, but on Trials 16 to 20 the mature-young rats made significantly fewer errors and had lower time scores than the aged rats ($p < 0.01$). The aged rats also made significantly more perservative errors than the mature-young rats did ($p < 0.001$).

Conclusion

The major finding of these experiments was that age differences in learning were obtained for a task with a high degree of complexity, but not for relatively simple tasks. The 14-unit T-maze represents a minimum level of difficulty for basic studies of the learning process and variables that may reduce maze acquisition differences between mature-young and aged rats.

Abstract **28**

Age Differences in the Effects of Starvation

LEONARD F. JAKUBCZAK, Ph.D.

"Age Differences in the Effects of Terminal Food Deprivation (Starvation) on Activity, Weight Loss and Survival of Rats," *Journal of Gerontology*, 1967, *22*, 421-426.

Information about the relationship between age and the drive-inducing function of food deprivation is needed to further understanding of the relationship between age and various behaviors such as age and learning performance. Some studies have indicated that the degree to which a given *duration* of food deprivation induces drive is directly related to growth rate, and thus is inversely related to age; however, these studies did not include old adults. This study investigated the effects of food deprivation on the activity of rats over their entire life span, and also compared the utility of relative body weight loss with hours of deprivation as alternative ways of specifying the intensity of drive in the study of age differences in behavior.

Method

SUBJECTS: Five age groups (2-, 3-, 6-, 11-, and 26-month-old) of experimentally naïve Sprague-Dawley male rats, with at least 16 rats per age group, were randomly assigned to control or experimental conditions.
PROCEDURE: After a three-week period of adaptation to Wahmann activity wheels, food was totally withdrawn from the experimental animals while the control group had continual access to food. Number of wheel revolutions, body weight, and survival were determined at 14:00 daily for each rat throughout both the predeprivation and deprivation periods.

Results

With increasing deprivation, each rat increased its running activity to a maximum, which was followed by a rapid terminal decline. Thus it was possible to determine initial activity, maximum activity, increase per day to maximum activity, days to maximum, and weight loss at maximum. To control for age differences in growth rate, the mean percentage of increase in body weight of the control Ss on a particular day was added to the percentage weight loss of each experimental S.

Initial and maximum levels of activity, the increase of activity per day to maximum, and the percentage of weight loss decreased with age to six months but were not related to age thereafter. Days of deprivation to maximum activity levels and the survival time increased with age to six months but did not vary among older groups. The age groups did not differ for percentage of weight loss at maximum activity, the percentage of weight loss at death, the relationship between percentage of weight loss and maximum activity, or the relationship between percentage of weight loss and survival time.

These results suggest that percentage of body weight loss is a more comparable way of specifying degree of need and drive resulting from food deprivation in rats of different ages than is duration of deprivation.

Abstract **29**

Environment Effects on Avoidance Behavior

BARBARA A. DOTY, Ph.D.

"The Effects of Cage Environment Upon Avoidance Responding of Aged Rats," *Journal of Gerontology*, 1972, *27*, 358-360.

There is evidence that external environmental stimulation early in life facilitates subsequent performance on a variety of tasks. The effects of similar treatments applied later in the life-span are largely unknown, though it has been assumed that to be maximally effective, environmental manipulations must be conducted in the initial stages of development. This study was undertaken to determine whether the performance of aged rats is affected by prolonged exposure to "enriched" environment in mid-life. Because the behavior of aged organisms is sometimes characterized as rigid and stereotyped, it is of particular interest to determine whether environmental enrichment increases the behavioral "flexibility" of aged animals.

Method

SUBJECTS AND DESIGN: Ss were 18 male and 18 female Sprague-Dawley rats, 300 days old at the beginning of the experiment. Littermates were randomly assigned to an enriched or a control group. Half the Ss in each group were selected randomly for pretesting on learning tasks on which all Ss were tested after treatment. The enriched environments consisted of two wire, mesh-covered plastic toy swimming pools, 4 ft. in diameter, containing an assortment of dime-store toys and objects, and lined with cedar shavings. Nine male and nine female rats lived in same-sex groups in one of the two enriched environments for 360 days, beginning when they were 300 days old. The 18 control group Ss lived in same-sex pairs in standard 12-in.-square wire laboratory cages.

PROCEDURE: Data were collected throughout the experiment on food and water consumption and body weights. Prior to testing on the learning tasks, Ss were tested for gross behavioral responses (flinch and jump) to painful shock to determine whether these reactions alone are affected by age and enrichment.

Three avoidance learning procedures were used with the same order of task presentation for all Ss: discriminated (light-dark) active conditional avoidance, discriminated avoidance reversal, and passive avoidance. On the discriminated avoidance task, the Ss had to run to one of two compartments of a two-way shuttle box within 5 seconds after presentation of a light (CS) in one of the compartments to avoid shock to the feet (UCS). Running to the unlighted area was correct for the remaining animals. When the criterion of eight avoidances in ten trials had been met, reversal training began and the S had to respond to the alternate cue. When the S learned reversal to criterion (eight avoidances in ten trials) passive avoidance training was initiated. On this task, the S had to remain in the start compartment on the presentation of a light CS to avoid foot shock. Again, the criterion was eight avoidances on ten consecutive trials. Ss ran 30 trials a day on each task until criterion was reached. One day elapsed between training on successive tasks.

Results

Treatment groups did not differ for pain-threshold responses or for food and water consumption. However, the Ss in both of the enriched groups weighed less ($p < .05$) than the control rats at posttesting, perhaps because of greater opportunity to exercise freely.

Mean avoidance responses performed by all groups for the three avoidance learning tasks are shown in Table 1. The main components for the 2 x 3 x 2 analyses of variance were pretesting, task, and environment (cage versus enrichment).

Table 1.
Mean Trials Run to Criterion by All Ss
on Three Avoidance Tasks

Treatment Group	Pretest Scores			Post-test Scores		
	Driscriminated Avoidance	Avoidance Reversal	Passive Avoidance	Discriminated Avoidance	Avoidance Reversal	Passive Avoidance
Enrichment - Pretested	53.6	92.6	24.6	58.3	78.4	27.6
Enrichment - No Pretest				53.2	83.3	25.4
Control - Pretested	54.2	97.3	28.3	61.3	114.6	40.2
Control - No Pretest				64.8	127.4	38.7

The only significant effect of pretesting on posttest scores was on the posttest performance of the control group rats for the discrimination reversal task. Both pretest and posttest performance varied substantially with the type of learning task (p<.001); the passive avoidance task was the easiest, followed by the discrimination task and the reversal problem. Environmental enrichment with and without pretesting resulted in superior posttest performance on the discrimination reversal and passive avoidance problems; it failed to alter discriminated avoidance responses.

Rats in the enriched groups also made fewer posttest errors than the control group animals on the discrimination reversal and passive avoidance tasks. Rats in both control groups made more incorrect avoidances (performing the previously rewarded response) than did the enriched group animals.

The avoidance data demonstrate that environmental stimulation facilitates the performance of aged rats on a response reversal task, and to a lesser extent on a passive avoidance problem. Perhaps living in laboratory cages impairs the rat's capacity to shift his behavior in recognition of new reinforcement contingencies.

Abstract **30**

Age Changes in Aversive Learning in Rats

CARL I. THOMPSON, Ph.D. and THOMAS R. FITZSIMONS, M.D.

"Age Differences in Aversively Motivated Visual Discrimination Learning and Retention in Male Sprague-Dawley Rats," *Journal of Gerontology*, 1976, *31*, 47-52.

The results of several studies suggest that as rodents approach old age their performance on active avoidance tasks deteriorates. However, when Ray and Barrett (1973) counted the number of correct initial responses in a discrimination situation, regardless of whether an avoidance had occurred, they found that year-old rats performed as well as younger rats. They suggested that avoidance scores may reflect performance factors rather than learning decrements. This reopened the question concerning whether aging animals suffer any actual learning deficits on shock-motivated discriminations. The present study explored whether the correct initial choice measure might reveal age-related differences when rats much older than the year-old rats used by Ray and Barrett served as subjects.

Method

SUBJECTS: The subjects were 43 male albino Sprague-Dawley rats of the following ages: three mo. (post-pubescent, N = 7), seven mo. (young adult, N = 11), 12 mo. (middle-aged, N = 14), and 24.5 mo. (senscent, N = 11). All were experimentally naïve.

Apparatus: Animals were trained in a four-unit discrimination box, consisting of a start box, four two-choice discrimination units, and a goal box. The grid floor was connected to a scrambled shock source. Within each of the two-choice compartments, either of the two exit passageways could be kept dark or could be lighted.

PROCEDURE: On the first day, Ss were given a 15-minute habituation period to explore the discrimination box with all barriers removed and all exit passages illuminated. Pretraining, administered on the second day, involved training the S to escape from a blocked alley by administering a brief train of shocks whenever he came into contact with a blocked exit until he escaped through an open alley.

Discrimination training began 24 hours after pretraining. On each trial one randomly chosen exit in each discrimination unit was lit, and a barrier was placed across the oppposite darkened exit. A brief shock was administered every five sec. until the rat had left the start box and, after a ten sec. delay, every five sec. at the choice point if the rat was not moving, and continually, as long as the rat was in an incorrect alley. Thus, the rat could avoid the shock entirely if he moved within five sec. and then took no longer than ten sec. to make each of the four successive discriminations. No attempt was made to monitor whether shock was avoided. Only the correctness of the initial response at each choice point was recorded.

Each S had ten trials, with a total of 40 discriminations a day. The criterion for learning was 11 correct responses within a series of any 12 consecutive discriminations.

Eight days after the 11/12 criterion was reached rats were tested for retention of discrimination, and the training procedure continued until an 11/12 criterion was reached again.

Results

Figure 1 presents the mean number of trials to criterion for the four age groups for both learning and relearning the discrimination task to criterion. Trials to criterion increased with advancing age, both for learning ($p < 0.01$) and relearning ($p < 0.02$). These results indicate that although senescent rats eventually meet criterion on a shock-motivated light-dark discrimination task, they learn this discrimination at a slower rate than younger animals. This deficit appears even when the correct initial response measure is used. In addition, eight days after having reached the learning criterion, older rats appear to retain less of what they have learned.

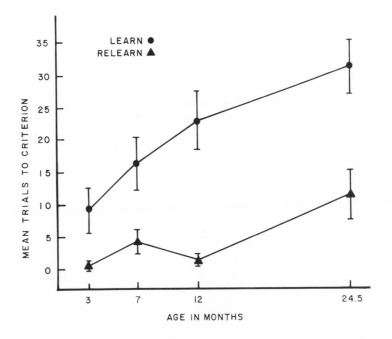

CHAPTER V

Memory

Abstract 31

In Search of Early Memories

DAVID SCHONFIELD, M.A.

"In Search of Early Memories." Paper presented at the International Congress of Gerontology, Washington, D.C., 1969.

The assumption that with advanced age there is a greater decline in memory for recent events than for remote events is based largely on hearsay evidence, because the recall of "old" memories reflects a biased sample of the population of past incidences. Choice of which remote memory to recount is ordinarily left to the recollector. On the other hand, the inability of older persons to recall specific items of recently acquired information tends to be emphasized, whereas the wealth of knowledge retained tends to be ignored. To investigate the effects of age on memory for remote events, a roughly equivalent population of remote events for younger and older people is needed. The names of one's own school teachers seemed to serve this purpose. The question posed for this study was "Do we remember more, less, or as many names of our own teachers as we grow older?"

Method

SUBJECTS: The Ss were 195 noninstitutionalized persons, with a minimum of 25 Ss in each decade from 20 to 70 and over 70 years of age. No attempt was made to equate Ss in the different decades.

PROCEDURE: Each S was tested individually and was asked his age, when he had left school, number of teachers in each grade, sex of each of the teachers that had been mentioned and, the important question, the names of his teachers. Notes were taken on teachers who had taught more than one grade, and if one grade had more than one teacher. Ss were also asked to name teachers they had met since their school days.

Results

Results were based on the proportion of names recalled to possible number of recallable names. Separate calculations were made for Grades I to VI and for all grades, as some Ss did not go beyond the sixth grade, and primary schools seemed to resemble each other more than high schools did. Because the sixty-year-old group included a disproportionately high number of professional teachers, and because teachers were more likely than others to have encountered the names of their own former teachers during their careers, the recall scores were also examined with all teacher Ss excluded.

Table 1
Proportion of Possible Names Recalled

| Age | | Grades | | | | Excluding Teachers | | |
| | | I-VI | | All Grades | | All Grades | | |
	N	M	SD	M	SD	N	M	SD
20-29	46	.71	.32	.67	.26	42	.67	.26
30-39	25	.66	.36	.54	.51	22	.56	.32
40-49	31	.63	.39	.52	.33	29	.52	.34
50-59	39	.59	.35	.55	.31	33	.50	.31
60-69	28	.62	.32	.60	.28	13	.50	.30
70+	20	.54	.37	.53	.33	20	.45	.31

The results are summarized in Table 1. When all Ss were included, the rank order for mean recall was generally inversely related to rank order for age, with the exception of the 60-year-old group. However, the standard deviations were high, for in every age group some Ss earned perfect scores and some Ss remembered no names. The product moment correlations for age and proportion of names recalled, though significant, were only 0.15 for Grades I to VI and 0.20 for all grades. When teachers were excluded, there was a consistent loss by age groups in proportion of names recalled, with the exception of one tied mean score.

These results suggest there is some loss with age in the ability to recall previously well-known names. However, the evidence for ability to recall is more impressive than the evidence for forgetting.

Abstract **32**

Recall After Sixty Years

MANDORAH E. SMITH, Ph.D.

"Delayed Recall of Previously Remembered Material after Fifty Years,"*Journal of Genetic Psychology*, 1963, *102*, 3-4.

How well does one remember in late adulthood material that was well learned in childhood?

Method

SUBJECT: There was only one subject, who also served as the investigator.

Procedure: The 107 answers to the questions of the Westminster Shorter Catechism were learned so thoroughly that they were repeated perfectly at one sitting shortly before the S's thirteenth birthday. During the next ten years there was considerable incidental practice of the earlier portion of the catechism, but not of the latter part. The repetition of answers was undertaken again when the S was 47, 63 and 73 years of age. Apart from these attempts at repetition, and the practice on the earlier portion of the catechism until age 23, the only incidental practice was quoting from the Bible, as in naming the ten commandments. The 107 answers were scored for difficulty on a seven-point scale.

Table 1
Recall Scores at Different Ages

	Age and Date			
	13 (1900)	47 (1934)	63 (1950)	73 (1960)
Remembered	107	54	53	41
Prompted Once		44	39	32
Partly Forgotten		9	15	34

Results

Table 1 summarizes recall scores at different ages. Although by age 73, 34 of the answers required more than one prompting, none of the answers was completely forgotten. The answers that were partly forgotten tended to be the more difficult ones and those that had not received incidental practice during early adulthood. The decrease in recall score was more marked from age 63 to age 73 than from age 47 to age 63. Nevertheless, at age 73, 68 percent of the answers were recalled perfectly, with no more than one prompting.

Abstract 33

Recent Memory of Centenarians

BELLA BOONE BEARD, Ph.D.

"Some Characteristics of Recent Memory of Centenarians,"*Journal of Gerontology*,1968, 23, 23-30.

This study explored some of the parameters of recent memory after 100 years of age. The specific questions were: (1) How do 100-year-olds perform on standard memory tests? (2) What are the social and psychological correlates of maintenance of memory to extreme old age?

Method

SUBJECTS: The Ss were 62 men and 104 women selected from a larger sample of 485 persons over 100 years of age on the basis of completeness of social history taken in conjunction with another study. The sample population was representative of the 485 person pool of potential Ss. All but two of the centenarians were interviewed in their own homes. For some Ss there were several interviews.

Materials: Tests for recent memory included: (1) digits forward—five or more; (2) digits backward—four or more; (3) memory for previous meal—at least three items checked against actual menu; (4) naming of current President of the United States—last name; (5) three incidents that happened in the past week; (6) ability to perform tasks that require at least four steps in sequence, e.g., playing bridge, following a recipe, carpentry instructions or crochet pattern; evidence of actual performance or corroboration by others was required; (7) memory of interviewer's name—last name. Responses were classified as "good" if performance was at the designated level.

Tests for stored memory included: (1) designation of dates of World War I and the Spanish American War, with an error of no greater than five years; (2) memory for at least four lines of any song or poem; (3) interest in politics—naming party and candidates or platform.

Indications of social awareness included: (1) favors versus disfavors the new as compared to the old for at least two of changes in dress, manners, food preparation and gadgets; (2) writes letters or telephones family or friends at least once a week; (3) attends church or social events at least once a month.

Performance scores were assessed as a function of age, education, sex, and self-evaluation of health.

Data from a different study involving 402 persons aged 95 to 99 permitted a comparison between those over and those under 100 years of age.

Table 1
Tasks at the Designated Level of Competence

Task	Male %	Female %	Total %
1. Digits forward - 5 or more	62.2	59.1	60.3
2. Digits backward - 4 or more	57.0	46.4	49.8
3. Memory of previous meal - 3 items	78.2	81.0	80.7
4. President of U.S. - last name	87.4	74.2	81.8
5. Recount 3 recent incidents	84.3	80.4	81.6
6. Follow sequence of 4 or more steps	60.8	50.5	53.9
7. Remember interviewer's last name	46.7	53.3	50.0

Results

Table 1 gives the percentage of men and women able to perform specified activities designed to assess recent memory. Males performed significantly better than females on digits backward and naming the President. Persons with education beyond grammar school performed better than those with less education for all but the food at previous meal and three recent events items. Persons with good ratings for self-evaluation of health outperformed those with poor health ratings on all of the tests except digits forward. Within the age range studied there was an age difference for only one of the items; people 103 years and over remembered recent events better than those aged 100 to 102! Also, persons in the present study, all aged over 100, recalled more events of national importance than persons aged 95 to 99 in an earlier study.

Performance on the digits forward, digits backwards, and memory for the President's name tests was significantly related to one or more of the social awareness measures.

In general, persons who performed well on the recent memory tests also performed well on the stored memory tests. Persons who performed well on the digit forward and the digit backwards tests performed exceptionally well on the stored memory tests. These data suggest that recent memory is not a separate phenomenon but a function of memory in general.

A surprisingly large number of centenarians played bridge, chess and checkers, kept their own financial records, did their own shopping, and even made dresses and furniture, all following steps without assistance.

Abstract 34

Patterns of Declining Memory

JEANNE G. GILBERT, Ph.D. and RAYMOND F. LEVEE, Ph.D.

"Patterns of Declining Memory," *Journal of Gerontology*, 1971, *26*, 70-75.

Scientific investigations and popular observations have long noted that most cognitive abilities tend to decline with advancing age, and nowhere has this been more evident than in the area of memory. However, memory is not a unitary function. Because the amount of loss occurring with advancing age depends on the type of material used and the kind of learning or memory involved, memory impairment with aging should not be spoken of in a general way, nor can it be measured by using a single test, such as memory for design, digit span or paired associates, nor by combining diverse tests in which serious loss in a particular type of memory might be obscured by relatively good functioning in other areas of memory. In the present study it was hypothesized that, if diverse tests should be given to a group of the same individuals and measured separately, the pattern of differential loss would become more evident.

Method

SUBJECTS: Four hundred persons aged 20-34, 111 persons aged 35-49, 102 persons aged 50-59, and 103 persons aged 60-75. Age groups were equated for score on the vocabulary subtest of the Wechsler Adult Intelligence Scale.

Materials: The Guild Memory Test, composed of six separate subtests as follows: immediate recall of meaningful verbal material (two paragraphs); delayed recall (retention) of meaningful verbal material; immediate recall of newly-formed associations (paired-associates); delayed recall (retention) of newly-formed associations; immediate rote memory (memory span for digits); nonverbal memory (memory for designs).

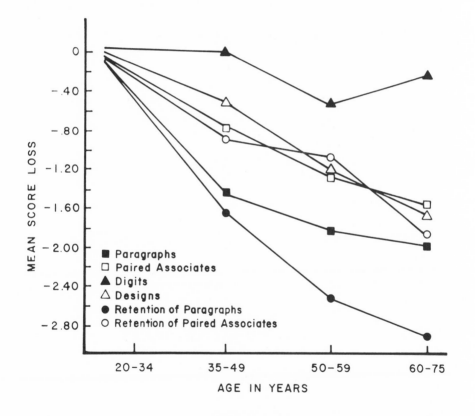

Results

Mean score loss in comparison to the 20- to 34-year-old group is presented graphically in Figure 1 for each of the other age groups for each of the six tests. The 35-49 age group earned significantly lower scores than the 20-34 age group on five of the six tests; only on the immediate rote memory (digit span) test was there no evidence of decline. In comparison to the 35-49 age group, the 50-59 age group earned significantly lower scores on four of the tests (the immediate recall of newly formed associations, immediate rote memory, nonverbal memory, and delayed recall of meaningful material tests) and slight but nonsignificant decline on the other two tests (immediate recall of meaningful verbal material and delayed recall of newly formed associations). In comparison to the 50-59 age group, the 60-75 age group performed significantly less well on only one of the tests (delayed recall of newly formed associations), slightly but not significantly better on one test (immediate rote memory) and showed a nonsignificant decline in score on the other four tests.

As Figure 1 and the statistical analyses indicate, the pattern of decline differs from test to test, with immediate rote memory varying relatively little as a function of age, whereas the age-related decline in score on the delayed recall of meaningful verbal material is very marked and progressive. These data suggest that for several types of memory there is a sharp decline after age 34 which continues at a slower rate during the 50's and at a still slower rate during the period from age 60 to age 75. The differential amount and pattern of decline from age 20-34 to age 60-75 emphasizes the importance of considering memory as a multi-faceted function rather than a unitary factor.

Abstract **35**

Differences in Interference Effects

IRENE M. HULICKA, Ph.D.

"Age Differences in Retention as a Functioning of Interference," *Journal of Gerontology*, 1967, 22, 180-184.

Are older people more susceptible than young people to interference from new learning on the recall of old learning? Although such an assumption has been offered as a partial explanation for a decline in memory efficiency, the alleged phenomenon has not been thoroughly investigated. It has been demonstrated with young people that interference effects vary inversely with the degree of learning and there is evidence that, in general, learning efficiency decreases with age. In most nonlaboratory situations, equal opportunity to learn rather than learning to criterion conditions prevail; hence, older people may learn the material less well and thus be more susceptible to interference effects. However, if material were learned to the same criterion, age differences in interference effects would perhaps be minimal. This possibility was investigated.

Method

Design: A 2 (age) × 2 (equal learning opportunity vs. trials to criterion) × (interpolated vs. no interpolated learning) design was used. In the equal opportunity to learn condition all Ss had six trials on List 1; the trials to criterion condition required one errorless trial on List 1. In the interpolated learning condition, Ss learned List 2 to criterion. All Ss relearned List 1 to criterion.

SUBJECTS: There were 80 Ss, 40 aged 65 to 85 years (mean = 70) and 40 aged 15 to 17 years (mean = 15.6); ten Ss were assigned to each of eight subgroups with matching by group for vocabulary score, education, and male-female distribution. Ss were recruited for a nominal fee from the community. One young and 12 elderly Ss were replaced for failure to reach criterion in 15 trials, inability to comprehend instructions, visual impairment or very low vocabulary score.

Materials: Each of the seven paired-associates for List 1 (OL) consisted of an occupational title and a one-syllable surname, e.g., TEACHER - WOOD, DOCTOR - BATES. List 2 (IL) used the same occupational titles with different surnames, e.g., TEACHER - CARR, DOCTOR - HUFF. Ss were told that the investigation concerned the problem some people have in remembering names. They were asked to assume they had moved to a new town and had to learn the names of people in different positions. For List 2, they were asked to assume they had again moved and had to learn a new set of names. Ss seemed to enjoy the task, whereas in preliminary testing with meaningless paired associates (e.g., TL - INSANE) many older Ss had complained.

PROCEDURE: Ss were tested individually and practice lists were administered. For all conditions, flip cards were used to present the stimulus alone for six sec. or until the S responded, and the stimulus and response together for five sec. The inter-trial and inter-list intervals were two sec. and one min., respectively. Items within lists were randomized. Ss were told whether there would be 6 trials or trials would continue to one perfect repetition. The recall and relearning of List 1 began exactly 30 mins. after completion of trials on List 1.

Table 1
Means for Number Correct or Trials to Criterion

| | List 1 | | List 2 | Relearn | List 1 |
| | | Correct | | | Correct |
	Trials	T1-6	Trials	Trials	T1
Equal opportunity groups					
Interpolated learning					
Young		32.7	2.4	1.7	5.9
Old		30.4	5.8	5.2	3.4
No interpolated learning					
Young		32.7		1.8	6.2
Old		29.6		3.9	5.8
Trials to criterion groups					
Interpolated learning					
Young	3.1		2.4	3.0	4.5
Old	6.4		7.7	6.2	3.4
No interpolated learning					
Young	3.2			2.2	6.0
Old	8.5			2.9	5.5

Results

Table 1 summarizes the results. For both learning conditions, the interpolation of List 2 lowered recall scores (number correct on Trial 1 for relearning of List 1) for both age groups. Under the equal opportunity condition, the interpolation of new material between learning and recall had a differentially negative effect on the recall scores of the elderly Ss (age × condition interaction, $p < 0.01$). However, under the learning to criterion condition, the effects of the interpolation of List 2 on the recall of List 1 were not related to age. These results suggest that when material is learned to the same criterion, older Ss are not more susceptible to interference than young Ss.

Number and types of errors were also examined. During the relearning of List 1, for the equal opportunity, interpolated learning condition, older Ss made proportionately more interference errors (List 2 responses) than the young, but there were no age differences for proportion of interference errors under the corresponding learning to criterion condition. The error data thus also support the hypothesis that observed age differences in interference effects probably reflect the differential degree of original learning rather than increased susceptibility to interference with advanced age.

Several investigators have reported that older people tend to make more "no response" errors than young people do, and this observation has been interpreted as reflecting increased cautiousness with age. In this study, although the absolute number of errors made by old people in the three learning phases (List 1, List 2, and relearning List 1) was greater than that of the young, the proportion of errors of the "no response" type was actually somewhat lower than for the young. A substantial response interval (six sec.) may account for the relatively low proportion of "no response" errors by older people. Perhaps slowness rather than cautiousness may account for the higher proportion of "no response" errors in other studies.

Although these results suggest that degree of original learning rather than aging *per se* accounts for age differences in interference effects, ordinarily older people function under the equal opportunity rather than the learning to criterion condition, and hence, interference may indeed be a salient factor in explaining observed age differences in recall.

Abstract 36

Age Differences in Retroaction

DAVID ARENBERG, Ph.D.

"Age Differences in Retroaction," *Journal of Gerontology,* 1967, 22, 88-91.

Although interference has been used frequently as an explanatory concept to account for age differences in learning and retention, the relationship between verbal retroaction and adult age has not been subjected to much study. (Retroaction refers to the effect of an interpolated task on the recall or relearning of previously learned material.) One set of investigators reported small or no age differences in retroaction and another reported significant differences. One of the operational differences between these two studies was in the length of the anticipation interval (time available to make a response). Several studies of verbal learning indicated that the faster the items are presented, the larger the age differences become. In the present study two anticipation intervals were used. It was hypothesized that an age difference in retroaction would be found at the short anticipation interval, but at the long anticipation interval the age difference would be smaller if it occurred at all.

Method

SUBJECTS: The Ss were 24 young men aged 30 to 39 years (mean = 35.1) and 24 older men aged 63 to 77 years (mean = 71.4) who were randomly assigned to the short or long anticipation-interval condition. Eleven of the old Ss (nine in the short and two in the long interval condition) had to be replaced because of failure to meet the learning criterion within 52 trials. Because of this selection factor, the mean vocabulary score of the old Ss on whom completed data were collected exceeded that of the young Ss.

Materials: Each of the eight items for the original learning (OL) list consisted of two consonants serving as the stimulus and a two-syllable adjective serving as the response, e.g., TL—INSANE, SN—COMPLETE. For the interpolated list (IL) the same eight pairs of consonants served as stimuli, but the response elements were unrelated adjectives, e.g., TL-ORAL, SN-VULGAR.

PROCEDURE: The anticipation intervals were 1.9 sec. and 3.7 sec. for the short and long anticipation-interval groups respectively. For all Ss the inspection interval was 1.9 sec. and the inter-item (no display) interval 1.8 sec. At the slow condition, therefore, the interval during which the S could respond was 3.7 sec., and total time per item was 7.4 sec.; for the fast condition, these times were 1.9 sec. and 5.6 sec. Materials were displayed visually on a card-changing instrument which automatically controlled the intervals. Approximately two minutes elapsed between OL and IL and between IL and relearning. The criterion for OL, IL and relearning was one perfect trial plus one additional trial. An S who did not meet the OL and IL criterion within 52 trials was replaced.

Table 1
Means for Trials to Criterion

	OL	IL	Relearning	Adjusted Relearning
Short interval				
Old	20.5	20.4	11.9	11.3
Young	20.4	12.6	7.3	6.8
Long interval				
Old	19.3	10.8	6.7	6.3
Young	11.0	9.5	5.2	6.6

Results

The means for trials to criterion for both age groups for OL, IL and relearning are presented in Table 1. The selection of old Ss at the short interval (replacement of nine Ss who failed to meet criterion) resulted in no age difference in OL under that condition. Despite this selectivity, an age difference did emerge in relearning (p <0.02). No such age difference was apparent at the long interval. An analysis of covariance with OL trials-to-criterion as the covariate (adjusted relearning scores in Table 1), resulted in an interaction effect (p <0.02) which demonstrated a larger age difference in relearning at the short anticipation interval than at the long.

Although this study focused on retroaction, the difference in interpolated trials-to-criterion between the old and young groups at the short anticipation interval (p <0.02), with virtually no difference at the long interval, suggests that duration of anticipation interval also influences age differences in proaction.

These results demonstrated that age differences in retroaction were affected by the anticipation interval. Whether the critical factor was anticipation interval during OL, IL, relearning, or a combination thereof cannot be determined from these data.

Abstract **37**

Memory Storage and Aging

DAVID SCHONFIELD, M.A. and BETTY-ANNE ROBERTSON, Ph.D.

"Memory Storage and Aging," *Canadian Journal of Psychology*, 1966, *20*, 228-236.

Of learning's three stages—acquisition, retention, and remembering— it is the last, that of remembering, which is necessarily the dependent variable from which conclusions are drawn concerning the influence of independent variables at any of the three stages. A loss at the remembering stage may be interpreted as reflecting a deficit in acquisition, storage or retrieval. This study examined age differences in retrieval efficiency. The general prediction was that a test of memory that does not require retrieval from storage will show less of a loss with age than a test that requires retrieval. Specifically, it was predicted that the scores of the aged on a recognition test would be far superior to their scores on a voluntary recall test, because the act of recognition demands the matching of a stimulus to a stored trace but does not involve retrieval as such. It was further predicted that the older groups would show a greater difference between recognition and recall scores than younger groups would.

Method

SUBJECTS: The Ss were 134 noninstitutionalized persons aged 20 to 75 years with a minimum of 20 Ss in each decade between 20 and 60 and over 65 years of age. Approximately half the Ss were males and half females, but there were more males below 40 and more females over 40 years old. The Ss were students, university graduates, professionals, wives of professionals, and parents and grandparents of university students.

Materials: There were two lists (A and B) of 24 monosyllabic or bisyllabic nouns or adjectives equated for frequency on the Thorndike-Lorge count, number of words beginning with the same letter and other characteristics. The recognition lists consisted of the 24 words from lists A or B, each within a group of four other words selected with respect to association value with the original learning word.

PROCEDURE: For learning, the words were projected consecutively on a screen, each for four sec. As the word appeared on the screen, the S was required to read it aloud once. As soon as he had pronounced the last word on the list, he was instructed either to say as many of the words as he could recall in any order he wished, or was given the recognition list and told to underline the one word in each group of five words that he had seen previously on the screen. Recognition and recall tests were untimed.

Ss were tested individually for recognition on one list and recall on the other. Approximately half of the Ss performed the recognition task first, the recall task second. Approximately half the Ss were presented with list A for recognition and list B for recall, while the remainder had recognition on list B and recall on list A.

To provide information on the effect of recall on recognition of the same list, and the effect of recognition on the recall of the same list, Ss were given a subsidiary recognition test on list A after their recall of list A. Similarly, after recognition on list A, they were given a subsidiary recall test on list A. The same procedure was used aftr recognition or recall of list B.

Results

Lists A and B did not differ for either mean recognition or mean recall scores, an indication that the two lists were of equivalent learning difficulty.

Means for the two recognition scores (first and second lists) and the two recall scores (first and second lists) were almost identical, indicating that neither positive nor negative transfer occurred between the first and second memory tests, whether recall or whether recognition came first. It therefore

Table 1
Mean Recognition, Recall and Recognition Minus
Recall Scores by Age

Age	N	Recognition	Recall	Recognition Minus Recall
20-29	36	20.01	13.78	6.42
30-39	23	19.48	12.30	7.17
40-49	32	19.53	10.01	9.47
50-59	21	19.90	9.57	10.24
60+	22	20.09	7.50	12.59

seemed justifiable to combine all recognition results whether from list A or B and whether recognition preceded or followed recall, and to make a similar combination of all the voluntary recall results.

Table 1 presents the mean recognition and voluntary recall scores by age groups. There was little difference between age groups for recognition scores but there was a steady decline with age on the voluntary recall scores.

The results of the subsidiary experiment indicated that recognition was not facilitated by prior recall on the same list, and surprisingly, recall was hindered by recognition on the same list.

The findings support the hypothesis that aging causes special difficulties in retrieving memories from storage. Voluntary recall, which involves retrieval, showed a loss with age, whereas recognition, which does not require retrieval, showed no such deterioration.

Abstract 38

Age Differences in Recognition Memory

JOAN T. ERBER, Ph.D.

"Age Differences in Recognition Memory," *Journal of Gerontology*, 1974, *29*, 177-181.

A recall memory task requires a person to supply the material to be remembered, whereas a recognition memory task requires him to match information in memory storage with a test item. Although there is no agreement as to whether recall and recognition are inherently different processes, it has been proposed that recall involves both the storage and retrieval of information in memory, whereas recognition involves only storage and bypasses the need for retrieval. Several studies have reported a decline for recall memory with age but no corresponding decline for recognition memory. These findings may indicate that older people have less efficient retrieval processes than young people, but the results could also be due to the use of easier recognition than recall tasks, since the aged typically show a greater deficit on difficult than on easy tasks. This study further investigated the relationship between recognition memory and age by comparing two age groups on a difficult recognition task. Difficulty was manipulated by varying the list length and by using a five-alternative forced choice test instead of fewer alternatives as used in earlier research.

Method

SUBJECTS: Participants were 40 young (range 19-30, Mean = 23.3 years) and 40 older (range 65-75, Mean = 70.0 years) nuns. The age groups were comparable for years of education and WAIS vocabulary scores.

Materials: Two recognition lists, one of 24 words (short) and one of 60 words (long), matched for proportion of monosyllabic and bisyllabic words, were constructed from the AA words on the G list of the Thorndike-Lorge word lists. The five words for the recognition test were typed in a horizontal row on 5" x 8" index cards.

PROCEDURE: Subjects were tested individually, and all Ss were tested on both the long and the short list, with counterbalancing for order of list length. Study time per word was four seconds. An untimed recognition test was administered immediately after the presentation of the study list. After the recognition test for the second list, the S was asked to recall as many words as possible from the second list.

Results

Recognition: The young Ss earned higher recognition scores than the old Ss (80.70% versus 69.25%; p <.0002). Performance was better on the short than on the long list (81.52% versus 68.35%; p <.0001). The order of presentation of lists affected recognition score only in that subjects in both age groups performed better on the long list if it preceded rather than followed the short list. The Age x List Length interaction (evaluated for first list only to eliminate possible interference effects) was not significant.

Recall: (It was recognized that the recall test was not ideal, because Ss were exposed to another list and to two recognition tests prior to being tested for recall on the second list.) The young Ss earned significantly higher recall scores than the older Ss (25.85% versus 11.95%; p <.0001) and recall was significantly better for the short list than for the long list (25.22% versus 12.59%; p <.0001). The Age x List Length interaction was not significant.

The most important finding of this study is that age differences for recognition do occur when the recognition task is difficult.

Abstract **39**

Retention as a Function of Learning

IRENE M. HULICKA, Ph.D. and ROBERT L. WEISS, Ph.D.

"Age Differences in Retention as a Function of Learning,"
Journal of Consulting Psychology, 1965, *29*, 125-129.

When something is said to be remembered, the implication is that it has been learned and retained over a period of time. However, in many of the studies that have been interpreted as supporting the hypothesis that efficiency of memory functioning declines with age, the level of learning was not known. This study tested the hypothesis that age differences in retention scores may be due in part to age differences in amount learned.

Method

SUBJECTS: Forty older men (mean age = 68 years; range = 60-72) and 40 younger men (mean age = 38 years; range = 30-44) served as subjects. All were hospitalized veterans whose speech, hearing, vision and general physical condition were sufficiently good to permit participation.

Materials: The learning materials were nine paired-associates with a geometrical design serving as the stimulus and a three-letter masculine name as the response.

PROCEDURE: Ss within each age category were assigned either to an equal learning opportunity condition or a learning-to-criterion condition, with matching of groups for score on the vocabulary subtest of the WAIS. In the equal learning opportunity condition each S was given 15 learning trials, regardless of the number of correct responses. In the learning-to-critrion condition, training was continued to a criterion of one errorless trial. Retention was measured for all Ss 20 min. after completion of training and for most Ss after a one-week interval.

Results

Under the equal learning opportunity condition, the younger Ss made more correct responses during learning (p <.01) and earned significantly higher scores on both the 20 min. and one-week recall tests. However, the correlation between number of correct responses during learning and number of items recalled at 20 min. was .92. Analysis of covariance indicated that when differences associated with level of learning were partialled out, the age groups did not differ significantly for number of items recalled.

Under the learning-to-criterion condition the younger Ss required fewer trials (p <.05), but the differences in recall scores at 20 min. and one week after learning were negligible, with the older group having slightly higher mean recall scores on both occasions than the younger group. To investigate the possibility that the comparatively efficient retention of the older Ss was dependent on more frequent exposure to the material, with a consequent opportunity to overlearn particular items, the data were reanalyzed on the basis older and younger subgroups matched by individuals for trials to criterion. For these subgroups composed of 14 younger and 14 older Ss, mean recall scores for the younger Ss at 20 min. and one week were 7.79 and 6.50; for the older Ss the corresponding recall scores were 7.57 and 7.16.

Given equal learning opportunity, the older Ss learned the material less well; but relative to the amount they had learned, their recall was not inferior to that of the young. The older Ss required more trials to criterion, but once having learned the material to the same degree as the younger Ss, they recalled it equally well after intervals of 20 min. and one week.

Abstract **40**

Learning and Memory in Relation to Age

PHYLLIS A. MOENSTER, Ph.D.

"Learning and Memory in Relation to Age," *Journal of Gerontology*, 1972, 27, 361-363.

This study represents an attempt to determine whether the often-demonstrated deficit in cognitive ability in later years is more a function of learning variables or of memory variables. It also investigates the role of free associating to materials that have been learned as an aid to memory function. This study differs from most projects on memory in that a longer than usual retention interval was used, and the material to be remembered was the contents of meaningful paragraphs rather than the usual list of words, digits, or nonsense syllables.

Method

SUBJECTS: The Ss were 192 noninstitutionalized female volunteers, ranging in age from 20 to 94 years. Ss were categorized into five age groups (20-29, 30-39, 40-54, 55-69, and 70-94 years). All Ss under 70 had 17 to 18 years of education, those over 70 approximately 15 years. The age groups were statistically similar for vocabulary score of the WAIS, with mean vocabulary scores ranging from 16.76 to 17.56.

PROCEDURE: Each S was given a typed copy of a story consisting of several paragraphs from the Iowa Silent Reading Elementary Test, which was at approximately sixth-grade difficulty level. The material was typed on both standard size type and ¾-inch type to minimize the effects of visual difficulties. Immediately following reading of the paragraphs, each S answered a 20-question multiple-choice test covering the contents of the story. The score on this test was used as a measure of learning.

Within each age group 12 Ss were assigned randomly to each of three treatment conditions as follows: Control I—ten minutes were spent on unrelated tasks; Control II—ten minutes were spent on a related task, reading a selection similar to the original one; Experimental—the S was asked to spend ten minutes free associating outloud about the contents of the story. After the ten-minute interpolated task the same 20-question multiple-choice test, with a different ordering of questions, was readministered as a measure of memory for the story content.

Results

The age effect was statistically significant (p <0.001) for both learning and memory scores. The age effect was one of progressive decline beginning with the group aged 40-54. The pattern of decline was very similar for learning and memory scores. Indeed, for all age groups the mean memory score was almost identical with the learning score. Analysis of covariance with learning score as the covariant reduced the age effect in memory score to nonstatistically significant dimensions (p > 0.05).

Variations in the interpolated tasks did not have a statistically significant effect on memory scores; thus, free associatoin to the learned material did not serve as an effective aid to memory.

Abstract 41

Prose Recall and Recognition Memory

SUSAN K. GORDON, Ph.D. and W. CRAWFORD CLARK, Ph.D.

"Application of Signal Detection Theory to Prose Recall and Recognition in Elderly and Young Adults," *Journal of Gerontology*, 1974, 29, 64-72.

Age differences between young and elderly adults in long-term memory have been investigated primarily with relatively meaningless material, such as nonsense syllables, single words, or paired-associates. This study, by comparing recall and recognition performance, attempted to determine how older and younger adults differed on storage and retrieval processes in immediate and long-term (one week) retention of prose material. Signal Detection Theory was applied to recognition peformance in order to provide a more sensitive measure of recognition memory than could be obtained by examining number of errors without correction for guessing. Response criterion, an index of cautiousness, was also measured for prose recognition using this method of analysis.

Method

SUBJECTS: The sample consisted of 22 elderly (mean age = 71 years) and 22 young (mean age = 25 years) adult men and women, all of whom were attending college.

PROCEDURE: The prose materials were 15 short passages, each describing an issue involving opposing groups in a community project. The stories were based on a similar set of logical relationships among the groups. Each subject was given one of the 15 stories to read and then recall aloud. Recognition memory for the passage was assessed through 32 true-false questions, half of which were based on direct retention and the others requiring logical inferences to be made regarding the relationships described in the passage. These were administered directly following free recall for the passage. Delayed recall and recognition were tested one week following the initial presentation of the material.

Results

Content analysis was used for scoring taped recordings of immediate and delayed (one week) recall of the prose passage. Recognition performance was analyzed separately for those questions directly related to the passage ("factual") and those that were logical derivations ("deductive"). Multiple regression techniques were applied to recall and recognition data using age, sex, education, occupation, and score on the WAIS vocabulary scale as independent variables. Trial (immediate or delayed) also served as an independent variable, and memory scores were the dependent variables in separate analyses of recall, and factual and deductive recognition performance.

The elderly had significantly lower recall scores from the passages for both immediate and one-week retention intervals, although there was a considerably larger age difference on delayed recall. WAIS vocabulary scores were positively related to recall performance on both trials. Age and occupation were negatively related to both factual and deductive recognition memory scores, whereas vocabulary and recognition scores showed a positive association. The effects of sex and trial were relatively insignificant, compared to the other independent variables. The response criterion was not significantly related to any of the independent variables included in the analysis.

The results were interpreted as providing evidence for a storage deficit in the elderly which, in turn, resulted in poorer retrieval of information from long-term memory. Thus, the older persons appeared to have difficulty acquiring the type of information required in "everyday" verbal experiences. However, their ability to retain direct information was not substantially different from their retention of material that required the manipulation of logical relationships.

Abstract **42**

Retrieval from Short-Term Memory

TERRY R. ANDERS, Ph.D., JAMES L. FOZARD, Ph.D.
and TIMOTHY L. LILLYQUIST, Ph.D.

"Effects of Age Upon Retrieval from Short-Term Memory,"
Developmental Psychology, 1972, 6, 214-217.

There is considerable evidence that a deficit of short-term memory is associated with advanced age. Researchers have begun to focus on the question of which component or combination of components (registration, storage or retrieval) constitutes the locus of the age-related deficit. The goal of this experiment was to provide a direct assessment of possible age differences in the retrieval of information from short-term memory. Using young adult subjects, Sternberg in his studies of 1966 and 1969 found that the search process underlying retrieval from short-term memory is very fast (about 25 items per second), serial (i.e., it proceeds through memory one item at a time), and exhaustive (i.e., includes the entire list of alternatives even though the item in question may have appeared early in the list). This experiment was designed to measure these characteristics of the search process in young-, middle-, and old-aged individuals.

Method

SUBJECTS: There were ten young (M = 20.0, range = 19 to 21 years), ten middle-aged (M = 37.5, range = 33 to 43 years), and ten old (M = 68.1, range =58 to 85 years) subjects. Apart from five young female Ss, all Ss were males. None of the Ss were institutionalized, and all were assumed to be of normal intelligence.

Appartus: In front of each subject was a console, whose front panel contained three projectors, two mounted side by side toward the bottom of the panel, and one to the center and above the others. The digit lists were presented in the lower left projector, the warning signal (a green light) on the lower right projector, and the test digit in the top projector. Responses (yes or no) were made by depressing one of two lever switches. A control unit was programmed to present all stimuli and to record the location and latency of responses.

PROCEDURE: On each trial the S was visually presented with a list of one, three, five, or seven digits, one at a time, at the rate of one per sec. Following the presentation of the last digit, a warning light was shown for one sec., after which a test digit was presented and remained on until a response was made. The S's task was to determine whether the test digit had appeared in the preceding list, and to register his decisions as quickly as possible, by depressing either the Yes or No switch. The test digit appeared in the list on 50 percent of the trials. Half the Ss responded to the "yes" switch with their preferred hand, and half responded "no."

Results and Discussion

A linear relationship between search time and number of items in the list, with different equations for each age group, suggested that Ss of all age groups performed a serial search of the contents of memory. (The linear regression equations for search time (RT) were as follows: $RT = 623 + 39N$ for the young Ss; $RT = 619 + 63N$ for the middled-aged Ss; and $RT = 816 + 71N$ for the old Ss. N denotes the number of items in the list. In each case the linear regression of RT on N accounted for more than 98 percent of the variance.)

It appeared that all age groups conducted an exhaustive search during the retrieval of information from short-term memory, since the latencies for yes and no responses were not different. Logically, it would have to be assumed that the entire list be searched to determine that the item had not appeared; the equivalent latencies suggest an exhaustive search also preceded a positive response. This assumption is supported by the finding that in no age group were there any latency differences due to an item's location in the list.

The slope of the latency function allowed for a determination of speed of memory search. The young Ss searched through the contents of short-term memory at the rate of 25.6 items per sec. The middle- and old-aged groups' search speeds were 15.9 and 14.1 items per sec., respectively. The young Ss were significantly faster than the two older groups which did not differ in search speed.

For dimensions of performance not affected by number of items in the list, such as speed of motor response and decision time, the old Ss were significantly slower than either the young or middle-aged Ss.

For all age groups errors were very infrequent, an indication that Ss of all ages were equally successful at registering and storing the list materials.

It may be concluded that Ss of all ages studied employed a serial and exhaustive search, but that retrieval time increased with advancing age because of increased time required to search through the contents of memory and to initiate the search and/or to generate the response. The older Ss' slower search speeds may handicap their short-term memory performance by requiring time during which relatively greater amounts of forgetting would be expected to occur.

Abstract **43**

Retrieval from Primary and Secondary Memory

TERRY R. ANDERS, Ph.D. and JAMES L. FOZARD, Ph.D.

"Effects of Age upon Retrieval from Primary and Secondary Memory," *Developmental Psychology*, 1973, 9, 411-415.

Anders, Fozard and Lillyquist (1972) demonstrated age-related changes in the search process underlying the retrieval of information from short-term or primary memory. However, there is considerable evidence indicating that learning and memory difficulties associated with advanced age are most pronounced when the task demands exceed the capacity of primary memory, and performance relies heavily on the secondary memory system. Primary memory is conceptualized as a limited capacity system (about seven items) in which information can be held only briefly (less than a minute). Secondary memory is characterized as a larger and more permanent store; only information which has been successfully stored in secondary memory is available for recall after an extended period of time. This study explored the possibility of age-related deficits in the retrieval of information from secondary memory as well as from primary memory.

Method

SUBJECTS: There were eight young (M = 21.2, range = 20 to 23 years) and eight older (M = 55.5, range = 49 to 65 years) subjects. Apart from four young female Ss, all Ss were males. None of the Ss was institutionalized.

Apparatus: A computer was programmed to control all temporal and spatial dimensions of stimulus presentation and to record both the location and latency of the Ss' responses. Stimuli (letters and digits), about one in. high, appeared illuminated on a dark background. Responses were made by depressing one of two lever switches.

PROCEDURE: Testing took place on three consecutive days. Approximately 24 hours prior to testing on each day, the S was given a list of either one, three, or five items (either letters or digits) to memorize. These lists were memorized well in advance to ensure they had achieved storage in secondary memory. The secondary memory lists for a given S were consistently letters or digits, but the content (i.e., specific letters or digits) and length of list (one, three or five items) varied randomly from day to day. The primary memory lists also varied in length between one, three and five items, but the length and composition of these lists varied from trial to trial, i.e., the S saw a different primary list on each trial. If the secondary list was composed of digits, the primary lists were of letters, and vice versa.

There were 124 test trials per day. On each trial, the S was shown first the specific primary list, and then presented with a test item, of which half were digits and half were letters, and half of each type of item matched one from the appropriate primary or secondary list. The S's task was to decide whether the test item was an exemplar from either of the memorized lists (the secondary list for the day or the just-presented primary list) and to register his decision by pressing the switch labelled yes or the switch labelled no.

Results and Discussion

For primary memory, the results were similar to those reported earlier by Anders, Fozard and Lillyquist. For both age groups the temporal characteristics of positive and negative responses were basically identical, suggesting that the retrieval processes were exhaustive. A linear relationship between response times and the number of items in memory for Ss of both age groups (for young Ss, $RT = 680 + 23N$, and for the older Ss, $RT = + 45N$) suggested that their retrieval processes were serial. Search times of 43.5 items per sec. for young Ss and 22.2 items per sec. for older Ss were somewhat faster than in the earlier study, probably because of slower presentation rates. The ratio of approxmately 2:1 for search times for young and older Ss held for both studies. Again, for both age groups errors were infrequent, an indicaton that both age groups were successful at registering and storing the primary memory lists, and therefore the data provide an unconfounded assessment of retrieval processes.

Apart from the finding that the speed of search was slower for both age groups, the results for secondary memory more or less paralleled those for primary memory. Equivalent latencies for yes and no responses within age groups again indicated that the search was exhaustive. A linear relationship between response time and number of items in the list again indicated the search was serial (for young Ss, $RT = 596 + 69N$; for older Ss, $RT = 714 + 123N$). Search speed of the young Ss in secondary memory (mean = 14.5 items/sec.) was significantly faster than for older Ss (8.1 items/sec.). Again, the virtual absence of errors for both age groups allowed for the assumption that registration and storage were equivalent. Search speed decreased from primary to secondary memory at about the same rate for both age groups; the rate of search of the contents of secondary memory was approximately three times slower than the rate of search of primary memory.

Thus, in both primary and secondary memory retrieval, searches are serial and exhaustive processes. For both age groups search processes in primary memory are approximately three times faster than in secondary memory, and for both types of memory older Ss require approximately twice as much search time as young Ss. The extra time that older Ss require to search for, or to search for and report the first few items in memory, increases the probability that the items not yet searched for or reported will be forgotten before they can be retrieved.

Abstract **44**

The Effect of Hyperoxygenation on Cognitive Functioning

ELEANOR A. JACOBS, Ph.D., PETER M. WINTER, M.D.,
HARRY J. ALVIS, M.D. and S. MOUCHLY SMALL, M.D.

"Hyperoxygenation Effect on Cognitive Functioning of the Aged," *New England Journal of Medicine*, 1969, 281, 753-757.

Studies involving animal subjects have indicated that recent memory and learning are particularly sensitive to oxygen deprivation. Various psychological studies have demonstrated a high correlation between age and short-term memory deficit. Perhaps some of the underlying basic changes in the aging process may relate to an alteration in oxygenation to the tissues. This is the first known study concerned with the effect of increased arterial oxygen tension on cognitive functioning. Marked elevation of alveolar oxygen tension (P_aO_2) was accomplished by intermittent increase of inspired oxygen tension by administration of 100 percent oxygen in a hyperbaric chamber.

Method

SUBJECTS: Thirteen elderly male patients with a mean age of 68 years, all exhibiting clinical manifestations of intellectual deterioration, were studied. All were inpatients who had been hospitalized for several months to several years. All Ss were given a thorough physical exam in an attempt to eliminate persons for whom the experimental treatment was contraindicated.

Tests: Both pre- and posttreatment the Wechsler Memory Scale (WMS, with alternate forms), the Bender-Gestalt test (B-G) and Tien's Organic Integrity test (an abstract concept-perceptual test) were administered, prior to the experimental procedure, and approximately 12 hours after the experimental procedure was completed.

PROCEDURE: Each experimental S was treated for 90 minutes twice a day for 15 days at 2.5 atmospheres absolute. While at increased pressure, the Ss breathed 99 to 100 percent oxygen from a cyrogenic source. Each S served as his own control with pre- and posttreatment measurements.

A separate control procedure was used to eliminate methodologic bias in results (e.g., tester bias, increased attention to the patient, effects attributable to the environment or high barometric pressure per se). Ten patients were exposed in pairs, one experimental S who breathed 99 to 100 percent oxygen as described, and a control S who was treated identically except that he breathed ten percent oxygen in nitrogen resulting in approximately normal alveolar oxygen pressure. The study was a double blind one in that neither the patients, the investigator who scored the psychological tests, nor the ward personnel knew which Ss were in the control and experimental categories. During treatment, all Ss breathed through a mask. A trained attendant was with the Ss at all times in the hyperbaric chamber. After posttreatment testing had been completed, the five control Ss were given a series of 30 hyperbaric exposures breathing 100 percent oxygen.

Table 1
Mean Pre- and Posttreatment Psychological Test Scores

Group	Test	Pre-Test Mean	Pre-Test SD	Post-Test Mean	Post-Test SD	Level of Significance
Experimental (N = 13)	WMS	76.0	15.6	103.0	14.9	$p < 0.01$
10% oxygen	B-G	10.0	9.6	41.0	10.0	$p < 0.001$
	Tien's	25.0	11.7	49.0	12.4	$p < 0.01$
Control (N = 5)	WMS	80.3	18.4	78.0	18.1	N.S.
10% oxygen	B-G	6.0	4.9	15.0	11.4	N.S.
	Tien's	19.0	12.8	19.0	13.3	N.S.
Control (N = 5)	WMS	80.3	18.4	100.5	16.8	(not
10% osygen then	B-G	6.0	4.9	33.7	3.3	indicated)
100% oxygen	Tien's	19.0	12.8	45.0	10.6	

Results

Mean scores of psychological tests conducted before and after the experimental procedures are presented in Table 1. The experimental group breathing 100 percent oxygen showed uniform and large posttreatment increases in scores, whereas the control Ss on low oxygen showed no significant improvement. When the control Ss were given a second series of hyperbaric exposures, this time with 100 percent oxygen, their scores showed essentially the same degree of improvement that was noted in the original experimental Ss.

Analysis of blood samples revealed large increases in arterial PO_2 for the experimental group under hyperoxygenation, whereas control patients on ten percent oxygen at the same pressure retained arterial PO_2 near the normal range.

The results indicate that the psychological symptoms of gross senility can be markedly and reliably alleviated by intermittent oxygenation and that the effects persist much longer than can be explained purely on the basis of elevated brain-tissue oxygen tension.

Abstract **45**

Hyperbaric Oxygen and the Aged

ALVIN I. GOLDFARB, M.D., NEIL J. HOCHSTADT,
JULIUS H. JACOBSON, M.D. and EDWIN A. WEINSTEIN, M.D.

"Hyperbaric Oxygen Treatment of Organic Mental Syndrome in Aged Persons," *Journal of Gerontology*, 1972, 27, 212-217.

Jacobs, Winter, Alvis and Small reported that aged persons with measurable intellectual deficit derived transient benefit from 15 days' exposure to 100 percent oxygen at 2.5 atmospheres pressure twice a day for 90 minutes. This finding contradicts the current belief that there is little or no potential for change in the cognitive functioning of patients accurately diagnosed as having that psychiatric condtion that reflects diffuse brain damage known as Brain Syndrome, Chronic or Organic Mental Syndrome, Chronic. This study represents an attempt to replicate the findings of Jacobs and her colleagues.

Method

SUBJECTS: Because of press reports about the use of hyperbaric oxygenation for the treatment of senility, there have been many requests for treatment. Of the first 20 who came or were brought for treatment, 16 patients (ten women and six men) met the criteria of the presence of organic mental syndrome and no clear physical contraindication. The patient sample included ten whose condition appeared to be due primarily to senile brain disease and six in whom vascular disease could be implicated. Mean age of the sample was 74 years, 5 months. The degree of organic mental syndrome by clinical estimate was mild in two persons, moderate in nine and severe in nine. The duration of the impairment ranged from two years to well over five. One patient with mild impairment volunteered for treatment; all others were brought by families. Treatment was completed by only ten patients because of unwillingness of six to continue the entire course.

PROCEDURE: All patients received routine physical and laboratory examinations. Before, during and after treatment each patient was evaluated by a neurologist, psychiatrist and psychologist. Tests used included the Wechsler Memory Scale, the Bender Gestalt and Tien's Organic Integrity Test, which were used by Jacobs and her collaborators, the Mental Status Questionnaire and Double Simultaneous Stimulation. The neurological examination included a measure of aphasic status, visuo-constructional tasks and evaluation of insight present.

Insofar as possible, the treatment procedure replicated that of Jacobs et al., i.e., 15 days' exposure to 100% oxygen at 2.5 atmospheres pressure twice a day for 90 minutes. However, six patients discontinued treatment and only nine of the patients both completed the treatment and were completely evaluated pre- and posttreatment.

Results

According to clinical evaluation by neurologists and psychiatrists, none of the patients exposed to hyperbaric oxygen improved in social or intellectual performance. Moreover, treatment was disliked by all patients and increase in physical activity, restlessness and aggressivity was noted in most by the seventh day.

Mean pre- and posttreatment Wechsler Memory Scale scores were 63.70 and 65.44 (n.s.). The increment in mean score was due almost completely to a change from 103 to 112 in one patient's score; that patient was considered to be suffering primarily from a depressive reaction rather than organic brain syndrome. Three other patients showed gains of one, two and six points, and four patients showed decrements of nine, four, two and one points.

Five of the nine patients showed no improvement on the Bender Gestalt test and four showed minimal increments. Mean score on the Tien's test dropped from 41.57 to 27.50, a negative change which would indicate, if the test is valid and reliable, that the treatment had a deleterious effect.

Conclusion: Neither the clinical evaluation nor psychological test results provided evidence of improvement as a result of treatment. Although the hyperbaric oxygen treatment did not benefit a randomly selected group of old persons with intellectual deficit of the type called organic mental syndrome, it may be of benefit to selected groups.

CHAPTER VI

Problem-Solving and Creativity

Abstract **46**

Problem-Solving in Young and Old Adults

DAVID ARENBERG, Ph.D.

"Concept Problem Solving in Young and Old Adults,"
Journal of Gerontology, 1968, 23, 279-283.

Does ability to solve reasoning problems differ between young and old adults? Is within-problem performance related to age? Although most problem-solving studies other than concept-formation studies have found differences due to age, clear-cut differences among age groups have not been found for number of correct solutions of concept problems. Perhaps the absence of age differences in the concept problem-solving studies resulted from the matching of age groups for nonverbal intelligence. This study was designed to answer four questions: (a) Is reasoning performance of men 60 years or older inferior to performance of young men when age groups are not matched for nonverbal intelligence? (b) Is such an age difference found for all concept problems with one-element solutions or only for certain types of such problems? (c) Is negative information preceded by positive information more conducive to errors for old than for young men? (d) Is redundant information more conducive to errors for old than for young men?

Method

SUBJECTS: Forty-two men were recruited from two nonprofit employment services. Half the Ss were 17 to 22 years old, and half were 60 to 77. Ss were excluded if they did not achieve a minimum raw score of 27 on the vocabulary test of the WAIS or if they could not understand instructions for the problem-solving task (three older Ss were replaced). Means for the vocabulary scores were 52.8 for the old and 41.0 for the young. Although the old were favored with respect to vocabulary score, data from another study which provided nonverbal measures of intelligence for many of the participants indicated that the young group was superior to the old on that measure.

PROCEDURE: Initially an attempt was made to use concept problems with the dimensions of color, form and number, modeled after those of Bruner, Goodnow and Austin (1956). However, preliminary work indicated that the task was too abstract for the old Ss and the problems were converted to the poisoned food problems used in this study.

For each of the ten problems, the same nine foods appeared across the top of a worksheet. The S was told that one of the foods was poisoned and his task was to identify the poisoned food. The experimenter read three foods for each meal and indicated whether the diner lived or died after eating the meal. The S was required to record this information in order to minimize the memory component. Ss were required to cross out foods that could be eliminated and to write adjacent to each meal the possible solutions. An example of a problem (Problem 5) is presented in Table 1. A positive instance (died) indicated that the poisoned food was included in the meal; a negative instance (lived) indicated that the poisoned food was not included; and a redundant instance provided no new information. The order of instances in problems were as follows: Problems 1 and 10. +, +, +; 2 and 9. +, −; 3 and 8. −, −, −, −, −; 4 and 6. +, +, + R, +; 5 and 7. +, −, − (R), + (R), −. A key error was defined as the earliest error followed by no correct performance. Evaluation of within-problem performance was made by identifying the kind of information (positive, negative, positive redundant, or negative redundant) provided by the meal which resulted in each key error.

Table 1
A Problem with Its Solution

Meals	Lived or Died	Instance	Possibly Poisoned Foods
Tea, Lamb, Corn	Died	+	Tea, Lamb, Corn
Coffee, Lamb, Rice	Lived	−	Tea, Corn
Milk, Beef, Rice	Lived	−(R)	Tea, Corn
Tea, Beef, Corn	Died	+(R)	Tea, Corn
Coffee, Veal, Corn	Lived	−	Tea

After a practice problem (and clarification if necessary) the ten problems were presented in fixed order. Whenever a solution was reached, the problem was terminated, even if all meals had not been presented.

Results and Discussion

The mean number of correct solutions was 7.6 for the young and 4.5 for the old ($p < 0.001$). However, the superiority of the young in comparison to the old varied with the type of problem. The old group was not more susceptible than the young to errors when negative information was preceded by positive information (Problems 2 and 9, $+$, $-$); ten old men and eight young men made at least one key error on the negative instance. In the fifth and seventh problems ($+$, $-$, $-(R)$, $+(R)$, $-$) ten old and 13 young men made at least one error on a negative instance; thus, in these problems which contained positive and negative information, the performance of the older Ss was not inferior to that of the young on negative instances. Redundant errors were, however, age related. For the fourth and sixth problems ($+$, $+$, $+(R)$, $+$) the old Ss committed five errors on redundant instances, whereas no such errors were committed by the young. Also, on the fifth and seventh problems ($+$, $-$, $-(R)$, $+(R)$, $-$), three old and three young Ss committed errors on the negative redundant instance and five old and no young men made errors on the positive redundant instance.

It had been hypothesized that the old group would commit more key errors than the young when negative information followed positive information, since it was expected that the old would be more likely than the young to continue a previous mode of operation. The hypothesis was not confirmed. Although the findings of earlier studies are consistent with the hypothesis, examination of the procedure followed in the other studies suggests that the observed age differences were probably due to a memory factor rather than to a reasoning factor. Apparently, when negative instances are presented in the context of positive instances, age differences in performance do not result unless some additional memory load is imposed by task procedures.

Redundant information did result in more key errors for the old than for the young. Perhaps the preponderance of nonredundant information throughout the study established a set to eliminate at least one food after each meal, and the old may have been more prone to eliminate a food even when such behavior was contra-indicated.

Although recent studies of concept problem-solving in which groups were matched on nonverbal intelligence did not show age differences in number of correct solutions, age differences did result in this study in which age groups were not matched. Moreover, these differences occurred in spite of the fact that the old group was superior to the young for vocabulary score.

Abstract **47**

A Longitudinal Study of Problem-Solving

DAVID ARENBERG, Ph.D.

"A Longitudinal Study of Problem-Solving in Adults,"
Journal of Gerontology, 1974, *29*, 650-658.

Although reasoning is one of man's most cherished behaviors and problem-solving has been used in the laboratory to study reasoning, there have been few cross-sectional and apparently no longitudinal studies of problem-solving behavior and aging. The cross-sectional studies involving problem-solving of the concept-identification type have not consistently found age differences, but both of two cross-sectional studies that used logical problems of the type used in the present study have reported age differences. The present study, which involved both cross-sectional and longitudinal components, was designed to examine age differences and age changes in analyzing and synthesizing information in performance of problems that involved reasoning.

Method

SUBJECTS: The initial sample consisted of 300 men, predominantly well-educated and middle class, who ranged in age between 24 and 87 years (20-39, N = 45; 40-49, N = 79; 50-59, N = 80; 60-69, N =47; 70+, N = 49). Six years later (mean interval = 6.7 years), 224 men returned and attempted to solve logically equivalent problems. Reasons for nonreturn included withdrawal (45), death (23), and illness (5).

PROCEDURE: In all problems a display of ten lights was used and in each problem a set of logical relations between lights was defined by the experimenter. A problem disk displayed with each problem showed by arrows which lights were related. Each arrow could have one of three possible meanings: (a) effector, (b) combinor, (c) preventor. The S's task was to turn on a Goal light, which required discovery and utilization of the relationships depicted by the arrows.

The experimentor used a sample problem to introduce and explain the rules and procedures for solving this type of problem. He also illustrated a system for recording all input-outcome events to provide a written record available for review, thus minimizing the memory factor. After explanations on the sample problem were repeated as often as requested, a practice problem was administered, and again explanations were given and questions answered.

After solution of the practice problem, the S proceeded to Problem I and if time permitted to Problems II and III. There were no time limits throughout the procedure, except that the entire procedure could not last longer than one-half day, a limitation which prevented some Ss from attempting Problems II or III. Between 45 and 120 min. were used for the sample and practice problems, and up to 150 min. for the experimental problems.

The dependent measure was the number of uninformative inputs. Each input could be evaluated as potentially informative or uninformative depending on the pool of information available at that point in the S's solution. The uninformative inputs could be further categorized as overtly redundant, directly inferable or indirectly inferable.

Results

The cross-sectional results based on the initial sample showed an unequivocal decline in reasoning performance with age. The proportions of correct solutions declined monotonically with age; a substantially higher proportion of men under 60 than over 60 solved each of the three problems. There was a general increasing trend with increased age for mean number of uninformative inputs, with the largest increments between the 30's and 40's and between the 50's and 60's. In Problem I, the decline in reasoning effectiveness was due to both overtly redundant and directly inferable inputs. In the second and third problems the declines were almost totally attributable to overtly redundant inputs. A measure of "non goal-directed" behavior also showed an increasing monotonic relationship with age, suggesting that the old may be poor at formulating and adopting an effective strategy.

In the longitudinal analysis, mean age changes were limited to subjects who were initially in their 70's. For men over 70 the number of uninformative responses increased, primarily in the form of overtly redundant responses. Repetition of the same input or a variation of an earlier attempt should not be attributed to memory difficulties, since the S maintained a written record of every input-output event. In essence, the very old men were ineffective because they did not make use of the information available from earlier input-output events.

It is of interest that for men over 70, problem-solving effectiveness in the initial session seemed to be related to survival. Of the 36 men who solved Problem I, 17 percent died; of the 13 men who did not solve Problem I, 46 percent died during the six-year interval.

Abstract **48**

Cognitive Strategy Training

GISELA LABOUVIE-VIEF, Ph.D. and JUDITH N. GONDA, M.A.

"Cognitive Strategy Training and Intellectual Performance in the Elderly," *Journal of Gerontology*, 1976, *31*, 327-332.

Often age-associated deficits in performance of intellectual tasks are interpreted in terms of a maturational model emphasizing biological decrement. In contrast, the present study conceptualized reduced intellectual performance in the elderly as an experiential deficit which can be reversed by concentrating on the training of certain component skills. Specifically, this study examined the effect of strategy training on the intellectual performance of the elderly. Moreover, it examined the transfer effect of strategy training and its long term facilitative effect.

Method

SUBJECTS: The 60 female Ss ranged in age from 63 to 95 (mean age = 76 years). They were recruited from a housing development and were paid for participation. Ss were randomly assigned to four training groups of 15 each.

Materials: The training task was the Letter Sets Task, which presents the S with five sets of four letters in each item. The task is to find the rule that relates the four letters in each set to each other, and to mark the one that does not fit the rule. This task of inductive reasoning was selected because age-associated deficits on tasks of this type have traditionally been interpreted as evidence of a biological decrement.

The transfer task, Raven's Standard Progressive Matrices, is, like the Letter Sets Test, a marker of inductive reasoning.

PROCEDURE: The study consisted of three phases: *Training, Immediate Posttest* and *Delayed Posttest*. There were four training groups: *Cognitive Training, Anxiety Training, Unspecified Training,* and *No Training*. Training was given on one form of the Letter Set Test and the Immediate and Delayed Posttests were given on an alternate form of the Letter Set Test. The Immediate Posttest followed directly after the training and this was followed by the Transfer Test. The Delayed Posttest consisted of the administration of the Training and Transfer Test approximately two weeks (10 to 28 days) after the Immediate Posttest. Ss were tested individually in their homes.

The instructional training (cognitive and anxiety) involved modeling and overt-to-covert fading of self-instructional statements as a means of developing self-control. Initially, the experimenter modeled the solution of the first six training items, following a standard set of verbalizations. The verbalizations were intended to draw the S's attention to all possible rules which could be used in the solution of the tasks, e.g., alphabetical order and variations thereof (forward, backward and alternate), duplications and triplications, and vowels vs. consonants. The experimenter checked each item against the rule, verbalizing the specific way in which the item was or was not an instance of the rule. Ss were instructed to work on the next six items in exactly the same way the experimenter had done, and the experimenter prompted the S as necessary. The S solved the remaining three subsets, the first while talking aloud, the next while whispering and the last covertly. The Cognitive and Anxiety Training groups were treated alike with respect to strategy training for problem solution; however, the Anxiety Training group also included procedures designed to overcome anxiety and to cope with failure, e.g., statements to be modeled such as: "Think before I give up," "Go slowly, keep on trying," and "Now I know how it works."

In the Unspecified Training condition Ss worked on the Training Task with only standard instructions. The No-Training group worked on an irrelevant task, a verbal fluency test.

Results

The number of correctly solved items was computed for each S separately for the two times of testing for both the Training and the Transfer Tasks. In comparison to the No-Training group, the Cognitive and Anxiety Training groups performed significantly better on the Immediate Posttest. On the Delayed Posttest, significant effects were obtained for the Anxiety and Unspecified Training groups. On the Transfer Task, the Unspecified Training group performed better than the No-Training group on both the Immediate and Delayed Posttests, and the Cognitive Training group outperformed the No-Training group on the Delayed Posttest. The Anxiety Training had no significant transfer effect on either Posttest, but this might have been because the very oldest Ss happened to have been randomly assigned to the Anxiety Training group (mean ages were 80 years for Anxiety, 76 years for Cognitive and Unspecified, and 74 years for the No-Training group).

Discussion

The results indicate that it is possible, through training, to produce significant increments in the performance of the elderly. Moreover, these effects showed some generalizability across tasks as well as time. The finding of any training effects offers an argument against the traditional interpretation that intellectual aging decrements are irreversible. Moreover, the unexpected finding that the Unspecified Training, i.e., simple practice, produced the strongest effects argues against the view that the elderly are deficient in initiating task-relevant behavior components.

Abstract **49**

Age and Creative Productivity

WAYNE DENNIS, Ph.D.

"Creative Productivity between the Ages of 20 and 80 Years," *Journal of Gerontology*, 1966, *21*, 1-8.

This paper examines age changes in productivity of persons engaged in scholarship, the sciences and the arts.

Method

The sample included 738 scholars, scientists or artists, all of whom had lived to age 79 or beyond. A requirement for the inclusion of each S was the availability of a relatively complete dated record of his works. Data on productivity was derived from highly respected and comprehensive source books such as the *Royal Society of London's Catalog of Scientific Literature, 1800-1900*. Data limitations included variations in historical period, lack of uniformity among different groups of Ss for degree of eminence, and inequality of units of productivity for the different groups. The data pertained to frequency rather than quality of contributions at different ages.

Results

Table 1 summarizes by separate disciplines the percentages of total works between the ages of 20 and 80 which were done in each decade. In each group the output of the 20's was considerably less than the output of the

Table 1
Percentage of Total Works Between Ages 20-80
Which Were Done in Each Decade

	N	N	20's	30's	40's	50's	60's	70's
					Age Decade			
Scholarship	Men	Works						
Historians	46	615	3	19	19	22	24	20
Philosophers	42	225	3	17	20	18	22	20
Scholars	43	326	6	17	*21*	*21*	16	19
		Means	4	18	20	20	*21*	20
Sciences	Men	Works						
Biologists	32	3456	5	22	*24*	19	17	13
Botanists	49	1889	4	15	22	22	22	15
Chemists	24	2420	11	21	*24*	19	12	13
Geologists	40	2672	3	13	22	*28*	19	14
Inventors	44	646	2	10	17	18	*32*	21
Mathematicians	36	3104	8	*20*	*20*	18	19	15
		Means	6	17	*22*	21	20	15
Arts	Men	Works						
Architects	44	1148	7	24	*29*	25	10	4
Chamber Mus.	35	109	15	*21*	17	20	18	9
Dramatists	25	803	10	27	*29*	21	9	3
Librettists	38	164	8	21	*30*	22	15	4
Novelists	32	494	5	19	18	*28*	23	7
Opera Comp.	176	476	8	30	*31*	16	10	5
Poets	46	402	11	21	*25*	16	16	10
		Means	9	23	*26*	21	14	6

Note: Maximum values are shown in italics.

30's. For the scholars and scientists, age 20 to 29 was the least productive decade, less productive in all disciplines than age 70 to 79. Only in some of the arts were the 20's more productive than the 70's. For most disciplines, the period 40-49 was either the most productive or almost the most productive decade. Only in one field (chamber music) were the 30's higher in output than the 40's. In all other cases in which the 40's were not the most productive years, greatest productivity was achieved in the 50's or 60's. For scholars as a whole, the 70's were as productive as the 40's and the 60's were actually more productive. The scientists however, as a combined group, showed a slight decline from the 40's through the 50's and 60's with a marked drop in the 70's. The decline in productivity in the arts was considerably greater than in science. Only in the arts, as a combined group, was productivity in the 70's lower than in the 20's. The contrast between the steady output of scholars and the steep decline in the arts is sharp. Between

70 and 79, scholars increased their previous output by 25 percent, scientists by 18 percent and persons in the arts by only 6 percent.

Discussion

For the sample studied, scholarly productivity was maintained at a high level through the 60's with only a slight decline in the 70's, and scientific productivity was also maintained at a high level through the 60's but there was a marked decline in the 70's; however, artistic productivity declined progressively from a peak in the 40's to a relatively low level in the 70's. The proposed interpretation is that the output curve rises earlier and declines more severely because productivity in the arts depends primarily on individual creativity. Scholars and scientists require a longer period of training and a greater accumulation of experience and of data than do artists. The use of accumulated data and, perhaps also, assistance from others, permit the scholar and scientist to make more contributions in their later years than do those in music, art and literature.

CHAPTER VII

Self-Perceived and Attributed Age Differences

Abstract **50**

Age Parameters of Young Adult, Middle-Aged, Old, and Aged

PAUL CAMERON, Ph.D.

"Age Parameters of Young Adult, Middle-Aged, Old and Aged," *Journal of Gerontology*, 1969, 24, 201-202.

When is one old, or middle-aged? This study investigated the normative usage of the terms young adult, middle-aged, old and aged.

Method

SUBJECTS: The 571 participants included 253 males and 318 females; 472 whites and 99 non-whites; 248 below the age of 30, 248 between the ages of 30 and 59, and 75 over 59. The sample was not random but was sufficiently haphazard to include a wide range of those in the linquisitc community.
PROCEDURE: After pointing out that though everyone uses the terms "young adult," "middle-aged," "old" and "aged," we really don't know what ages are meant in most people's use of the word, the respondents were asked "What is the youngest a person can be and still be a 'young adult?' The oldest he can be?" Similar questions were posed for each of the other categories.

Results

The majority of respondents indicated that young adulthood extends from 18 to 25, middle age from 40 to 55, old age from 65 to 80 and agedness occurs at 80. A 15-year gap typically occurred between young adulthood and middle age, and a ten-year gap occurred between middle age and old age. There was a tendency for the parameters of the categories to rise somewhat with the age of the respondent.

Abstract 51

Perceptions of the Onsets of Adulthood, Middle Age and Old Age

JEAN DREVENSTEDT, Ph.D.

"Perceptions of Onsets of Young Adulthood, Middle Age and Old Age," *Journal of Gerontology*, 1976, *31*, 53-57.

This study tested the prediction that both age and sex of the perceiver, as well as the sex of the perceived, are significant variables in the judged age at which people reach young adulthood, middle age and old age.

Method

SUBJECTS: The young subjects, all university students, consisted of 134 women (mean age = 19.3 years) and 145 men (mean age = 19.5 years). The older Ss were 41 women and 30 men, distributed approximately equally within the age ranges 60 to 65, 66 to 70, 71 to 75 and over 75. The older Ss were recruited from senior citizens centers.

PROCEDURE: As part of a larger study, the Ss were asked: "At about what age do you consider a male becomes a 'young man' in American society? A female, a 'young woman'?" The same questions were asked for "middle-aged man," "middle-aged woman," "old man" and "old woman." Ss were also asked how many years they thought the average American man and woman lived.

Table 1
Mean Ages Perceived as Onsets of Young, Middle-Aged
and Old Adulthood Stages

Stages	Young Males	Young Females	Old Males	Old Females
		Respondents		
Young manhood	17.99	18.89	20.07	20.29
Young womanhood	17.77	18.19	18.70	18.54
Middle-aged manhood	36.24	38.63	42.23	44.32
Middle-aged womanhood	35.59	37.92	40.33	43.49
Old manhood	62.05	63.86	68.33	72.07
Old womanhood	60.70	62.86	67.83	71.95

Table 2
Percentage of Respondents Labeling "Middle Age" at Age 35
and Under and "Old Age" at Age 65 and Under.

Life Stage	Age of Onset	Young Women (N = 134)	Young Men (N = 145)	Older Women (N = 41)	Older Men (N = 30)
		Respondents			
		%	%	%	%
Middle-Aged Man	35 & Under	44.8	57.9	12.2	23.3
Middle-Aged Woman	35 & Under	47.8	58.6	19.5	33.3
Old Man	65 & Under	72.4	82.8	24.4	46.7
Old Woman	65 & Under	72.4	85.5	19.5	43.3

Results

As indicated in Tables 1 and 2, the results confirmed the hypothesis that the older respondents would perceive both middle and old age as occurring chronologically later than did young respondents. Although it had been predicted that women respondents would perceive people reaching middle and old age earlier than men would, the data in Table 1 indicate that women generally perceived the onsets as occurring later than did the men. The results supported the hypothesis that sex of the perceived would also be a significant variable, with men rather consistently viewed as reaching transition points later than women. Since respondent groups were generally similar in judgments of relative longevities of the sexes, there was no evidence that differential judgments of longevity biased the results.

Abstract **52**

Devaluation of Old Age

CLARA COLLETTE-PRATT, Ph.D.

"Attitudinal Predictors of Devaluation of Old Age in a Multigenerational Sample," *Journal of Gerontology*, 1976, *31*, 193-197.

Of the three major developmental stages—youth, middle age, and old age—the latter, old age, is consistently said to be devalued and negative in American society. Gerontologists have posited a variety of possible explanations of negative attitudes toward old age. (1) Negative attitudes reflect basically negative feelings toward the negative concomitants of old age: poor health, financial insecurity, social isolation and death. (2) The elderly lack the ability or opportunity to reflect the American values of productivity, achievement and independence. (3) Age stratification that divides American society may foster in younger people stereotypes and misinformation about the elderly. This study investigated the viability of each of these three major explanations of devaluation of old age.

Method

SUBJECTS: Three age groups were used, including 123 *young adults* aged 18 to 29 years (52 males, mean age = 23.6 years and 71 females, mean age = 22.4 years), 90 *middle-aged adults,* aged 30 to 59 years (40 males, mean age = 42.8, 50 females, mean age = 41.7) and 108 *older adults* aged 60 years and older (40 males, mean age = 73.0 and 68 females, mean age = 72.8). All were volunteers from educational, recreational or social groups.

PROCEDURE: Attitudes were indexed by using the following seven semantic differential scales which have high loadings on the evaluative factor: good-bad, optimistic-pessimistic, complete-incomplete, timely-untimely, positive-negative, successful-unsuccessful, and important-unimportant. The target concepts to be evaluated were those factors identified as possibly affecting attitude toward and/or devaluation of old age. These factors were as follows: poor health, social isolation, death, financial insecurity, achievement, independence, and personal productivity. In addition, the three developmental stages, old age, middle age and youth, were evaluated.

Attitudinal score of an S toward a target concept was computed as the mean of his scores for that concept on the seven evaluative scales; the lower the mean score, the more positive the attitude it reflected. A score for attitude toward "age in general" was obtained by averaging each S's attitudes toward youth, middle age and old age. A devaluation of old age score was obtained by subtracting from the individual's attitude toward old age score the mean age in general score that S's age group.

Information was also solicited from each S concerning age, sex, marital, occupational and educational status and degree of contact with other age groups, including for the young and middle-aged Ss, contact with parents and grandparents.

Table 1
Attitudes Toward Concepts for Young, Middle-Aged
and Older Adult Subjects

Concept	Young	Middle-Aged	Older	P
Achievement	2.08	2.05	2.16	N.S.
Independence	2.21	2.07	2.05	N.S.
Personal productivity	2.38	2.01	2.24	N.S.
Poor health	5.02	5.02	4.49	<.05
Financial insecurity	4.58	4.72	4.31	<.05
Social isolation	4.70	4.93	3.88	<.05
Death	3.79	3.56	2.86	<.05
Youth	2.36	2.42	1.96	<.05
Middle age	2.71	2.51	2.10	<.05
Old age	3.51	3.34	2.47	<.05
Age in general	2.87	2.76	2.16	<.05
Devaluation of old age	.65	.59	.31	<.05

Results

Table 1 summarizes mean attitudinal scores of the three age groups toward the target concepts (lower scores reflect more positive attitudes). There were no age differences for the cultural value concepts of achievement, independence and productivity. The elderly Ss were less negative than the other age groups toward poor health, social isolation, financial insecurity, death, youth, middle age, old age, age in general and devaluation of old age. The middle-aged Ss were most negative toward social isolation and financial insecurity. The young Ss were most negative toward poor health, social isolation, death, middle age, old age, age in general and devaluation of old age.

Females were less negative toward death than males in all age groups. Older females showed the least negative attitudes toward social isolation, and older males showed the most positive attitudes toward youth. Other sex and age by sex effects were not significant.

Although all of the age groups devalued old age, young and middle-aged Ss devalued old age almost twice as much as the older Ss did. Regression equations were calculated to identify predictors of devaluation of old age. For the young sample, the four best predictors were attitudes toward poor health, achievement and death, and association with young friends. For the middle-aged group three predictor variables were significant: attitudes toward death, independence and poor health. For the older adults, only attitudes toward personal productivity and poor health were efficient predictors of devaluation of old age.

Although the results provide some support for each of the explanations posited in the introduction, the first explanation received the most support. Negative attitude toward poor health was the most consistent predictor to devaluation of old age in that it contributed to devaluation for all age groups. For the middle-aged and young sample, a negative attitude toward death was also predictive of devaluation. One of the cultural values was predictive of devaluation for each age group, achievement for the young, independence for the middle-aged, and personal productivity for the elderly. However, peculiarly, negative rather than positive evaluations of these concepts was associated with devaluation of old age. The age stratification explanation was not supported; for young people *low* association with young friends was related to devaluation of old age.

Abstract **53**

Medical Student Attitudes Toward the Elderly

DOMENIC V. CICCHETTI, Ph.D., C. RICHARD FLETCHER, Ph.D., EMANUEL LERNER, M.A. and JULES V. COLEMAN, M.D.

"The Effects of a Social Medicine Course on Attitudes of Medical Students Toward the Elderly: A Controlled Study," *Journal of Gerontology*, 1973, *28*, 370-373.

This study attempted to determine whether a course in medical ecology, focusing upon the problems of aging, changes the attitudes of first-year medical students toward the elderly.

Method

SUBJECTS: The experimental group consisted of 91 first-year medical students enrolled in a course on social medicine which focused on problems with the aged. There were 18 weekly lectures covering the health care system; human ecology in the behavioral sciences; individual adaptations to aging; housing, poverty and welfare problems of the aged; the film "Wild Strawberries"; and several lectures and discussions on how to conduct interviews with the aged living in the community. Each student, working as a team with another student, had to interview at least one community-living older person. The interview guide focused on social participation, membership in organizations, friendship patterns and attitudes toward neighborhoods, neighborhood housing, work, retirement, economic status, health, disability, loneliness, morale, future planning and death.

The control group consisted of 89 first-year medical students enrolled the following year in a similar 18-week course in social medicine, which did not, however, stress the problems of the elderly.

PROCEDURE: On the first and last days of the course, students in both groups responded to a questionnaire designed to assess their attitudes toward and knowledge of the aged. Specifically, the items pertained to the psychological characteristics, influence, role and value to society, physical environment and medical treatment of the elderly.

Results

On the pretest the experimental and control groups differed significantly on only one item; more of the control Ss than the experimental Ss indicated that elderly patients are more likely than other patients to be called crocks. On the posttest approximately two-thirds of both groups indicated that elderly patients are likely to be called crocks, but it was impossible to determine whether the respondents themselves were classifying elderly patients as "crocks" or merely agreeing that others tend to classify aged patients in this fashion. On the posttest significantly more of the control group than of the experimental group agreed that elderly patients have emotional-social problems; there was a nonsignificant decrease from pre- to posttest for number of experimental subjects agreeing with this statement. The two groups differed significantly for amount of change from pre- to posttest responses on only two items. Members of the experimental group slightly strengthened their attitude that withdrawal of the elderly is socially determined, whereas the control group's attitude was slightly weakened on the second testing. Also, the experimental group attributed a higher suicide rate to the elderly after the course than the control group did; this change was probably determined by the learning of a social fact rather than by an attitudinal change.

On both pre- and posttests, the majority of members of both groups expressed a negative preference for elderly patients and reacted unenthusiastically to the prospect of becoming geriatricians.

This study did not provide evidence of positive attitude change toward the elderly as prospective patients as a consequence of a course on social medicine stressing the problems of aging.

Abstract 54

Age Concept in Women

CAROL A. NOWAK and LILLIAN E. TROLL, Ph.D.

"Age Concept in Women: Concern with Youthfulness and Attractiveness Relative to Self-Perceived Age," Paper presented at the Meetings of the Gerontological Society, Portland, Oregon, 1974.

This study explored age differences in concern with attractiveness and youthfulness and the relation between these concerns and a woman's age-concept. In accordance with Kastenbaum's multiple-age theory, the following age-concepts were examined: look-age, feel-age, do-age and interest-age. There were two general hypotheses: (a) Concern with attractiveness should show a different chronological age pattern than concern with youthfulness; namely, that concern with youthfulness should increase steadily with age, whereas concern with attractiveness should peak in middle age. (b) There should be greater disparity among the various aspects of the age-concept in middle age than at any other age. These hypotheses were based on the assumption that the middle-aged woman must come to grips with a host of negative expectations associated with aging in our society, which inspire concerns about isolation, uselessness and attractiveness. It was further assumed that young women should be less concerned with youthfulness than with attractiveness, and less concerned with either than middle-aged and older women would be. Older women—over 65—may have relinquished concern about attractiveness but might, in our youth-oriented society, still be concerned with youthfulness.

Method

SUBJECTS: The sample consisted of 90 white, middle-class women between the ages of 15 to 74 who were registered volunteers at a research center. There were 15 Ss in each of the following age categories: 15 to 24, 25 to 34, 35 to 44, 45 to 54, 55 to 64, and 65 to 74 years. Single women were over-represented in the age range from 15 to 44.

PROCEDURE: An adaptation of Kastenbaum's (1972) "Ages of Me" questionnaire was used to measure concern with youthfulness and attractiveness. From six different kinds of questions estimates can be made of how old the woman thinks she looks and feels, along with the age level of her daily activities and her attitudes and interests.

Results

Concern with youthfulness started in the youngest age period studied— adolescence—and exceeded concern with attractiveness at all ages. Concern with youthfulness increased regularly with chronological age, though the increase tended to decelerate during the forties and fifties.

Concern with attractiveness was curvilinear with age, and was highest among middle-aged women.

Disparity among the four age concepts studied increased with age and was greatest among the oldest subjects rather than the middle-aged ones. Moreover, the deviation of each of these age-concept scores from the subject's chronological age increased with age. The deviation was particularly marked for "feel" and "interest" ages.

Abstract 55

Self-Perception Among Older People

CAROLINE E. PRESTON, M.A. and KAREN S. GUDIKSEN, M.D.

"A Measure of Self-Perception Among Older People,"
Journal of Gerontology, 1966, 21, 63-71.

How do old people see themselves and their world? On what variables do these perceptions depend? What techniques can be used to explore how old people perceive themselves?

Method

SUBJECTS: Two hundred and forty-two persons over 65 years of age representing a broad range of socio-economic conditions participated on a volunteer basis. Mean age was approximately 75 years. There were 175 females
and 67 males. All were sufficiently cooperative, oriented, and free of sensory, motor, pain or weakness deficits to respond meaningfully to individual, structured interviews. Ss were recruited from two retirement homes
with high affluence requirements, one retirement home with modest financial requirements, two senior citizens clubs, and from out-patients in a
screening clinic which provided medical care for indigent people.

Materials: One of the test instruments was a 110-item true-false Questionnaire with 53 statements describing potential gratifications or satisfactions, and 57 items describing potential frustrations or disappointments in
past or present life conditions or anticipations for the future. The items
were based on statements made by 120 persons over 65 years of age who had
been asked to verbalize their attitudes about their current and past lives.
Also, a 64-item Interpersonal Adjective Check List was administered twice,
first for the S to indicate whether the descriptive phrases were true or false
for himself, and then as applied to "most people my age." Form I of the
Wechsler-Bellevue Vocabulary Subtest was administered and biographical
information was obtained.

Results and Discussion

Examination of Vocabulary scores, educational attainment, professional
achievement, and income status warranted a trichotomous arrangement of
Ss, with Ss from the two affluent retirement homes placed in the high
category with respect to socio-economic and achievement variables and
current financial and intellectual resources, Ss from the Clubs and modest
retirement home in the average category, and those from the out-patient
clinic in the low category because of low achievement variables and meager
current financial and intellectual resources.

Questionnaire scores and Adjective Check List scores (self-ratings and
ratings of other older people) were not different among the two affluent
retirement homes, clubs, and the modest retirement home, but Ss from
these sources did differ significantly for all three scores from Ss recruited
from the out-patient clinic. Thus, persons with high and average financial
and intellectual resources and patterns of achievement responded very
similarly with respect to affirming gratifications or denying frustrations,
and also with respect to ascribing positive attributes or denying negative
attributes both in themselves and in others of their age. By contrast, persons
from the out-patient clinic, who were low in achievement variables and had
meager financial and intellectual resources, responded in a distinctly different and more negative manner. This evidence suggests that, whereas

affluent or upper-middle-class status is not a necessary condition for positive response patterns among older people, indigence or lower-class status is such a condition for negative response patterns.

Subgroups were formed of 28 Ss whose scores on the Questionnaire were at least one S. D. above the mean, and 28 Ss whose scores were at least one S. D. below the mean. For ease of analysis, Questionnaire statements were assigned to three categories dealing with Relationships, Somatic Factors and Interests. Examination of the proportion of statements in each category which elicited significantly different endorsement rates among the high—as compared to the low-scoring Ss—indicated that the negative Questionnaire statements (.70) accounted for much more than the positive statements (.32) to the high-low differences. Thus, the low scorers endorsed many more of the negative statements than the high scorers did, whereas the difference between high and low scorers for endorsement of positive statements was slight, although the high scorers did endorse more positive statements. Negative Somatic statements had the highest discriminatory functions; .83 of'these were endorsed significantly less by high than by low-scoring Ss. The corresponding figures for negative Relationship and negative Interest statements were .69 and .53. The most important difference between high and low scorers for positive items was for positive Relationships (.47), with positive Somatic Factors (.27) and positive Interest (.24) discriminating less well among the Ss. Thus, high and low scorers differed more with respect to frustrations than gratifications.

Abstract 56

Objective Versus Perceived Age Differences in Personality

INGE M. AHAMMER, Ph.D. and PAUL B. BALTES, Ph.D.

"Objective Versus Perceived Age Differences in Personality: How Do Adolescents, Adults and Older People View Themselves and Each Other," *Journal of Gerontology*, 1972, 27, 46-51.

Many studies have been conducted to assess objectively measurable differences between age groups on various dimensions of personality, and to determine how older people are perceived by young people. Relatively little information is available about how older people perceive young people, and about the self-perceptions of members of one age group and perception of that age group by members of other age groups. The present study was designed to investigate perceived age differences in some personality dimensions across a wide age range. The hypothesis was that Ss in different age groups would exhibit highly similar (self-reported) behavior but would perceive each other as being different.

Method

SUBJECTS: Forty white, middle to middle-upper-class Ss, 20 male and 20 female, from each of three age ranges: adolescents (15-18), adults (34-40), and older people (64-74).

Materials: Forty items pertaining to Affiliation, Achievement, Autonomy and Nurturance were selected from the Jackson Personality Research Form. A nine-point rating scale ranging from extremely undesirable (1) through neutral (5) to extremely desirable (9) was used to obtain desirability judgments.

Design: Five male and five female Ss in each age group were assigned to each of four instructional groups as follows: (1) Personal Desirability: Ss were asked to indicate how desirable or undesirable they personally considered a given behavior; (2) Cohort-Desirability: Ss were instructed to how desirable or undesirable they thought individuals of their own age and sex would consider a given behavior; (3 and 4) Age-Desirability: Ss were asked to indicate how desirable or undesirable they thought individuals of a specified target age (15-18, or 34-40, or 64-74) would consider a given behavior (i.e., separate groups of adolescents rated either adults or old people, etc.). The Personal Desirability instruction was intended to indicate objective age differences, the Age-Desirability was assumed to measure perceived age differences, and the Cohort Desirability was included primarily as a control instruction to explore a potential method effect associated with other perception conditions.

Results

The Personal Desirability ratings for Affiliation were high for all age groups but significantly lower for adults than for adolescents and old people. For Achievement, Personal Desirability ratings were also high but significantly lower for adolescents than for adults and old people. Age groups did not differ for Personal Desirability ratings for Autonomy or Nurturance; Autonomy ratings for all age groups were slightly in the negative direction, while ·Nurturance ratings were slightly positive. None of the differences between Personal Desirability and Cohort-Desirability were significant for any of the dimensions.

Differences between Personal Desirability and Age Desirability ratings for Affiliation and Achievement did not approach significance, reflecting congruency between self-perceptions and other age group perceptions on these two dimensions. However, significant differences were obtained between Personal Desirability and Age Desirability scores for both Autonomy and Nurturance. Adults perceived adolescents as valuing Autonomy higher than they actually did and both adolescents and adults perceived older people as evaluating Autonomy as significantly less desirable than older people viewed their own age group or described themselves. Moreover, older people were perceived by both adolescents and adults as judging Nurturance as more desirable than older people actually did in self-reports. The results with respect to Autonomy and Nurturance support the proposition that perceived age differences may exist even though no actual age differences are obtained when self-reports or descriptions of one's own peer groups are considered.

In this study, the adult group was never misperceived, in that Age-Desirability ratings corresponded to Personal-and Cohort-Desirability ratings for the adult group. Adolescents were misperceived by the adults only on the Autonomy dimension, whereas the older group was misperceived by both adolescents and adults with respect to both Autonomy and Nurturance. Thus, the adult group could be described as never misperceived but often misperceiving, whereas the older group could be described as often misperceived but never misperceiving with respect to the dimensions evaluated.

Abstract 57

Adolescent Misperceptions of the Aged

GISELA LABOUVIE-VIEF, Ph.D. and PAUL B. BALTES,Ph.D.

"Reduction of Adolescent Misperceptions of the Aged," *Journal of Gerontology*, 1976, *31*, 68-71.

This study attempted to modify the perceptions adolescents hold about the elderly, in the direction of achieving greater consistency between the self-descriptions of elderly people, and the perceptions of elderly people by adolescents.

Method

SUBJECTS: The subjects were 40 adolescent girls (mean age = 15 years and 9 months) sampled randomly from the class rosters of grades nine to 12 in a small community. The girls were randomly assigned to four training groups of ten each. Each of the girls was randomly matched with one of ten elderly women (mean age 74.7) selected as examples of relatively advantaged aged persons who might serve as models for successful aging.

PROCEDURE: The procedure involved a pretest, a training session and posttests. The measurement instrument was the Personality Research Form (PRF; Jackson, 1967) which has two parallel forms (A and B) with no item overlap. Each form contains 14 personality scales. During the pretest, elderly Ss completed both forms of the PRF under self-endorsement instructions. Adolescent Ss completed form A under instructions to simulate the response pattern of a typical (but hypothetical) elderly woman. Examination of response patterns indicated that the greatest discrepancies between the self-descriptions of the elderly Ss and the adolescent simulations were for Aggression, Dominance and Nurturance. Therefore, these three characteristics were selected as training targets.

Training was given four weeks after the pretest. It consisted of providing feedback as to how the elderly women had responded under self-endorsement. Training items were selected from form B to avoid item specific acquisition and to produce a clear distinction between assessment and training items.

For *Specific Training,* items were selected from the three scales on which the elderly were most misperceived. The girls were trained to answer 30 test items in exactly the same way as a matched elderly counterpart had done previously. For *General Training* the 30 items that the girls learned to answer in exactly the same way as their elderly counterpart did were composed of two items randomly selected from each of the 15 PRF scales. This condition was included to examine the possibility that only feedback pertaining to stereotype perceptions *per se* would be effective in changing attitudes. For *No Feedback Training* the Ss were presented with the same training items as the Specific Training group, but did not receive information feedback about the elderly women's self-endorsement. The *No Training* group did not participate in any experimental activity between pre- and posttests.

Posttests were administered to the adolescent on form A of the PRF immediately after training and two weeks later.

Results and Discussion

Table 1 summarizes the scores for self-description by the elderly and the simulations of the elderly by the adolescents on the subscales of the PRF. The simulations of the adolescents were significantly higher than the self-endorsements of the elderly for Aggression, Dominance, Exhibition, and Nurturance, and significantly lower for Achievement. Analysis of the change in posttest scores from pretest scores indicated that Specific Training markedly increased accuracy of perception with respect to Dominance. This training effect was well-maintained during the second posttest, two weeks after training.

Table 1

Pretest Discrepancies Between Adolescents' Simulations of the Elderly and Self-Endorsements of Elderly Subjects

| | Mean Scale Score | | | |
Scale	Adolescent Simulations	Elderly Subjects	Difference	Probability
Achievement	10.98	13.30	−2.32	<.05
Affiliation	15.75	15.90	−0.5	
Aggression	5.25	2.90	+2.35	<.01
Autonomy	5.65	6.90	−1.25	
Dominance	7.13	2.90	+4.23	<.01
Endurance	10.18	11.40	−1.22	
Exhibition	7.43	5.10	+2.33	<.05
Harm avoidance	16.68	15.70	+0.98	
Impulsivity	6.98	6.10	+0.88	
Nurturance	15.65	13.80	+1.85	<.01
Order	15.00	14.80	+0.20	
Play	8.25	8.60	−0.35	
Social recognition	11.15	9.20	+1.95	
Understanding	9.80	11.80	−2.00	

Although the training was effective on only one of the three target dimensions, the results suggest some optimism with regard to the possibility of affecting changes in attribution of the aged by the young, especially since the intervention effort was small, and the outcome was maintained over a two-week period.

Abstract **58**

Life-Span Person-Perception

KENNETH H. RUBIN, Ph.D. and IAN D. R. BROWN, M.A.

"A Life-Span Look at Person Perception and Its Relationship to Communicative Interaction," *Journal of Gerontology*, 1975, *30*, 461-468.

Young adults typically perceive the elderly in a less positive light than they see themselves or the middle-aged. When the perceiver makes attributional judgments about a stimulus person, he assumes a set of expectancies related to the perceived. However, few data exist concerning the relationship between attribution of psychological traits to various age groups and the perceivers' behaviors toward their perceptual targets. The following experiments were designed to investigate expressed attitudes of young adults about the intellectual abilities of various age groups, and to examine one mode of behavior, that of verbal communication, toward these age groups.

Experiment I

This experiment differed from most previous person-perception investigations in that it used seven target populations (infants, preschoolers, preadolescents, adolescents, and young, middle-aged and elderly adults) and in that it considered both specific and general categories of intellectual skill rather than personality characteristics.

Method

SUBJECTS: Two hundred forty-three introductory psychology students, including 131 males and 112 females, with a mean age of 21.08 years.

Materials: During the first few minutes of a regular class meeting the respondents were asked to rate the seven target persons (aged 18 months, and 5, 10, 15, 20, 40 and 75 years) on their ability to perform the following specific tasks: (1) to classify a picture of an adult male into five separate categories; (2) a water conservation task; (3) to find one's way to a goal by using a map; (4) to solve a 100-piece puzzle; (5) to solve a three-digit long division problem; (6) to live alone and care for oneself; (7) to discuss a moral issue. Rating choices were: 1 = unable, 2 = able with difficulty, 3 = moderately able, 4 = easily able to solve the problem. Respondents were also asked to rank order the seven age groups from "most" to "least" with regard to (8) general knowledge and (9) possession of problem-solving ability. Respondents were told that target persons were "healthy, of average intelligence, middle-class and noninstitutionalized."

Results

The respondents perceived middle-aged and young adults as the most intellectually able group across questions 1—7, followed by the elderly, adolescents, preadolescents, preschoolers and infants. The same trend held for responses to items 8 and 9, except that on question 8 (general knowledge) the elderly did not differ significantly from young adults and on question 9 (problem-solving ability) the elderly versus adolescent comparison was nonsignificant. Thus, elderly adults were seen quite consistently as less intellectually competent than young and middle-aged adults. However, the elderly were not viewed in a negative vein since overall they were perceived as being moderately to easily able to perform all tasks.

Experiment II

This experiment was designed to discover whether college students who were found to view the elderly as less intellectually competent than younger adults would behave in a manner consistent with their attitudes. Specifically, this study examined ways in which university students modified their speech when communicating rules and objectives of a simple game to listeners of different ages. It was hypothesized that the complexity of game explanation would be least when the listener was a young child or elderly person, intermediate for an adolescent listener, and greatest for a peer or middle-aged adult.

Method

SUBJECTS: Sixty undergraduate students (30 males and 30 females) who had participated in Experiment I. Twelve subjects (six males and six females) were randomly assigned to communicate to each of the preschool, preadolescent, adolescent, middle-aged and elderly groups.

Materials: A simple game consisting of dowels and discs used to construct a pyramid. The "listeners" consisted of 12 black ink drawings representative of six different age levels and of both sexes.

PROCEDURE: Each S was seen individually. He was informed that the experimenter would demonstrate a game, and then he would have to explain the game to some other people. The experimenter demonstrated the game nonverbally until the S indicated he understood the rules. The S was then required to explain the game verbally to a listener from another age group and also to a peer age-group listener. There was counterbalancing for listener order. The explanations were tape recorded and subsequently analyzed for: (1) mean number of words per utterance (a greater number of words reflecting greater complexity); (2) number of utterances; (3) number of sentences: (4) number of game rules cited.

Results

Communicative complexity, as measured by mean number of words per utterance, was significantly greater when the listener was a middle-aged adult than when he was a child or an elderly person. On the remaining measures of verbal interaction, there was a nonsignificant trend toward curvilinear complexity with age. The results provided partial support for the hypothesis that a relationship exists between person-perceptions and behavior toward those perceived.

CHAPTER VIII

Life Satisfaction and Adjustment to Aging

Abstract **59**

Personality and Aging

ROBERT J. HAVIGHURST, Ph.D.

"Personality and Patterns of Aging," *Gerontologist*, 1968, *8*, 20-23.

Considering that a great many people after sixty-five have good enough health and enough income to support a life of happiness and satisfaction, why are some of these people unhappy and dissatisfied? Have they been unhappy all their lives? Are they unhappy due to remedial present situations?

Neither of the two most prevalent theories of successful aging, the *activity theory* and the *disengagement theory*, are satisfactory because they obviously do not explain all the phenomena of successful aging, yet both have some facts to support them. The activity theory implies that except for the inevitable changes in biology and health, older people are the same as middle-aged people, with essentially the same psychological and social needs. Decreased social interaction results from the withdrawal by society from the aging person, and the decrease in interaction is against the desire of most aging men and women. The person who ages successfully stays active and manages to resist the shrinkage of his social world. He maintains the activities of middle age as long as possible and uses substitutes for work after retirement and for loved ones whom he loses by death.

In the disengagement theory (Cumming and Henry, 1961) decreased social interaction is interpreted as a process characterized by mutuality; both society and the aging person withdraw, and the aging person accepts and perhaps even desires the decreased interaction. The individual's withdrawal is assumed to have intrinsic or developmental qualities and is accompanied or preceded by increased preoccupation with self and decreased emotional investment in persons and objects. In this sense, disengagement is a natural rather than an imposed process. According to this theory, the older person who has a sense of psychological well-being, i.e., is aging successfully, will usually be the person who has reached a new equilibrium characterized by greater social distance, altered types of relationships and decreased social interaction.

Since some people are satisfied with disengagement while others are satisfied with a high degree of social engagement, perhaps a theory of the relationship of personality to successful aging is needed. The beginning of such a theory was made by Reichard, Livson and Peterson (1962), who rated 87 men, 42 retired and 45 working, on "adjustment to aging" and on 115 personality variables. A "cluster analysis" of personality ratings identified men highly similar to one another. The "high on adjustment to aging" group included three types, labeled Mature, Rocking Chair and Armored. The "low on adjustment to aging" group included two types labeled Angry and Self-Haters. Some of the Ss did not fit into any type.

The Mature group was characterized by a constructive rather than an impulsive approach to life. The Rocking Chair group tended to take life easy and depend on others. The Armored men defended themselves actively from dependency, avoided retirement and disliked idleness. The Angry men were generally hostile, blamed others, were fearful of death and were downwardly mobile socially. The Self-Haters rejected and blamed themselves, were depressed and looked forward to death as a release. Each type made different behavioral adjustments to aging. Thus, though the Rocking Chair and the Armored types both adjusted successfully to aging, one group was disengaged while the other was active.

In this investigation, data from the Kansas City Study of Adult Life were analyzed to test empirically the disengagement and activity theories and to relate personality and role activity to life satisfaction in old age.

Method

SUBJECTS: The Ss were 159 men and women, aged 50 to 90, from the upper-working to upper-middle class. Institutionalized and chronically ill people, and those with a psychiatric diagnosis, were excluded. Ss were interviewed intensively over the period 1956 to 1962. By the end of the study there was a 45 percent attrition rate; 27 percent was due to deaths, 12 percent to geographical moves, and the rest to refusals, usually because of reported poor health.

PROCEDURE: Interviewees were rated on 45 personality variables reflecting the cognitive and affective aspects of personality. On the basis of the sum of role activity scores for 11 common social roles (e.g., worker, parent, spouse, citizen) respondents were categorized into high, medium and low activity levels. A composite score for life satisfaction or psychological well-being was derived from five scales recording the extent to which a person finds gratification in everyday activities, regards life as meaningful, feels that he has succeeded in achieving major goals, has a positive self-image, and maintains happy and optimistic moods and attitudes. Respondents were categorized as having high, medium and low life satisfaction.

Results

Neither the disengagement nor the activity theory was adequate to account for the observed relationships between activity and life satisfaction scores. Although engagement in common social roles was negatively related to age, generally those more active at the later ages had higher life satisfaction scores, but there were many exceptions.

Factor analysis was used to extract personality types. Four major types emerged, labeled integrated, armor-defended, passive-dependent and unintegrated personalities. An analysis based on personality, role activity and life satisfaction dimensions was applied to data from the 59 persons aged 70-79. Fifty of these were clearly in one of the eight patterns of aging presented in Table 1.

The *reorganizers* are competent people, engaged in many activities, who reorganize their lives to substitute new activities for lost ones. They fit the American ideal of "keeping active, staying young." The *focused* individuals

Table 1
Personality Patterns in Aging

Personality Type	Role Activity	Life Satisfaction	N
A. Integrated (reorganizers)	high	high	9
B. Integrated (focused)	medium	high	5
C. Integrated (disengaged)	low	high	3
D. Armored-defended (holding-on)	high or medium	high	11
E. Armored-defended (constricted)	low or medium	high or medium	4
F. Passive-dependent (succorance-seeking)	high or medium	high or medium	6
G. Passive-dependent (apathetic)	low	medium or low	5
H. Unintegrated (disorganized)	low	medium or low	7

have well-integrated personalities and medium levels of activity. They tend to focus their time and energy in one or two role areas. The *successful disengaged* have low activity levels with high satisfaction. They have voluntarily reduced role commitments and have high self-esteem, with a contented "rocking chair" position in life. The *holding-on* people hold on to the activities of middle age as long as possible, and as long as they do, they have high satisfaction. The *constricted* individuals differ from the focused group in having less integrated personalities. Their reduced role activity and constricted social interactions are presumably a defense against aging. The *succorance-seeking* individuals are successful in getting emotional support from others and thus maintain medium levels of activity and life satisfaction. The *apathetic* people have low role activity combined with medium or low life satisfaction. Presumably, they have never given much to life and never expected much. The *disorganized* category includes those who have deteriorated thought processes and poor emotional control. They barely maintain themselves in the community and at the most have medium life satisfaction.

Patterns of aging are probably established and predictable by middle age. These data support the hypothesis that personality is a pivotal dimension in describing patterns of aging and in predicting relationships between level of activity and life satisfaction.

Abstract **60**

Disengagement in Old Age

AARON LIPMAN, Ph.D. and KENNETH J. SMITH, M.A.

"Functionality of Disengagement in Old Age," *Journal of Gerontology*, 1968, 23, 517-521.

This study tested Cumming and Henry's hypothesis that disengagement from normal adult roles by old people is as functional for the personality system as it presumably is for the social system. Specifically, it questioned the contention that, for the individual, the most functional *method* of preparation for death (the "normal" way to grow old) is to disengage. Functionality was estimated in terms of the morale of the aged person.

Typical disengagement implies that as a person grows older his level of disengagement from the social system increases. Atypical or deviant disengagement patterns would occur if individuals who are younger exhibit the disengagement characteristic of older people, or, conversely, if older persons exhibit an engagement pattern characteristic of younger persons.

Method

Criteria: In order to isolate typical and atypical patterns of disengagement, the population was dichotomized into high and low engagement levels. The four indices of engagement were those used by Cumming and Henry, i.e., (1) Role count (median = 8); (2) Social participation (median = 3.5); (3) Social life space (median = 15); (4) Perceived life space (median = 1).

SUBJECTS: To be included in the study population each respondent had to be above, equal to, or below the median on *all four criteria*. Of the original sample of 765 older individuals living in low-cost public housing, only 281 met the criteria. The age range of the sample was 60 to 81. The sample included males and females, whites and blacks, white-collar and blue-collar workers, native born and foreign born, and variations with respect to marital status, religious affiliation, years of education, and perceived health and adequacy of income status.

Of the group, 157 individuals could be described as disengagers (below the median on all four indices), and 124 as engagers (equal to or above the median on all four indices). When such groups of high and low engagers were further dichotomized according to age (younger median = 69; older median = 79 years), the age by engagement status distribution presented in Table 1 was obtained.

Successful aging measure: The criterion of successful aging was the

Table 1
Morale, Age and Disengagement

Age and Engagement Category	Mean Morale	SD	N
Younger - 74 or under			
Typical - engaged	18.9 a	3.1	65
Atypical - disengaged	17.7 b	4.0	75
Older - over 74			
Typical - disengaged	17.3 c	4.0	82
Atypical - engaged	19.4 d	3.0	59

a vs. b - P < 0.05   c vs. d - P < 0.01

maintenance of an optimal level of morale as assessed by the following morale scale items:

Do you regret very much the chances you missed during your life to do a better job of living?

Would you say you are satisfied with your way of life today?

Do you find a great deal of unhappiness in life today?

Do you feel that these days a person doesn't really know whom he can count on?

Do you feel that in spite of what some people say, the lot of the average man is getting worse, not better?

Do you feel that it is hardly fair to bring children into the world with the way things look in the future?

Do you often feel there is just no point in living?

Do you feel that things keep getting worse and worse for you as you get older?

Items were scored from 1 to 3 with 2 for "don't know" answers, yielding maximum and minimum morale scores of 24 and 8.

Results

Table 1 presents the mean morale levels for the four patterns of disengagement under investigation. These data indicate that maintenance of high morale was not associated with typicality of the disengagement pattern, but rather with the level of engagement. Higher morale was more characteristic of those people who were more engaged, regardless of age.

Separate analyses were conducted to investigate relationships between typicality of the disengagement pattern and each of education, occupation, race, sex, perceived health and adequacy of income. Engagement varied as a function of occupation (there was a higher proportion of engagers and a lower proportion of disengagers in manual occupations than in nonmanual occupations), and race (proportionately more non-whites than whites were engaged). Morale varied as a function of race (whites had higher morale than non-whites), perceived health and adequacy of income. However, the general relationship between high morale and engagement was maintained, regardless of variations in age, occupation, health, income, sex or race. The finding that engaged rather than disengaged older persons have higher morale suggests that the general applicability of the disengagement theory should be examined critically. It would appear that inculcation and internalization of an activist value system is not necessarily reversed in old age.

Abstract **61**

Disengagement and the Stresses of Aging

MARGOT TALLMER, Ph.D. and BERNARD KUTNER, Ph.D.

"Disengagement and the Stresses of Aging," *Journal of Gerontology*, 1969, 24, 70-75.

According to the original promulgation of the disengagement theory, disengagement is an inevitable, universal, self-perpetuating, gradual and mutually satisfying process prepared for in advance by society and the individual. These alterations are accompanied by concomitant changes in the perception of life space and by increasing self-absorption and lessening of ego energy. This study raises the issue that certain factors other than aging, namely, stress-inducing environmental and circumstantial disturbances, have social consequences which have been attributed to disengagement. If the changes that purportedly reflect disengagement can be shown to appear at variable times during the life span of the individual and can be related to extrinsic assaults, either social or physical, or to unusual occurrences in life history, then disengagment may be viewed as an extrinsic rather than an intrinsic process. It is suggested that rather than age *per se* it is what transpires as time elapses that forces the individual to change his life style and perhaps to disengage.

Method

SUBJECTS: The sample of 101 women and 81 men ranged in age from 50 to 89. The Ss were selected to encompass all marital statuses and a wide range of health statuses, extending from the physically active and employed to the institutionalized disabled.

PROCEDURE: Each S was interviewed for approximately 90 minutes. The prepared schedule of questions allowed for the use of the same measures of social engagement as were used in the formation of the disengagement theory. These were as follows: role count (an index of the number of roles in which an individual is involved); interaction index (density of interaction determined by amount of each day spent in normatively governed interaction with others); social life space measure (composite of density and variety of interactions within a monthly period). Additional questions were used to establish a health index.

Each S was scored for stress from 0 to 3 depending on the number of the following stresses he had experienced: illness, widowhood and retirement.

The stress index was then correlated with each of the engagement measures.

Results

There was a decline in engagement score as stresses rose from 0 to 1 and again from 1 to 2; no further decrease in engagment was noted as stresses increased from 2 to 3. The one stress and two stress groups were nearly identical in age (mean ages 67.3 and 68.0) but had very different engagement scores; the three stress group was older (mean age 72.4) but did not show less engagement than the two stress group.

Correlational analyses indicated that marital status, residence and working status all showed as high or higher relationships with engagement measures as age did. Income status, the scoring of which was completely independent of the engagement measures, had a larger effect on engagement than age. Health appeared to have a much more powerful effect on engagement than any other factor including age. Partial correlations indicated that all of the association between age and engagement measures can be accounted for by the correlation between working status and engagement and the tendency for fewer older people to be employed.

The results provide substantial support for the hypothesis that disengagement among the aged can be predicted to occur as a concomitant of physical or social stresses which profoundly affect the manner in which the life pattern of the person is redirected. It is not age that produces disengagement, but the impact of physical and social stress which may be expected to increase with age.

Abstract 62

Age Changes in Activities and Attitudes

EDMAN B. PALMORE, Ph.D.

"The Effects of Aging on Activities and Attitudes,"
Gerontologist, 1968, *8*, 259-263.

Does aging reduce activities and attitudes? Are decreases in activities related to decreases in satisfaction? Is there a persistence of life style among the aged? This paper discusses longitudinal findings relevant to these and other questions.

Method

SUBJECTS: One hundred twenty-seven (out of 256) volunteers in a longitudinal study of aging were interviewed at approximately three-year intervals until they had completed four waves of interviews. When interviewed the fourth time they ranged in age from 70 to 93, with a mean age of 78. Fifty-one were men and 76 were women. All were ambulatory and noninstitutionalized. Analysis of selection and attrition factors indicated that the panelists were a social, psychological and physical elite among the aged and became more so through time.

PROCEDURE: The Inventory of Activity and Attitudes questions were read to the Ss as part of a longer social history. The Activity Inventory consisted of 20 questions dealing with five areas of activities: health (physical capacity to act); family and friends (frequency of contacts); leisure (ways of spending time, hobbies, reading, organizations); economic (amount of housework and lack of economic restrictions on activities); and religious activity (attendance at religious services, listening to them on radio or TV, reading religious literature). Maximum score per subscale was ten, with higher scores indicating more activity.

The Attitude Inventory consisted of 56 agree-disagree items about the S's satisfaction with eight areas of his life: health, friends, work, economic security, religion, usefulness, family and general happiness. The score in each area could range from zero to six with higher scores indicating more satisfaction.

Results

The men had almost no overall reduction over the ten years in either activities or attitudes. The women had significant but quite small (less than 7 percent) reductions in both activities and attitudes. Table 1 summarizes the activity and attitude scores for women only at the four points in time. Changes in total activities were significantly and positively correlated with changes in total attitudes. This means that those who reduced their activities as they aged tended to suffer reduction in overall satisfaction, and, conversely, those who increased activities tended to enjoy an increase in satisfaction. There was a clear tendency for these aged people to persist with the same relative levels of activities and attitudes as they grew older.

The lack of substantial reduction in activities is contrary to the commonly held assumption that most people become less active as they age. It is also contrary to disengagement theory which asserts that marked withdrawal from activities is the modal pattern of aging. Moreover, the positive correlation of activity with attitudes contradicts predictions from the disengagement theory and supports the activity theory of aging, which has been stated as the "American formula for happiness in old age: keep active."

Table 1
Mean Activity and Attitude Scores for Women Only
at Four Points in Time

	Time 1	Time 2	Time 3	Time 4
Activities:				
Health	2.5	3.2	2.6	2.5
Family and friends	5.9	6.1	5.5	5.3*
Leisure	7.7	7.2	6.6*	6.3*
Economic	7.4	7.5	8.1	8.4*
Religious	6.7	7.1	6.4	6.7
Total	30.1	31.1	29.4*	28.8
Attitudes:				
Health	4.0	3.8	3.7	3.6*
Friends	4.5	4.4	4.5	4.3
Work	3.9	3.8	3.7	3.5*
Economic security	3.8	3.9	4.6*	4.0*
Religion	5.5	5.6	5.7*	5.6
Usefulness	4.6	4.3	4.4	4.1*
Family	4.7	4.8	4.9	4.8
Happiness	4.2	4.1	3.6*	3.6*
Total	35.3	34.6	34.2*	33.3*

*Difference between this score and score at Time 1 is significant at the .01 level.

Abstract 63

Future Commitments and Successful Aging

DAVID SCHONFIELD, M.A.

"Future Commitments and Successful Aging: I. The Random Sample," *Journal of Gerontology*, 1973, *28*, 189-196.

This study tested the hypothesis that future commitments are associated with successful aging. The hypothesis is relevant to two prevalent ideas about problems of the aged—that they tend to live in the past and that they do not have enough to do.

Method

SUBJECTS: One hundred females over the age of 65 (mean age—72.36) were interviewed. The sample was selected on a fairly random basis; residents in institutions and housing projects were excluded. Participants were paid a small fee.

Measurements: (a) *Future Diary:* The S was asked to list special commitments during the following seven days; committed hours included time traveling to and from an appointment. The score was:

$$\frac{\text{committed hours}}{\text{hours awake} \times 7} \times 100$$

(b) *Usual Day:* The score was:

$$\frac{\text{hours spent in active pursuits}}{\text{hours awake}} \times 7 \times 100$$

Active pursuits included domestic work, active hobbies and active social activities, and excluded such behaviors as eating, sleeping, watching TV, reading, and passive social activity (no preparation required).

(c) *Future Activity Index:* The score was the sum of the scores for the Usual Day and Future Diary, which represented the percentage of time during the following seven days committed to activities requiring effort and planning.

(d) *Tri/Scales (XOB):* These scales were designed to measure success in aging with respect to ten dimensions: happiness, financial situation, health, activities, family relationships, pleasure from companions, housing, clubs and organizations, transportation, and usefulness. For each dimension, the respondent rated herself with an X on the nine-point scale in comparison to the anchor point of five for the average Canadian. She then rated older people in general on the same scale with an O, followed by a rating for her own best year with a B.

The adjusted score for each Tri-Scale dimension was computed from the formula $4X-2B-0+24$, and a total Tri-Scale score was computed by averaging the adjusted scores. (The rationale for the formula is of interest. Self-assessed deterioration is estimated by the discrepancy between the best days (B) and present status (X) and to give this discrepancy heavy weight, $2(B-X)$ is subtracted from present status (X). Self-assessed present superiority to older people in general should add to feelings of success, whereas a comparative inferiority should reduce such feelings; hence, $(X-O)$ is added. The constant of 24 is added to avoid negative numbers. Thus, the measure of successful aging on each Tri-Scale is: $X-2(B-X) + (X-0) + 24 = 4X-2B-0+24$.)

(e) *MAGI (Personality):* Five scales, each consisting of six questions, were used to estimate neuroticism, introversion, depression, rigidity and aggression.

Results

A significant correlation ($r = .43$; $p<.001$) between Future Activity Index and total adjusted Tri-Scale scores confirmed the hypothesis of an association between future commitments and successful aging. The Future Activity Index also correlated significantly with four separate Tri-Scales—Happiness, Health, Ease of Transportation and Challenging Activities. The Future Activity Index did not correlate significantly with any of the MAGI personality scores.

The Usual Day score was negatively correlated with age ($r = -.41$; $p<.001$) and the Future Diary was positively correlated with socioeconomic status ($r = + .52$; $p<.001$). The implication is that everyday active pursuits are reduced in the very old, while socioeconomic status is conducive to special appointments or breaks in the monotony.

Figure 1 shows the mean present (X), best year (B) and old people in general (O) ratings for each of the separate Tri-Scales. In general, the

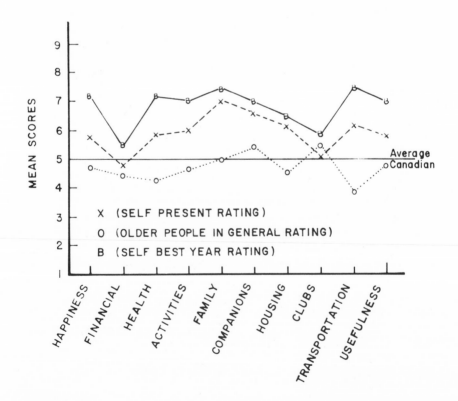

respondents rated their present status well below their best year, and old people in general well below their own present status. The greatest deterioration from the best year to the present was for Happiness, Health, Activities, Transportation and Usefulness. There was relatively little deterioration from best year to present for Family, Companions and Housing.

The separation of B, X and O scores for Transportation emphasizes the importance played by mobility in the lives of the elderly and identifies transportation as an area to which elderly people would give high priority in planning for an aged population. On the other hand, the fact that these older people rated the importance of clubs and organizations lower for themselves at present than for old people in general might justify questions about the current emphasis on group activities and clubs for the elderly.

Abstract **64**

Life Purpose in Old Age

GENE ACUFF, Ph.D. and DONALD ALLEN, Ph.D.

"Hiatus in 'Meaning': Disengagement for Retired Professors," *Journal of Gerontology*, 1970, 25, 126-128.

It has been suggested that a primary task for our society in caring for the aged is that of giving positive meaning to their place in society. What are some of the variables related to the degree of life meaningfulness experienced by older people? This study focuses on items significantly related to "meaning" experienced by emeritus professors in a southeastern state.

Method

SUBJECTS: All male professors (N = 188) who had retired from four-year colleges and universities in the state were mailed a questionnaire. One hundred and nine (71 percent) of those contacted returned usable questionnaires. The mean age of the respondents was 73 years.

Materials: The major test instrument was the Purpose in Life Scale constructed by Crumbaugh and Maholick (1964). It contains 20 items with each item varying along a seven-point continuum from highly positive to highly negative. Typical items are: "In life I have no goals or aims at all [1]—very clear goals and aims [7]"; "I am a very irresponsible person [1]—a very responsible person [7]"; "Every day is new and constantly different [7]—exactly the same as any other [1]."

Biographical and other personal information was also solicited from each respondent by means of a 67-item questionnaire.

Results

Purpose in Life scores (PIL) were not significantly related to age, community, socio-economic status or social participation variables. PIL scores were significantly related to professional characteristics, bereavement experienced, health evaluation, religious patterns and general life attitudes. Persons who earned high scores on the PIL tended to miss a sense of professional usefulness (in contrast to low scorers who missed peers or income more than usefulness), continued participation in professional organizations, were high in family affection and had extended-family rather than nuclear-family orientations, had not experienced multiple bereavements, evaluated their own health and the health of spouse positively, held an important religious philosophy, reported definite future plans and had a clear perception of what is worthwhile in life. Conversely, persons with low PIL scores tended to have discontinued participation in professional organizations, were low in family affection, had nuclear-family orientations, had experienced multiple bereavements, had negative health assessments, etc.

These findings suggest the appropriateness of comparing various categories of people for PIL scores and attempting to identify correlates of PIL for various populations.

Abstract **65**

Reminiscing and Ego Integrity

WILLIAM BOYLIN, B.A., SUSAN K. GORDON, Ph.D.
and MILTON F. NEHRKE, Ph.D.

"Reminiscing and Ego Integrity in Institutionalized Elderly Males," *Gerontologist*, 1976, *16*, 118-124.

The theory of ego development proposed by Erikson suggests that in old age, reminiscing is an important aspect of ego integrity, the state of positive adjustment in later life. The relationship between these two processes was assessed in the present study through measuring the amount of reminiscing that older institutionalized men reported in themselves, and correlating this with their scores on a measure of the three adult ego crises included in Erikson's theory: intimacy, generativity, and ego integrity. Although previous studies on reminiscing have suggested that older persons benefit from the experience of reevaluating their past lives, this hypothesis has not been empirically related to Erikson's criteria of positive acceptance within the individual of the aging process.

Method

Elderly males residing in a domiciliary unit of a Veterans Administration Hospital comprised the sample. These 41 men were given a questionnaire measure to ascertain the amount, affect (positive or negative), and time (childhood, adolescence or adulthood) of self-reported reminiscence. Ego adjustment was measured by a modified and expanded version of a scale devised for assessing the first six of Erikson's life stages in college students. The questions were administered in a relatively short (15 to 30 minutes) semi-structured interview.

Results

Scores on frequency, affect, and time of reminiscing were intercorrelated with each other and also with the summed scores of each of the three ego adjustment subscales, age, and educational level of the resident. The amount of reminiscing was found to be positively related to scores on the ego integrity subscale alone. Ego integrity scores were also positively correlated with negative affect of reminiscing. These findings were interpreted as indicating that the older men in the present study were engaged in a process of life reviewing, which emphasized the critical aspects of their past experiences. One might hypothesize that this was a temporary period which would be overcome as earlier conflicts became resolved in the life review process. The failure to find the relationship between positive affect and frequency of reminiscing observed in previous studies was considered to reflect dissatisfaction with being institutionalized. Indeed, the results on time of reminiscing suggested that the elderly men in this sample were thinking more frequently about their younger days of childhood and young adulthood than of old age.

Item analyses of the ego adjustment scale scores were also performed in order to determine which questions were most strongly related to the ego stage which they were designed to represent. Twelve out of the 20 items designed specifically for this study were highly correlated with their sub-scales alone. These results indicated that these subscales were useful in assessing ego adjustment in elderly institutionalized men. Further research would be needed to determine the reliability and content validity of these subscales.

The observed relationship between ego integrity and reminiscing adds to the evidence from earlier work linking reminiscing to adaptation in old age. Furthermore, the possibility that such reminiscing may be at least temporarily negative has implications for providing support during what may be a difficult period of adjustment for the older person.

Abstract 66

The Use of Leisure Time

ERIC PFEIFFER, M.D. and GLEN C. DAVIS, M.D.

"Use of Leisure Time in Middle Life," *Gerontologist*, 1971, *11*, 187-195.

This research addressed questions about allocation of time by middle-aged and older individuals with special emphasis on the use of free time.

Method

SUBJECTS: The subjects were 261 men and 241 women ranging in age from 46 to 71 years. Of the men, 98 percent were married and two percent were widowed or had never married. Of the women, 71 percent were married and living with spouse, 18 percent were widowed, six percent were separated or divorced, and five percent had never married. Eighty-one percent of the men and 49 percent of the women were employed.

PROCEDURE: A trained interviewer gathered information on three categories of leisure behavior: (a) a diary-like assessment of how time is typically spent; (b) an assessment of vacation behavior; (c) attitudes toward and satisfaction derived from leisure activities.

Results and Discussion

Ss on the average were able to account for 96 waking hours per week (range, 48 to 151 hours). Employed persons could account for more hours than nonemployed persons. Table 1 presents the mean number of hours spent per week by men and women on a variety of activities. There were age-related increases for time devoted to TV (women only), reading, and socializing (women only). One of the most marked sex differences was amount of time devoted to socializing. Volunteer work was not a major activity for these individuals.

Only 15 percent of the men and 20 percent of the women said they had not taken a vacation during the preceding year. Most vacations varied from one to four weeks (mean = 2.8 weeks) and about 91 percent of the vacations had involved travel. Vacations seem to be a highly institutionalized, almost mandatory type of leisure behavior.

Seventy-one percent of the men and 65 percent of the women expressed satisfaction with amount of available free time, 23 percent of the men and 28 percent of the women complained of shortage of free time and six and seven percent of the men and women respectively said they had too much free time. A disproportionately high percentage of men in the 66 to 71 age range complained about too much free time, while the greatest proportion of complaints about too little free time were from women aged 51 to 55 years.

More than half of the employed respondents, 52 percent of the men and 55 percent of the women, indicated that they derived greater satisfaction from their work than from their leisure activities. Only 13 percent of the men and 16 percent of the women indicated that they derived greater satisfaction from leisure activities than from work. In response to the question: "If you did not actually have to work for a living, would you still work?" 90 percent of the men and 82 percent of the women said "yes." Almost all men (97 percent) aged 66 to 71 indicated a preference for continued employment.

These results suggest that for the age groups studied, ours is a work-oriented, not leisure-oriented, culture. This conclusion has important public policy implications.

Table 1
Mean Hours Spent Per Week

Activity	Men	Women
Working	36.8	34.5
Eating	9.8	9.8
Personal care	7.7	8.4
TV	11.6	13.2
Reading	8.3	9.0
Sport hobby	3.9	3.4
Sport in person	0.6	0.3
Church and meetings	2.3	2.9
Volunteer work	0.7	1.1
Socializing	4.8	7.2
Activity around house	5.7	3.6
Other (specified)	0.7	0.6
Just sitting around	3.3	2.6

Abstract **67**

Association Activity and Life Satisfaction

STEPHEN J. CUTLER, Ph.D.

"Voluntary Association Participation and Life Satisfaction: A Cautionary Research Note," *Journal of Gerontology*, 1973, *28*, 96-100.

It is generally assumed that interaction in voluntary associations relates to the psychological well-being of the elderly. It is posited that association membership functions to maintain or expand life space, to promote feelings of efficacy, and reduce social isolation, and thereby to increase life satisfaction. However, many studies have demonstrated that both life satisfaction and voluntary association participation vary as a function of health and socio-economic status. This research investigated whether voluntary association participation bears any residual relationship to the life satisfaction of the aged after statistically controlling for the effects of health and socio-economic status.

Method

One hundred seventy noninstitutionalized respondents aged 65 or older were interviewed. The median age of the sample was 74. Included were 121 females, 49 males, 137 whites and 33 non-whites. The Neugarten, Havighurst and Tobin Life Satisfaction Index (1961) was administered and the sample was dichotomized into low and high life satisfaction subgroups at the approximate midpoint of the frequency distribution. The index of voluntary association participation was based on membership in each of 16 types of voluntary associations, subjective estimate of degree of involvement, and self-report on frequency of participation. Participants were divided into three approximately equal groups designated as having high, medium and low participation. The estimate of socio-economic status utilized the Hollingshead two-factor index, and subjective assessment of health status was obtained.

Results

The relationship between life satisfaction and level of participation was significant (p<.05) as were the relationships between life satisfaction and socio-economic status (p<.001) and life satisfaction and health (p<.001). However, the relationship between life satisfaction and participation in voluntary organizations when the effects of socio-economic status and health were controlled failed to achieve significance. In short, after the effects of status and health are accounted for, voluntary association participation bears at best a weak and statistically nonsignificant relationship to life satisfaction. It seems reasonable to conclude that voluntary associations self-select as members persons who are initially more satisfied with their life situation by virtue of their health and status characteristics.

Abstract **68**

Membership and Attrition in a Senior Center

JAMES E. TRELA, Ph.D. and LEO W. SIMMONS, Ph.D.

"Health and Other Factors Affecting Membership and Attrition in a Senior Center," *Journal of Gerontology*, 1971, 26, 46-51.

The recent proliferation of associations designed exclusively for the aged suggests that rather than withdrawal from society's secondary structure, older people reorient (or are expected to reorient) their associational activities in response to their changing age status. Whether such organizations are thought of as political aggregates, recreation centers, vehicles for the distribution of needed services, or integrating links between the aged individual and larger society, their effectiveness may often be contingent on their ability to involve a significant proportion of the population they purport to serve or represent. Although their numbers are growing, these organizations face unique problems of recruitment and attrition; the majority of older people do not affiliate with aged peers in voluntary associations exclusively for the aged.

This paper focuses on several dimensions of senior-center membership, including the following: the effectiveness of a systematic attempt to incorporate new members; reasons for joining; deterrents to membership and participation; and reasons for termination of membership.

Method

Seven hundred nineteen persons aged 62 and over were contacted by members during a senior-citizen-center recruitment campaign. Prospective members were visited, advised of the resources and availability of the center and invited to become members. Of those contacted 248 joined. Subsequent interviews were held with 210 of the new members and 110 persons who failed to join. The interview refusal rate was 5 percent for members and 21 percent for nonmembers. The interviews focused on areas such as health, physical mobility and factors governing the decision whether to join the center. One and two years following the interview most of the interviewees responded to brief mail questionnaires focusing on membership status and contingencies of change.

Results

Of those contacted by recruiters, 35 percent, exclusive of the house-bound, eventually became members. Reasons for joining included the following: "sounded good" (38 percent); outside activities (48 percent); companionship including statements which reflected preparation for the potential loss of spouse (12 percent); the persuasive influence of volunteers though some of these indicted they paid fees for charitable reasons or to terminate "pestering" with no intention of participating (more than one third). The most frequently given reasons for not participating more actively or not joining were as follows: none (39 percent and 36 percent for members and nonmembers respectively); competing activities and interests (50 percent for both groups); ambivalence toward organizational activity, including noninterest in handicraft and other activities and distaste for exclusive association with age peers (45 percent and 43 percent); poor health (9 percent and 19 percent); and transportation (10 percent and 1 percent). The member and nonmember groups differed significantly only with respect to health and transportation variables.

The favorable health status of members in comparison to nonmembers, as determined by self-judgments, was supported by the death of 7.7 percent of the members versus 17.7 percent of the nonmembers within a two year period.

Although recruitment of new members was relatively successful (35 percent of those invited), the attrition rate of those who became members was very high. During the first year 22 percent terminated their membership and 38 percent terminated membership in the second year. For the 106 individuals for whom reasons for termination could be identified, the distribution of reasons was as follows: competing activities and interests (31.1 percent); poor health (16.0 percent); death (15.1 percent); moved from community (14.2 percent); center did not meet expectations (12.3 percent); plan to rejoin (11.3 percent). The emphasis on competing activities and interests is noteworthy; one half the individuals interviewed indicated that competing activities interfered with participation or membership, and of those who subsequently terminated membership almost one third did so because of competing activities.

Abstract **69**

Age-Grading in Social Interaction

GORDON L. BULTENA, Ph.D.

"Age-Grading in the Social Interaction of an Elderly Male Population," *Journal of Gerontology*, 1968, *23*, 539-543.

Do the aged tend to interact with each other increasingly as they grow older, and with younger people decreasingly? Cultural trends provide considerable justification for suggesting that the frequency of contact between the aged population and younger persons is decreasing, and the aged are thereby coming to consititute a subculture. The plurality of factors underlying the emergence of an aged subculture can be subsumed under two broad categories: (a) historical changes in the collective structural position of the aged in society, and (b) changes in the individual's role set accompanying his movement through the life cycle.

The first hypothesis tested by this study is that older persons interact more with each other than with persons of a younger generation. Confirmation of this hypothesis would offer evidence as to the contemporary impact of cultural trends which are viewed as having isolated the aged as a societal subgroup. The second hypothesis tested is that advancing age among the elderly brings an increased prominence of horizontal, as vis-à-vis vertical, social ties in extended family, kinship, and community groups. This hypothesis taps the saliency of the aging process as a precipitant of social isolation from younger persons.

Method

SUBJECTS: A sample of 434 retired men was selected randomly from six communities ranging in size from a small rural community to a city of 170,000 population. Persons in congregate-care facilities such as retirement units or nursing homes were excluded.

PROCEDURE: Information was obtained on the frequency of each respondent's face-to-face contact with spouse, children, grandchildren, siblings, relatives and friends. Only contacts that regularly occurred on a daily basis or at least once a week were included in the analysis. The age of each of the interactants was determined.

Results

The 434 respondents averaged 1.6 contacts per day and 3.4 contacts per week (each contact represented a different person). Sixty-seven percent of the daily contacts and 59 percent of the weekly contacts were with persons aged 60 or older. Thus, there was confirmation of the hypothesis that the majority of daily and weekly contacts of these retirees were with older persons.

In order to test the second hypothesis, the respondents were categorized in two age groups, those aged 65 to 79 years (N = 328) and those aged 80 years and over (N = 106). Table 1 summarizes nature and frequency of contacts reported by respondents in the two age categories. The "very old" retirees had a greater proportion of their social contacts crossing generational lines than did their younger counterparts. Moreover, the absolute number of contacts with younger people was higher for the very old group than for the younger old group. Although these data do not support the argument that advancing age is associated with greater confinement of social relationships to age mates, they may reflect the decreased availability of like-aged family members and/or increased need for assistance from younger people. Eight percent of the persons aged 65 to 79 years reported no regular daily contact, in contrast to 14 percent of the respondents aged 80 years and over.

Table 1
Proportion of Respondents Having Contact
with Specified Persons, by Age

| | Age | | | |
| | 65 - 79 (N = 328) | | 80 or older (N = 106) | |
Persons interacted with	Daily	Weekly	Daily	Weekly
Spouse	77*	77*	58	58
Child	23	44	31	68*
Grandchild	2	6	8*	16*
Sibling	6	22*	4	11
Other relative				
60 or older	4	13	5	8
younger	2	7	8*	8
Friend				
60 or older	13	40	15	33
younger	7	19	4	13
No contact	8	2	14	4
Average number of contacts	1.6	3.5	1.6	3.2
Average number of contacts with older people	1.0	2.2	.9	1.5
Average number of contacts with younger people	.6	1.3	.7	1.7
Proportion that older persons comprise of all contacts	71	63	57	47

* differences between age groups are significant at p < 0.05.

Abstract **70**

Recreation and Successful Aging

THOMAS J. DeCARLO, Ed.D.

"Recreation Participation Patterns and Successful Aging,"
Journal of Gerontology, 1974, *29*, 416-422.

This study examined the relationship between recreative activities and successful aging in persons over 60 years of age.

Method

SUBJECTS: The participants were 23 male and 37 female members of like-sexed twin pairs who were the surviving participants of an extensive longitudinal study of twins.The age range was 79 to 91 years (Mean = 85.5 years). All Ss were noninstitutionalized, white, literate and English-speaking. Co-twins had been reared together. The sample was generally representative of the aged population with respect to education, class and marital status.

PROCEDURE: The current physical health and mental health of the participants was assessed by a standardized battery of examinations administered by physicians. Intellectual functioning was assessed by means of a Composite Intellectual Index. A Geriatric Life History Interview Schedule was used to obtain both current and retrospective data about the Ss' recreative pursuits. A Recreative Activity Schedule (RAS) was used to classify information about recreative activities. Participation was classified with respect to *stage* (childhood, 12 to 20 years; young adulthood, 21 to 39 years; middle age, 40 to 59 years; later life, 60 years and above; and current) and *frequency* (often, occasionally and never). Type of participation was classified according to behavioral elements as sensory-motor, cognitive, or affective. Participation was also classified as regular or sporadic.

Successful aging was evaluated by means of criteria established by physicians and psychologists as follows: (1) good successful aging—able to carry on daily routine; absence of more than mild illnesses; absence of chronic brain syndrome; psychological test score more than .5 SD above the S's mean score; (2) fair successful aging—moderate incapacity to carry on daily routine as a result of past or present illness; mild chronic brain syndrome; psychological test score between .5 SD below and above the S's mean score; (3) poor successful aging—presence of marked debility or incapacitating illness; severe chronic brain syndrome; psychological test score below .5 SD from S's mean. Appropriate numerical scores were assigned to ratings for recreative activities and successful aging.

Results

Table 1 presents the correlations among successful aging criteria and total life recreative activity. A correlation of .28 or higher denotes a significant relationship. These data suggest a positive relationship between continued participation in recreational activities and successful aging. The relationship between cognitive activity and intellectual performance is quite strong, and there is a moderate relationship between affective activity and mental health. Motor activity did not significantly relate to physical health and failed to show a strong relationship with successful aging. Of the three types of recreative activities, the cognitive activities were most strongly related to successful aging. An analysis of the relationship between frequency of activity and successful aging suggested that individuals who engage in a high degree of activity with regularity will age more successfully than those whose engagement is of low degree and sporadic.

Table 1
Correlations Among Criteria of Successful Aging and
Total Life Recreative Activity

| Activities | Criteria of Successful Aging | | | |
	Physical Health	Mental Health	Intellectual Performance	Total Criteria
Motor	.11	.34	.19	.29
Cognitive	.28	.28	.52	.48
Affective	.01	.30	.28	.30
Total	.14	.45	.42	.48

Abstract 71

Sexual Behavior In Senescence

ADRIAAN VERWOERDT, M.D., ERIC PFEIFFER, M.D.
and HSIOH-SHAN WANG, M.D.

"Sexual Behavior In Senescence," *Geriatrics*, 1969, 24, 137-154.[1]

This study examined the effects of age, sex and marital status on degree, incidence and patterns of sexual activity and interest in a group of 254 men and women ranging in age from 60 to 94. The data were obtained from three separate studies carried out at intervals of approximately three years.

Method

SUBJECTS: All subjects were participants in a comprehensive longitudinal study which investigated many aspects of behavior and physiological status. None of the Ss was institutionalized. Data were collected on 254 Ss in Study I, 190 Ss in Study II, and 126 Ss in Study III. The decline was principally due to death and serious illness.

PROCEDURE: The data on sexual behavior were gathered as part of each S's medical history and were elicited during a structured interview conducted by a psychiatrist. The interview focused on the following: (1) enjoyment of intercourse in younger years (none, mild, very much); (2) sexual feelings in younger years (none, weak, moderate, strong); (3) enjoyment of intercourse at present (none, mild, very much); (4) sexual feelings at present (none, weak, moderate, strong); (5) present frequency of intercourse (none, monthly, bimonthly, weekly, more than once a week); (6) if intercourse has stopped, when stopped? (less than a year ago, 2 to 5 years ago, 6 to 10 years, 11 to 20 years, more than 20 years ago); (7) reason for stopping intercourse (death of spouse, illness of spouse, illness of self, loss of interest of spouse, loss of interest of self, loss of potency of spouse, loss of potency of self). The interviewer tried to obtain answers in the Ss' own words and then scored responses according to the system outlined above. Not all Ss answered all questions.

Results

The data indicated that age and degree of sexual activity (frequency of

1. Abstracted from *Geriatrics*, © 1969, by the New York Times Media Company, Inc.

intercourse) are not related in a strictly linear fashion and that one or more intervening variables exist, probably age-related infirmities or physical illness or both. At the time of Study I when the mean age of the respondents was 68.8 years, the mean frequency of sexual activity was approximately once a month; approximately six years later at the time of Study III it had decreased almost 50 percent. The incidence of sexual activity (the proportions of Ss with sexual activity or interest) declined from a level of more than 50 percent during the early sixties to 10 to 20 percent during the eighties. The degree of sexual interest was more intimately related to aging than activity was; strong degrees of interest did not occur beyond age 75. However, the incidence of sexual interest did not show an age-related decline; mild to moderate degees of interest tended to persist into the eighties. In Study III 76 percent of the men and 30 percent of the women indicated sexual interest; the corresponding percentages for the subsamples aged 78 years and older were 72 and 29 percent. In general, the incidence of interest was higher than that of activity. This discrepancy was more prominent in male Ss and tended to increase with age.

Marital status had little effect on the activity and interest of aging men; indeed, the relatively few unmarried men had higher proportions of sexual activity than married men did. Unmarried women had a negligible amount of sexual intercourse but about 20 percent of the female Ss reported sexual interest. The sexual activity and interest of men was greater than that of women, regardless of marital status, but with advancing age, marital status became less important in its effect on activity.

For men, generally, patterns of sustained activity and interest were relatively typical for the sixties, decreasing activity and interest for the mid-seventies, and continuously absent activities and interest beyond that age. However, patterns of rising activity and interest occurred in 20 to 30 percent of the men, regardless of age, and including men in their eighties. Only 27 percent of the men reported the absence of sexual interest. Only 16 percent of all women studied showed a rising or sustained pattern of sexual interest, while 74 percent and 10 percent reported the absence or diminution of sexual interest.

For men, the activity-interest discrepancy was greater than for women, and the discrepancy tended to increase with advancing years i.e., male sexual activity after age 75 tends to decline more rapidly than sexual interest does. This discrepancy implies the probability of increased psychological stress.

Abstract **72**

Sexual Behavior in Middle Life

ERIC PFEIFFER, M.D., ADRIAAN VERWOERDT, M.D.
and GLENN C. DAVIS, M.D.

"Sexual Behavior in Middle Life," *American Journal of Psychiatry*, 1972, *128*, 1262-1267.[1]

This study was designed to provide additional information about the incidence of sexual behavior in late adulthood, and about antecedents to differences in the incidence of sexual behavior.

Method

SUBJECTS: The subjects were 268 men of whom all but four were married (two were widowers and two had never married), and 241 women of whom 170 were married, 44 were widowed, 14 were separated or divorced and 13 had never married. The Ss ranged in age from 46 to 71. They were chosen randomly from membership of a medical insurance plan, and were representative of the middle and upper socio-economic strata.

PROCEDURE: The data on sexual behavior were gathered as part of a medical history questionnaire. The questions were almost identical to those used in an earlier study by the same investigators (Verwoerdt, Pfeiffer and

Table 1
Current Frequency of Sexual Intercourse in Percentages

Age Group	number		none		Once a month		Once a week		2-3 times a week		+3 times a week	
	M	F	M	F	M	F	M	F	M	F	M	F
46 - 50	43	43	0	14	5	26	62	39	26	21	7	0
51 - 55	41	41	5	20	29	41	49	32	17	5	0	2
56 - 60	61	48	7	42	38	27	44	25	11	4	0	2
61 - 65	54	44	20	61	43	29	30	5	7	5	0	0
66 - 71	62	55	24	73	48	16	26	11	2	0	0	0

Wang, 1969). It was predicted correctly that the paper and pencil technique would reduce embarrassment and thereby increase the yield of data.

Results

Table 1 summarizes the reported frequency of sexual intercourse in percentages. The frequency of sexual relations was lower for women than for men in all age categories, and for both sexes there was a significant ($p < 0.001$) decline in sexual activity with increasing age. The pattern for expressed level of sexual interest followed the same age and sex trends as the sexual activity data, except that the proportion of both men and women expressing strong sexual interest was somewhat higher for the oldest age group than for the next-to-the-oldest group. This suggests that persons who survive beyond the late sixties may represent an elite group. Overall, only 25 percent of the men and 19 percent of the women reported no awareness of decline in sexual interest. For both sexes, the proportion reporting no decline of interest decreased with age. Fourteen percent of the men in comparison to 42 percent of the women reported cessation of sexual relations. The time given for cessation ranged from within the last year to more than 20 years ago, with a greater proportion of women stopping at an earlier age. Twenty-nine percent of the men and 90 percent of the women attributed reasons for cessation to the spouse (death, separation, illness, loss of interest or inability to perform). The general finding that men blame themselves and women blame their partners for cessation held even after death of and separation from spouse were removed from analysis.

Abstract 73

Social Profile of the Black Aged

IRA F. EHRLICH, D.S.W.

"Toward a Social Profile of the Aged Black Population in the United States: An Exploratory Study," *International Journal of Aging and Human Development*, 1973, 4, 271-276.

This paper reported an exploratory, descriptive study on the social functioning of elderly black men and women. It replicated an earlier study with a sample of elderly white people.

Method

SUBJECTS: The participants were a stratified random sample of the black residents in two new, federally funded, high-rise age-segregated public housing units. People who had an income of less than $1,200, were in self-determined poor health, or who were white (less than ten percent of the total residents) were excluded. The average age of the sample was 75.1 years, 71 percent were female, 63 percent were widowed, 82 percent had no more than junior high school education, and the average income was low ($2,000; 1972).

Method: Questionnaires were administered on an individual basis by white interviewers. The major instruments were the Neugarten, Havighurst and Tobin Life Satisfaction Scale (LSA) and a questionnaire based on a modification of Cumming and Henry's interaction index, role count and life space concepts.

Results and Conclusions

Mean role count was 4.95 out of a possible seven roles. Females, married persons, and persons with higher education tended to have higher role counts. Also, ten of the 14 octogenarians had five or more role counts.

The mean LSA score was 11.9 out of a possible 20. Life satisfaction score correlated positively with income, education, former occupational status, marital status and perceived health.

The life space score, based on cumulative frequency of contacts between the respondents and children, relatives, friends and others on a monthly basis, indicated that more than half (56 percent) of the respondents had a relatively normal range and frequency of contacts. However, most of the other respondents could be described from their life space score as either excessively isolated or almost frenetically active.

In comparison to a comparable sample of elderly white people interviewed in the earlier study, these black respondents had lower role count, life space and life satisfaction scores. Perhaps some of the differences between the samples could be accounted for by: (1) perceived health, since the whites tended to give more positive self-ratings for health; (2) income, since the modal income for whites was higher than for blacks, or (3) religious preference, since four-fifths of the black sample were Protestant in comparison to one-half of the white sample.

Abstract **74**

Correlates of Life Satisfaction

JOHN N. EDWARDS, Ph.D. and DAVID L. KLEMMACK, Ph.D.

"Correlates of Life Satisfaction: A Re-examination," *Journal of Gerontolgy*, 1973, *28*, 497-502.

Intensive investigation has been conducted for more than a decade concerning the biological, psychological, and sociological correlates of individual well-being, of which life satisfaction is one component. It has been demonstrated that life satisfaction scores correlate significantly with many variables including age, health, socio-economic status, marital status, work status and size of the community. The general purpose of this study was to identify which, if any, of the many variables related to life satisfaction are the most efficient predictors of it, and what combination of factors is most successful in explaining the variance in experienced satisfaction.

Method

SUBJECTS: The data were secured using a census enumeration district quota sample, resulting in proportionate representation of males and females aged 45 to 64 and those 65 and older residing in a Virginia four-county area.

Measures: Life satisfaction, the dependent variable, was measured by employing ten items from the Life Satisfaction Index modified by Adams (1969). The 22 independent variables grouped into six major categories are listed in Table 1.

Results

The first column of Table 1 indicates the correlation between life satisfaction score and each of the independent variables. Eleven of the 22 variables correlate significantly with life satisfaction, with income, education, voluntary association, church-related activities and perceived health showing the strongest relationships. Neither of the informal familial participation variables correlated significantly with life satisfaction. The second column lists partial correlations between life satisfaction and the remaining 19 variables when the socio-economic variables were treated as control variables (i.e., their effects were removed statistically). When the effects of socio-economic

Table 1
Relationship of Selected Variables with Life Satisfaction

	Correlation with Life Satisfaction	Partical Correlation with Life Satisfaction Controlling for Status	Beta Coefficients to Predict Life Satisfaction
Socio-economic status			
Education	.24*	—	.11
Income	.33*	—	.34*
Occupational status	.12	—	.12*
Background characteristics			
Age	−.14*	−.05	−.06
Sex	−.01	−.04	−.01
Marital status	.14*	.07	.10
Family size	.10*	.02	−.01
Time in area	−.07	−.01	−.05
Community size	−.02	−.08	−.12*
Retired (head of household)	−.06	−.06	−.08
Formal participation			
Voting	.05	−.08	−.14*
Voluntary association	.24*	.12*	.09
Church-related activities	.19*	.15*	.14*
Informal familial participation			
Visit relatives	.06	—	.02
Visit children	.02	−.02	−.03
Informal nonfamilial participation			
Visit neighbors	.16*	.18*	.14*
Phone others	.13*	.14*	.11*
Number of neighbors	.09*	.09*	.11*
Number of friends	.04	.04	−.01
Health			
Perceived health	.19*	.12*	.16*
Number of ailments last month	−.06	−.02	.04
Number of ailments last year	−.07	−.03	.01

*p < .05

variables were removed, life satisfaction scores correlated significantly with none of the background variables, and again with none of the informal familial participation variables. Life satisfaction scores did correlate significantly with two of the formal participation variables, three of the informal nonfamilial participation variables and perceived health.

Column 3 of the table presents beta coefficients which reflect the amount of change expected in the dependent variable for one standardized unit change in the independent variable when the remaining independent variables are held constant. The beta coefficient thus provides a measure of the relative contribution of each predictor in accounting for life satisfaction.

These data indicate that the primary determinant of life satisfaction is socio-economic status, especially family income. Perceived health is also an important predictor, as are the nonfamilial participation variables, particularly the combination of extent and intensivity of neighboring. One of the implications of these data is that because socio-economic status is a prime determinant of life satisfaction, no study of life satisfaction should fail to take this variable into consideration.

Abstract **75**

A Revision of the PGC Morale Scale

M. POWELL LAWTON, Ph.D.

"The Philadelphia Geriatric Center Morale Scale: A Revision," *Journal of Gerontology*, 1975, *30*, 85-89.

A number of morale scales have been constructed in an attempt to assess the inner states of older people. Lawton (1972) devised the Philadelphia Geriatric Center (PGC) Morale Scale on the assumption that morale was multidimensional rather than unidimensional, and that a really useful scale required easier response formats and wording than many of the previously used scales have. The 22 items in the original scale were subjected to a principal-componenet analysis and yielded six factors, as follows: Attitude Toward Own Aging, Agitation, Dissatisfaction, Acceptance of Status Quo, Optimism, and Surgency.

Other investigators subsequently used the same items with a different population. Their analysis indicated that some of the original PGC factors were either unstable or specific to the initial sample. This investigation involved a further analysis of the PGC on new subjects.

Method

SUBJECTS: The 22-item PGC scale was administered to 1,086 tenants of housing for the elderly and community-resident elderly people. For the tenants a random sample was drawn, and for the community-residents probability sampling was used. The mean age of the Ss was 72.6 years; 72 percent were female, 32 percent were married and living with spouse; 76 percent were white, and almost all were functionally independent, and of low income status. Only 828 of the Ss completed the entire PGC scale.

Results

On the basis of analyses involving five combinations of subject group and item pools (item pools were varied by deleting specific items), three stable factors emerged. These factors, Agitation, Attitude Toward Own Aging, and Lonely Dissatisfaction, and the items best representing them, are presented in Table 1. These new data suggest that three stable factors can be derived from a smaller subset of the original PGC Morale Scale. This aggregate pool of 17 items has been labelled the Revised PGC Morale Scale.

The data from the PGC scale, along with work by other investigators using other scales, support the idea that there ware identifiably separate aspects of what has been called morale or life satisfaction.

Table 1
Stable Factors That Emerged from New Analyses of PGC, with Scale Items[1]

Factor 1 - Agitation

*Little things bother me more this year (No)
*I sometimes worry so much that I can't sleep (No)
 I have a lot to be sad about (No)
*I am afraid of a lot of things (No)
*I get mad more than I used to (No)
 Life is hard for me most of the time (No)
*I take things hard (No)
*I get upset easily (No)

Factor 2 - Atittude Toward Own Aging

*Things keep getting worse as I get older (No)
*I have as much pep as I had last year (Yes)
 Little things bother me more this year (No)
*As you get older you are less useful (No)
*As I get older, things are better/worse than I thought they would be (Better)
 I sometimes feel that life isn't worth living (No)
*I am as happy now as when I was younger (Yes)

1. High morale responses indicated in parentheses.

Factor 3 - Lonely Dissatisfaction

*How much do you feel lonely? (Not much)
*I see enough of my friends and relatives (Yes)
*I sometimes feel that life isn't worth living (No)
*Life is hard for me much of the time (No)
*How satisfied are you with your life today? (Satisfied)
*I have a lot to be sad about (No)
 People had it better in the old days (No)
 A person has to live for today and not worry about tomorrow (Yes)

*Items selected as best representing factors 1, 2, or 3 respectively.

CHAPTER IX

Age and Personality Attributes

Abstract 76

Senility or Garden-Variety Maladjustment

FRANCES M. CARP, Ph.D.

"Senility or Garden-Variety Maladjustment?" *Journal of Gerontology*, 1969, *24*, 203-208.

Senility is a particulary ill-defined term which is frequently used in reference to older people. It has long been known that some of the symptoms of senility are actually functions of anxiety. Anxiety, maladjustment, and neuroticism are basic dimensions of personality throughout the life span. Behaviors labeled "senile" may not be limited to the old. A behavioral test of senility may differ primarily in name from other tests used to assess anxiety or neuroticism or maladjustment in younger people. A difference in the title of the tests that are administered to persons of different ages, rather than difference in people at those ages, may result in the erroneous conclusion that certain age differences exist. If we are to understand aging, it is necessary to separate the lifelong from the age specific.

This study tested the possibility that behaviors judged to reflect senility are not specific to later life. The Senility Index from the Chicago studies on "adjustment in old age" was selected as the compendium of "senile signs." The goal was not to criticize the Index, but rather to clarify the nature of the set of behaviors which many investigators assume to be associated with growing old. It was predicted that the "senile signs" do not vary as a function of age, but rather are positively related to introversion, social ineptness and low self-esteem, and negatively related to ego strength and intellectual competence.

Method

SUBJECTS: The older Ss were 295 people with an average age of 72 years at first contact (range 52-92 years), who lived independently in an urban community. They were relatively representative of their age group with respect to education, income and socio-economic status. The younger Ss were 270 resident undergraduates in a private college. Their average age was 20 years (range 17-25 years). The age groups were comparable for IQ score but the younger Ss had higher educational and income levels; most of the old lived at or below the poverty line, whereas the families of the young financed a private college education.

PROCEDURE: Twice at an interval of about 18 months, the Senility Index was filled out for each older S by an interviewer who had spent many hours with him collecting biographic, demographic and attitudinal data. Each college S was rated on the Senility Index items (presented without a title) by his roommate with whom he had lived for at least six months. A socio-metric questionnaire, self-report data on personality and behavior traits, and interviewer ratings were used to obtain additional information about the older Ss.

Results

Within the old group (53-94 at a time of second testing) there was no relationship between Senility Index score and age ($r = -.05$). Score change over the 18-month period was not significant. The younger group had a statistically significant higher proportion of "senile" signs than the older group (college mean = $31.15 \pm .96$; older mean = $14.59 \pm .94$; $t = 12.35$, df = 563, $p < 0.01$). These findings suggest strongly "senile signs" are not specific to old age and do not increase as a function of age.

Correlations of the Senility Index scores of the older Ss with measures of personality-behavior traits suggest that "senile signs" indicate maladjustment, neuroticism, anxiety or low ego strength. High scorers tended to be neurotic, negativistic, dissatisfied, socially inept persons with unrealistic and unfavorable views of themselves. They tended to be low in intellectual competence and ego strength. There was no evidence that high scores were associated with advanced age.

To say that college undergraduates are "more senile" than people with a mean age of 72 is unrealistic; however, it would be reasonable to conclude that younger people exhibited more signs of maladjustment than the older people did. These results emphasize the need to test age specificity and also to assess the appropriateness of labels assigned to sets of behaviors.

Abstract 77

Aging and Individual Differences

GEORGE L. MADDOX, Ph.D. and ELIZABETH B. DOUGLASS, M.A.

"Aging and Individual Differences: A Longitudinal Analysis of Social, Psychological and Physiological Indicators," *Journal of Gerontology*, 1974, *29*, 555-563.

This study explored the relationship between age and individual differences. Some theorists have assumed that whereas children and adolescents become more differentiated through their development, adults become increasingly more alike as they approach the common denominator of death. Other theorists, utilizing a life-span perspective, have claimed that individual differences in life style and intellectual functioning observed in the middle years are accentuated in late life. Contradictory conclusions have been difficult to assess because of the lack of adequate reliable data.

Attempts to determine whether heterogeneity in populations remains stable, increases, or decreases in the later years of life must take into account a number of methodological considerations including the following: (a) a distinction, not possible in simple cross-sectional studies, must be made between age differences and age changes; (b) selective survival; (c) sampling bias, since less able people tend to have higher refusal rates for initial testing and retesting; (d) a possible terminal drop in functioning shortly before death; (e) the distinction between intra-individual and inter-individual variability; (f) males and females may exhibit different patterns of differentiation with age. In this study particular attention was paid to considerations (a), (b) and (e).

Two hypotheses were investigated: (a) Individual differences do not decrease with age. Variability on a variety of indicators is at least maintained, if not increased, in late life; (b) Individuals tend to maintain the same rank on a variety of indicators in relation to age peers throughout the later years of life.

Method

SUBJECTS: Data were derived from a continuing longitudinal investigation of human functioning at Duke University. The sample was composed of 106 current survivors of an original panel of 271 persons ranging in age from 60 to 94 at time of first testing; the mean age initially was 70. The social and economic characteristics of the sample reflected those of the Durham, North Carolina area. Six rounds of observation were available spanning an average of 13 years from observation 1 to observation 6. For various reasons (illness, scheduling difficulties, etc.) measurements on all variables are not available for all Ss at all times of testing.

Variables Assessed: A total of 19 variables were selected for examination. The physiological variables were as follows: physician's functional rating, performance status, weight, cardiovascular state, right and left visual acuity, binaural hearing loss, diastolic and systolic blood pressure, and blood cholesterol. The social/social psychological variables were as follows: life satisfaction, level of social activiy, self-health assessment, concern about health and depression. The psychological measures were verbal, performance, and full-scale scores of the WAIS and reaction time. Reaction time was used to asses intra-individual as well as inter-individual variability. Major comparsions were for differences in variability measures between Times 1-3 and Times 4-6.

Results

A comparison of Time 1 and Time 6 variance indicated that for the 15 variables that could be compared, there was no significant change for eight variables, an increase in variance for five, and a decrease in variance for two. The two variables that showed a decrease were self-health assessment, probably reflecting a tendency on the part of the elderly to minimize health difficulties, and diastolic blood pressure, a change that reflected medical treatment. An examination of group variances at all six times of measurement indicated that Time 1 variance was the smallest for six variables, and Time 6 variance was the greatest for six variables. Comparisons of Times 3 and 6 for all 18 variables indicated maintenance of variability for 16 and a significant increase in variability for two variables. The average of Times 1, 2 and 3 variance was smaller than the average of Times 4, 5 and 6 variance for 15 out 19 measures. Had mortality not been controlled in this study by withdrawing the data for Ss who died, the findings would have been different. When mortality was not controlled, variance did decrease in 10 out of 19 instances for Times 1, 2 and 3 to Times 4, 5 and 6. Intra-individual variability in Reaction time showed no clear pattern for change through time. These observations provided strong support for the first hypothesis.

Rank order correlations showed that those who scored high on a particular variable in earlier observations also tended to score high later and low scorers tended to remain low scorers; a confirmation for the second hypothesis.

Thus, when mortality within a defined sample is controlled, the variability of a number of social, psychological and physiological measures tend to remain stable through time.

Abstract **78**

Psychoneurotic Reactions of the Aged

EWALD W. BUSSE, M.D., ROBERT H. DOVENMUEHLE, M.D.
and ROBERT G. BROWN, Ph.D.

"Psychoneurotic Reactions of the Aged," *Geriatrics*, 1960, *15*, 97-105.[1]

This study investigated the prevalence and significance of psychoneurotic manifestations in a group of persons over 60 years of age who were reasonably well adjusted and living in the community.

Method

SUBJECTS: The subjects were 222 volunteers over the age of 60 who were maintaining a satisfactory level of social adjustment in the community. An attempt was made to control the selection system so that the sample was reasonably representative.

PROCEDURE: An eight-category classification system was developed with a number of symptoms listed within most of them. Each area of symptomatology specified descriptive cutoff levels to separate normal from disturbed functioning. The eight categories with their associated symptoms were as follows: A) Neurotic, nonorganic signs: Mood, Affect, Anxiety, Obsessions, Compulsions, Hypochondriasis, Self-condemnatory trends, Expansive trends; B) Functional psychotic signs: Delusions, Persecutory trends, Somatic delusions; C) Organic psychotic signs: Illusions, Perception, Intellectual function, Form of talk; D) Mixed organic and functional signs: Combination of B and C above; E) Probable organic, nonpsychotic signs: Motor activity, Form of talk, Speed of reaction, Appropriate to ideas, Insight into defects: (a) physical, (b) mental, judgment concerning: (a) general activities, (b) future plans; F) Mixed neurotic and probable organic, nonpsychotic signs: Combination of A and E; G) Normal: None of symptoms in categories A through F.

Each S was rated for each symptom type. For example, for anxiety the rating labels were as follows: slight situational anxiety, and no apparent anxiety for normal ratings and panic, acutely anxious, chronically anxious or apathetic for neurotic ratings. In assigning ratings, it was recognized that

1. Abstracted from *Geriatrics,* © 1960, by the New York Times Media Company, Inc.

certain psychic processes or defense mechanisms that are clearly detrimental to a younger adult may be necessary to maintain a satisfactory adjustment in the aged, e.g., denial may be used by older persons who are maintaining successful social adjustment to control anxiety resulting from realistic threats, whereas a younger person using denial in a similar manner would be considered poorly adjusted by most psychiatrists.

The neurotic group was further subdivided into mild and severe neurosis. The criteria for severe neurosis were as follows: (a) two or more neurotic symptoms from Category A; or (b) one symptom from affect (deeply depressed), severe obsessions, severe compulsions or severe hypochondriasis.

Results

According to this method of classification, only 89 of the 222 Ss could be considered normal. Of these, 17 demonstrated some recent memory loss and three some remote memory loss. (If both types of memory loss were present, Ss were rated as having organic mental signs and were not classified as normal.)

One hundred and nineteen persons were classified as having nonpsychotic mental disorders. Of these, 56 were considered neurotic (25 with severe neurotic reactions), 21 had relatively minor organic changes which impaired function, and 42 demonstrated evidence of both neurotic and organic pathology. Surprisingly, 14 of this community group were psychotic (seven organic, six functional and one a combination of organic and functional).

The psychoneurotic subjects were compared to the normal individuals in regard to various parameters including age, and physical, psychologic and social measurements. There was an inverse relationship between age and mental disorders, with many of the neurotics, particularly those with hypochondriac symptoms, in the younger ages. This observation suggests either a negative survival factor or the possibility that with advancing years better adjustment is attained. Those who were psychoneurotic were decidedly less social than those of the normal group and were apt to be hypochondriacal and depressed; however, their attitude toward work was not strikingly different from the normal group.

This study demonstrates that elderly people with varying degrees of psychoneurotic reactions may still be able to maintain a reasonably acceptable adjustment in society. Further investigation is necessary to identify the elements in society which permit adequate adjustment.

Abstract **79**

Structure of Self-Concept

ROLF H. MONGE, Ph.D.

"Structure of the Self-Concept from Adolescence Through Old Age," *Experimental Aging Research,* 1975, *1,* 281-291.

This paper reports an investigation of age differences over the major portion of the life-span in the connotative structure of the self-concept.

Method

SUBJECTS: The 4,540 Ss were distributed within age categories as follows: nine to 19 years, N = 2646; 20 to 34 years, N= 511; 35 to 49 years, N = 641; 50 to 64 years, N = 407; 65 to 89 years, N = 335. There were more females (2,741) than males (1,799) but the proportion of males to females was approximately equivalent across age groups. Most (2,062) of the Ss in the youngest age group were tested in 1963; the other 584 young Ss were tested in 1970. The adult Ss were tested between 1968 and 1971. All Ss were noninstitutionalized, community-dwelling individuals. The adults were recruited from various community organizations, the adolescents from schools.

Instrument: The instrument involved the presentation of seven-point semantic differential scales which were used by the S to rate the concept "My Characteristic Self" on 21 polar adjective pairs as follows: Superior-*Inferior;* Leader-*Follower; Smart*-Dumb; *Success*-Failure; *Sharp*-Dull; Valuable-*Worthless; Confident*-Unsure; Steady-*Shaky; Strong*-Weak; *Kind*-Cruel; *Nice*-Awful; *Friendly*-Unfriendly; Good-*Bad; Stable*-Unstable; Refreshed-*Tired;* Relaxed-*Nervous;* Satisfied-*Dissatisfied;* Healthy-*Sick; Happy*-Sad; Rugged-*Delicate; Hard*-Soft. The italicized pole was to the left on the instrument.

Results and Discussion

An earlier study had indicated that, for adolescents, the connotative structure of the self-concept could be described by four factors labeled Achievement/Leadership, Congeniality/Sociability, Adjustment, and Masculinity-Femininity. Using these four factors as a basis for comparison, it was determined through complex factor analytic techniques applied to the data from the current sample that a very substantial degree of agreement existed across age groups and between the sexes on the connotative structure of the self-concept as originally identified among the adolescents. This finding justified the calculation of one grand analysis on data from all Ss.

The definition of the components of self-concept that emerged were as follows:

Component I, Achievement/Leadership, is defined at one pole by the adjectives superior, leader, smart, success, sharp, valuable, steady and strong, and at the other pole was inferior, follower, dumb, failure, dull, worthless, shaky, and weak. Positive ratings suggest that the individual perceives himself as a capable, intelligent frontrunner, whereas negative ratings convey acceptance by the individual of the "loser" image.

Componet II, Congeniality/Sociability, is defined at the positive end by the adjectives kind, nice, friendly, good and stable. Positive ratings suggest an image of self as open to, pleased by, and responsive to social stimulation. The adjectives at the other pole (cruel, awful, unfriendly, bad, unstable) convey a decidedly misanthropic attitude, perhaps toward self as well as others.

Component III, Adjustment, is defined at the positive pole by refreshed, relaxed, satisfied, healthy and happy, versus tired, nervous, dissatisfied, sick and sad. The positive adjectives convey the image of a person comfortably accommodated to his or her environment, adjusted to the ups and downs of life, and in a state of inner psychic equilibrium.

Component IV was labeled Masculinity-Femininity because whereas Ss of the same sex and different ages used the adjectives similarly, the males and females generally disagreed about which pole was positive. Males tended to view the rugged, hard and, to a lesser degree, strong pole as positive, while females tended to view as positive the delicate, soft and, to a lesser degree, weak pole.

A score was computed on each component for each individual. Figure 1 presents the mean component on the four components by age and sex. As Figure 1 indicates, there were marked and significant differences as a function of age and sex for scores on all four components.

For Component I, Achievement/Leadership, males and females did not differ at the youngest age level; at all other ages there were large sex differences. There was a sharp rise for both sexes from the adolescent years into the years of young adulthood (20 to 34) in willingness to describe self in positive terms on the Achievement/Leadership component. Males continued to rate themselves highly, though there was a slight decline in late adulthood. Females aged 35 to 64 rated themselves lower on this component than did younger or older females. Perhaps the females aged 35 to 64 were so immersed in family matters or subordinated to their husband's career that they found the positive adjectives in this category inappropriate for self-description. The rise after age 65 for women may be due to an increased role in leadership due to the poor health, retirement or death of the husband.

The age trend in the Congeniality/Sociability Component is essentially flat from the adolescent years through the postretirement years. The significant rise in the postretirement years may be an artifact due to the fact that Ss in the 65 to 89 years group were largely recruited from social clubs and senior centers, settings that would be expected to attract congenial, sociable people. The alienated, lonely, incapacitated elderly were probably under-represented in the sample. At all age levels except postretirement, females earned higher scores for Congeniality/Sociability than males.

The decline in Adjustment (Component III) from the teens to young adulthood may reflect the anxieties and readjustments consequent to the establishment of self in marriage, family and vocation, with increases in adjustment in subsequent years as stability in these and other major arenas of life is achieved. The decline in postretirement years may result from loss of spouse, loss of significant roles and the lesser prestige involved in being retired as opposed to being a productive member of society. At all ages, males earned higher scores on the adjustment component than females, though in the postretirement group the sex differences are slight.

The age trends for Component IV (Masculinity-Femininity) suggest that

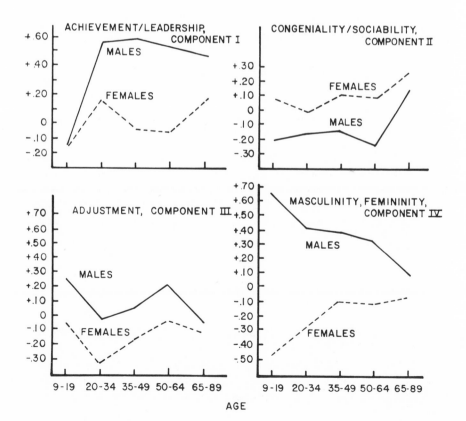

the need for males to hold themselves forth as "real men" is greatest during adolescence and declines fairly steadily therafter. Females tended to show a movement away from femininity (as defined by soft, delicate and weak) from adolescence until the mid -thirties, with the age curve remaining essentially unchanged from the mid-thirties until very late adulthood. The male-female differences were very great for the youngest age group but declined progressively to minimum but significant differences in late adulthood.

Abstract 80

Self-Concept and Altruism

KESTUTIS A.TRIMAKAS, Ph.D. and ROBERT C. NICOLAY, Ph.D.

"Self-Concept and Altruism in Old Age,"*Journal of Gerontology*, 1974, 29,434-439.

This study investigated the hypotheses that: (1) there is a negative relationship between self-concept and old age; (2) persons with a positive self-concept will demonstrate altruistic behavior to a greater degree than persons with a negative self-concept; (3) persons encouraged by conformity and public stimuli toward altruism will behave altruistically with greater frequency than persons discouraged by a lack of such stimuli.

Method

SUBJECTS: The subjects were 162 female tenants of a low-income senior housing project. The age range was 66 to 88 years, with 35 Ss in the 60's, 109 in the 70's and 18 in the 80's.
PROCEDURE: The Tennessee Self-Concept Scale (TSCS) was used to assess self-concept. It consists of 100 self-descriptive statements, to be answered on a five-point scale from completely true to completely false.

Altruism was defined as the S's choice to contribute some money which she might win in a lottery to the entertainment fund of the building in which she lived. It was scored according to the amount chosen to share with others if she were to win $100.

On the basis of TSCS score, Ss were assigned to High, Middle and Low Self-Concept groups. Ss in each of these three groups were then randomly assigned to three social-influence subgroups, with 18 Ss per subgroup.

All Ss were given a lottery ticket for $100, with the time of drawing scheduled for the end of the survey. They were told that the winner could keep the $100 or she could share with everyone in the building by contributing some or all of it to the entertainment fund. Ss in the *positive influence* condition were told that senior citizens are usually generous, and that the winner's choice would be made public to all. Ss in the *no-influence* condition were told that the choice was up to them, and that no one would ever know their decision. Ss in the *negative influence* condition were told that senior citizens usually need money and take it when it is offered, and that the choice would not be made public. All Ss were to place a card indicating their decision in a sealed envelope.

Results

The mean self-concept for the entire group as measured by the TSCS was significantly higher than the mean of a normative sample of 625 people of both sexes with an age range from 12 to 68 (381 versus 346; $p < 0.01$). Moreover, within the sample, the self-concept score increased somewhat with increased age. There was thus no evidence for the hypothesis that self-concept decreases with age.

Table 1
Altruistic Behavior of Elderly Women Under
Various Social Influences

| | Social Influence | | | |
Self-Concept	Positive	None	Negative	Row Total
High	69.44	56.11	30.00	51.85
Middle	41.11	36.11	31.67	36.30
Low	27.22	41.11	24.44	30.93
Column Total	45.93	44.44	28.70	39.69

Table 1 presents the mean of the amounts of money that members of the various subgroups indicated they would contribute if they won the lottery ticket. Both self-concept and social influence had significant impacts on altruistic behavior. Persons with high self-concept scores were more altruistic than those with low scores. The respondents under negative social influence were less altruistic than those under positive or no influence, but groups under positive and no influence did not differ significantly from each other. The effects of social influence varied somewhat in relation to self-concept; the high self-concept group was the most sensitive to social influence, whereas relatively low generosity was demonstrated by all self-concept groups under the negative social influence condition. The low self-concept group was almost equally generous (or nongenerous) under the positive and negative conditions and was most generous under the no-influence condition.

Abstract 81

Introversion and Egocentricity

PAUL CAMERON, Ph.D.

"Introversion and Egocentricity Among the Aged," *Journal of Gerontology*, 1967, 22, 465-468.

Although many theorists have predicted that egocentricity and introversion increase with age, the posited relationship lacks acceptable empirical evidence.

Method

SUBJECTS: There were four samples of Ss, as follows: a young sample (age range = 18-40, mean = 30.10) and an older residential sample (age range = 59+, mean = 70.05) obtained by a random area sampling technique, a cooperative-apartment dwellers sample (age range = 59+, mean = 72.24) randomly sampled from a federally-sponsored, church-related institution, and a hospitalized aged sample (age range = 59+, mean = 80.32) randomly drawn from those aged able to cooperate in two hospitals. The young and the residential aged samples had higher socio-economic status than the other two aged groups. There were 645 Ss, with approximately equal numbers of old and young, but more females than males. The refusal rate among all Ss was five percent.

Tests: One half the Ss were administered the Eysenck Extraversion Scale, and the other half were subjected to Consciousness Sampling which consists of interviewing Ss at various times of the waking day with the queries "what were you just thinking about (what was on the 'tip' of your mind?")" and after salutations and explanations, "what was the focus of your thinking (the main trend of your thought) over the last half hour?" Responses to these questions were coded later by trained raters, who approached each response with the question, "does this response indicate the S was contemplating his *own* or another's needs or want?" (interrater reliability = .89).

Results

The results indicated that typical aged females are more egocentric and introverted than young adult females, but there was no evidence of a difference between young and aged males. Young females were less egocentric than young males, and aged females on the whole tended to be slightly (but not significantly) less egocentric than aged males. There was no evidence of sex differences for introversion. The female cooperative-apartment dwellers were the most egocentric and extroverted aged.

Abstract **82**

Cautiousness with Advanced Age

Jack Botwinick, Ph.D.

"Cautiousness with Advanced Age," *Journal of Gerontology*, 1966, 21, 347-352.

Various types of data suggest a relationship between increasing cautiousness or conservatism and increasing age past adulthood. A study by Wallach and Kogan (1961) was aimed specifically at the problem of cautiousness in advanced aged. Wallach and Kogan used 12 "life situations," each involving a central character who faced two alternatives. The S made each choice for the central character by indicating the probability of success that was judged sufficient to select the more risky course. The elderly, in comparison to the young, required more certainty of outcome before the risky alternative was selected, i.e., the elderly responded in a more cautious or more conservative manner.

In the present study, the problem of cautiousness in advanced age was further analyzed by examining the interaction between age of S and age of central character as he copes with situations relatively unique to his age group. The Wallach and Kogan questionnaire involved central characters who were young adults and who coped with situations primarily within the experience of young people, e.g., the choice between alternatives such as: (a) a secure job with a modest income versus a job with an uncertain future, but a high income; (b) entering medical school versus a conservatory of music where the future is less certain but there is greater interest; (c) whether or not to marry when there is an indication of differences of opinion. In this study the questionnaire was extended to include "life situations" of people who are aged and face problems of the aged. Would the elderly Ss be relatively more cautious or conservative when the problems involve needs, values and attitudes of the aged? Would the opposite be the case for younger Ss?

Method

SUBJECTS: The Ss were white male and female volunteers recruited from a variety of academic and community groups. The older group included 23 men aged 67 to 86 (median = 73.5) and 24 women aged 67 to 84 (median = 76.5). The younger group included 63 men aged 18 to 32 (median = 20.0) and 48 women aged 18 to 35 (median 21.0). Ss were categorized into three educational levels (7-12 years, 13-15 years, and 16 years and over).

Materials: Twelve "life situations" which involve the needs of the elderly were constructed. Examples are as follows: (a) A widower after more than fifty years of marriage would like to ask a widow to marry him for comfort and companionship. His choice involves the fear of alienating good relations that exist between his son and himself; (b) The choice of an old man is between a home for the aged and continuing to live with his family. He has become a burden, a fact of which he is aware, even though his family has not verbalized discontent; (c) A 78-year-old man must choose between making a cross-country trip to see grandchildren he has never seen and wants to see before he dies and medical advice to avoid activity and excitement in order to prolong life. These "life situations" and those prepared by Wallach and Kogan with young people as central characters were randomly arranged in a 24-item booklet.

Each item had to be responded to by checking the probabiity of success that was acceptable before the desired but risky alternative would be selected. There were six probability levels to choose from: 1 chance in 10 of success, 3 in 10, 5 in 10, 7 in 10, 9 in 10, or not to choose this alternative no matter what the probabilies. The scores for each of the 24 situations were the probability levels indicated, i.e., 1, 3, 5, 7, 9 or 10 (the latter score given for the last alternative).

Results and Conclusions

In the initial analysis of variance, the S was represented by 24 scores, the probability level that he selected for each of the 24 situations. In the second analysis of variance, the S was represented by two scores, each being the mean of one of the two sets of 12 situations based on the stage of life of the central character. These scores were, of course, assumed to reflect degree of cautiousness. In both analyses, neither sex of S nor S's level of education was significantly related to score for cautiousness. In both analyses, age was statistically significant ($p < 0.01$). The older Ss were more cautious in their decisions than the younger Ss. Differences in cautiousness scores were associated with the differences among the 24 "life situations" ($p < 0.01$) and between the two sets of 12 situations ($p < 0.05$). Both the elderly and the younger Ss were more cautious in their decisions concerning young adult central characters than those concerning aged central characters. This tendency was greater among elderly Ss than among young Ss.

Responses were also analyzed for the number of times each probability level was chosen by each S. The prominent feature of this analysis was the tendency of elderly Ss to choose the number 10 alternative (would not choose this alternative no matter what the probabilities), and the tendency of young Ss to choose middle-value alternatives.

The results provide strong confirmation for the hypothesis that older people are more cautious than young people. Part of the increase in cautiousness with advanced age took the form of decisions not to choose the risky course of action, regardless of the likelihood of outcome. This suggests that older people may be disinclined toward making decisions or may be more willing than the young Ss to continue with involvements that are far from ideal (or both of these).

If it may be assumed that the "life situations" involving young and aged central characters were equally balanced with respect to risky and safe alternatives, then it can be concluded that the problems of the aged were solved with less caution than the problems of younger adults by both young and elderly respondents. Perhaps the young and old alike regarded the aged as having less to lose than the young with a gamble that went badly.

Abstract **83**

Rigidity and Age

SHIELA M. CHOWN, Ph.D.

"Rigidity and Age" in C. Tibbits and W. Donahue (Eds.), *Social and Psychological Aspects of Aging,* Columbia University Press, 1962, 832-835.

It is often assumed that there are age differences in rigidity or in adaptability to new situations; however, studies relating age to rigidity are rare. Different studies have used different definitions and measures of rigidity. Because rigidity-flexibility is not a unitary trait, the relationship between its several aspects and age may be expected to vary.

The aims of this research were, first, to find out whether overlap occurred between types of rigidity named by other workers and, second, to see what effects age had on performance in various rigidity tasks and on the relationships between these tasks.

Method

The Ss were 200 males, ranging in age from 20 to 82, recruited from a variety of sources. Eighteen tests of rigidity, selected from those used by other workers, and tests of nonverbal intelligence and vocabulary, were group administered to all Ss. Scores were factor analyzed to obtain eight factors which accounted for 63 percent of the variance.

Results

Four rigidity types, labeled spontaneous flexibility, personality rigidity, speed, and disposition rigidity, emerged as separate factors with no overlap. Spontaneous flexibility, adaptive flexibility and speed were all loaded highly on intelligence; adaptive flexibility was accounted for almost entirely by the intelligence measure. One aspect of personality rigidity was loaded negatively on the intelligence factor.

Verbal intelligence and one aspect of personality rigidity (liking for habit) were positively associated with aging. Nonverbal intelligence and two of the adaptive flexibility tests were negatively related to aging. Scores on these three tests and one other rigidity test (double alternation disposition) declined in an approximately linear fashion with age. Scores on other tests showed a curvilinear or inverted-U shape in relation to age.

These results suggest that much of what is regarded as "rigid" behavior in older people may be due to a decline in intelligence. Over and above the rigidity accounted for by low intelligence, there are various forms of rigidity that differ in extent from person to person, and these differences are only rarely linked to the age of the individual.

Abstract 84

Predictors of Social Conformity

RONALD L. KLEIN, Ph.D.

"Age, Sex and Task Difficulty as Predictors of Social Conformity," *Journal of Gerontology*, 1972, *27*, 229-236.

Although people over 65 represent a potentially strong political force, they apparently fail to demand those things which they say they desire and need. Various hypothetical explanations have been offered to account for this failure to strive for rights and needs by the older individual: disengagement, low energy level, change in social role, lack of social status, and lack of opportunity. Perhaps, however, the explanation may lie in the tendency of older individuals to conform. Laboratory studies have compared children, adolescents and young adults on measures of conformity, but whether the relationships found in such studies hold throughout adult age span is unknown.

The present study was concerned with the relationship of conforming behavior with age. It sought to answer the question: do age, sex and task difficulty act as predictors of social conformity in a laboratory perceptual judgment task?

Method

SUBJECTS: There were 72 Ss, of which 36 were young (16-21 years; mean age 18.3) and 36 were old (60-86 years; mean age 69.4). There were 18 males and

18 females in each age group. The young Ss were students in introductory psychology and the old Ss were students at the Institute of Lifetime Learning. All were volunteers.

Apparatus: A modified Crutchfield apparatus, which made it possible to test four Ss at one time in separate stalls, and enabled the E to introduce false information into the situation. The S's task was to judge which of two disks was the larger and to indicate his choice by turning the left switch which lighted a bulb if the left disk was perceived as larger, the right switch if the right disk was perceived as larger. For low task difficulty the two disks were in the ratio of 8:5; for high task difficulty the ratio was 8:7; for extreme task difficulty the radii of the two disks were nearly equal.

PROCEDURE: The Ss were first tested alone and then in the conformity situation. There were 36 trials in each situation. In the conformity situation the S was provided false information about the choices made by each of three other Ss before he made his own choice. On 24 of the conformity situation trials, the contrived report of the judgment of the three peers displayed a unanimous selection of the wrong member of the pair. The critical trials were either of low, high or extreme task difficulty.

The dependent variable was the number of times the S agreed with the contrived group consensus on the critical trials of the conformity situation minus the number of wrong choices on critical trials when tested alone.

Table 1

Mean Conformity Scores for Young and Old Ss at Each of Three Levels of Task Difficulty

	N	Low T.D.	High T.D.	Extreme T.D.
Young	36	0.67	1.67	7.00
Old	36	1.33	3.50	12.33

Results

Age groups did not differ for number of wrong choices when tested alone. Table 1 summarizes mean conformity scores for the two age groups. Mean conformity score for the old group was significantly higher than for the young group ($p < 0.001$). Females did not earn higher conformity scores than males ($p < 0.10$), though there was a trend in that direction. The higher the level of task difficulty, indicating greater stimulus ambiguity, the higher the mean conformity scores ($p < 0.001$). The age by task difficulty interaction effect was significant ($p < 0.01$). With increases in task difficulty, conformity scores increased for both young and old Ss, but there was a greater proportionate increase for the old Ss. The results thus suggest that in addition to showing a greater overall tendency to conform than young people do, the susceptibility of the older person to group pressure and social influence increases in situations in which the objective determinants of the judgment are indefinite or ambiguous.

Abstract **85**

Personality Changes with Age

ALLEN E. EDWARD, Ph.D. and DAVID B. WINE, Ph.D.

"Personality Changes with Age: Their Dependency on Concomitant Intellectual Decline," *Journal of Gerontology*, 1963, *18*, 182-184.

Although there seems to be a general assumption that personality variables change as a function of age, some research findings suggest that changes in level of intellectual functioning may be the important determinant of personality changes. The purpose of this study was to measure a broad range of personality and biographical characteristics and to adjust these measures for intellectual decline. The hypothesis was that personality changes that seem to be related to aging are not due to adding years *per se*, but are associated with intellectual decline.

Method

The Ss were 80 hospitalized men from 20 to 76 years old, including every fifth admittee to a VA General Medical and Surgical Hospital. All tests were administered individually. The tests were a comprehensive Biographical Data Questionnaire, the Comrey Personality Inventory (1961), consisting of 210 items which measure 35 personality variables, and The Raven Progressive Matrice (1958), a well-known intelligence test. Responses on the Biographical Data Questionnaire indicated that the sample group did not deviate markedly from normality except for higher scores on Chronicity of Illness and lower scores on Marital Consistency.

Results

The sample was rank-ordered in terms of age to form eight groups of ten Ss each (mean ages 29, 36, 41, 48, 58, 63, 69, 73). Mean scores on the intelligence test dropped significantly from the youngest to the oldest group (p<0.001) and a correlation of -0.55 was calculated between age and individual score on the Progressive Matrices. Nine of the 35 personality variables (Dependency, Need for Order, Conformity, Friendliness, Truth, Social Desirability, Cautiousness, Need for Approval, and Personal Grooming, correlated significantly with age, as did five of the six variables assessed by the Biographical Data Questionnaire (Chronicity of Illness, Financial Stability, Education, Job Stability, and Social Relationships). When the effect of intelligence was removed by analysis of covariance, only Need for Approval (p<0.05), Social Desirability, Financial Stability and Job Stability (p<0.01) retained the significant relationship with age, and Sociopathic Tendency and Vindictiveness (p<0.05) attained it.

The most striking outcome of these analyses was the fact that most of the personality patterns usually associated with the aging process were no longer evident. Measures of personality characteristics as Dependency, Need for Order, Conformity, Cautiousness and Personal Grooming seemed to change as a function *not* of growing older, but as a function of intellectual decline.

One cluster of personality traits, namely, a decrease in Vindictiveness and Sociopathic Tendencies and an increase in Need for Approval and a tendency to respond in a Socially Desirable manner varied as a function of chronological age, independent of intellectual decline. It may be that these changes reflect a reorientation of role in society toward a less competitive position, rather than a withdrawal from society.

Abstract **86**

Age And Conservative Opinions

FRANCIS D. GLAMSER, Ph.D.

"The Importance Of Age to Conservative Opinions: A Multivariate Analysis," *Journal of Gerontology*, 1974, *29*, 549-554.

A rather common stereotype is that conservativism increases with age. This study attempted to answer two questions. First, how important is age as an independent variable in explaining the relationship between age and conservativism? Second, how does age compare with other demographic variables in its explanatory power?

Method

SUBJECTS: A total of 118 faculty wives, from a randomly selected sample of 131, participated in this study. All adult age groups up to 65 were represented. The sample was homogeneous with respect to sex, social class, race, husband's occupation, marital status and present residence.

Materials: Conservativism was measured on a Likert-type summated scale, with items designed to assess attitude toward law enforcement, patriotism and race. Conservativism was defined as reflecting one or more of the following characteristics: attachment to traditional modes of thought, resistance to social change, and/or a low tolerance for nonconformity.

The relationship between conservativism as measured by scale score to the following variables was investigated: age, education, father's education, father's occupational status and community size.

Results

A multiple correlation of 0.50 between conservatism and the five variables (age, education, father's education, father's occupational status and community size) indicated that in combination these variables accounted for only 25 percent of the variance in conservative opinion. The multiple correlation of education and age with conservativism was 0.45, an indication that the contribution of the other three variables was very low. Age alone yielded a correlation of 0.28 and education alone an r of 0.40. Education was clearly a more important explanatory variable than age.

Table 1
Opinions on Combined Topics by Age

Age	Liberal	Moderate	Conservative
20-29	55%	39%	6%
50-65	21%	69%	10%

Table 1 summarizes opinions by age for the oldest and youngest sub-groups. The similarity of the two age groups for percentage of conservative ratings, and the very high number of liberal ratings by the young, suggest that the age differences are due to the high proportion of liberal attitudes of the young women rather than to marked conservativism on the part of the older women.

Abstract 87

Age and Political Attitudes

ELIZABETH B. DOUGLASS, M.A., WILLIAM P. CLEVELAND, Ph.D.
and GEORGE L. MADDOX, Ph.D.

"Political Attitudes, Age and Aging: A Cohort Analysis of Archival Data," *Journal of Gerontology*, 1974, 29, 666-675.

Do political opinions vary as a function of age? This paper explores the effect of age on political opinions as gauged from national surveys conducted in the period 1940 to 1970. The paper also addresses the conceptual and methodological problems typically found in studies of politics and age, with specific reference to the use of Gallup survey archival data, a discussion that cannot be summarized meaningfully and therefore will be excluded from this abstract.

Method

A careful review of the archival data indicated that responses from persons of different ages were available for two or more periods of time to three questions that varied from the general to the specific as follows: What do you think is the most important question facing this *country* today? What do you think is the most important question facing this *community* today? What do you think is the most important question affecting your *family* today? For all questions, a large proportion of the responses could be categorized as economic or financial; for the national question, there were also many foreign policy answers; for the community question, there were also a lot of no response or "don't know" answers. Responses to the family question tended to be particularly timebound in that, apart from family economic problems, highly popular answers at one time of testing would seldom be mentioned at another time of testing, e.g., answers pertaining to housing or moral problems. Only categories of responses that were made in large proportions at all times of testing were subjected to analysis.

Major response categories to each question were subjected to a type of multiple regression analysis to assess the effects of age, cohort (generation) and time of testing on expressed attitudes. The analysis allowed for control and assessment of the effects of sex and education, but neither of these variables exerted a strong differential effect on attitudes. In effect, the statistical analysis was directed toward the following questions: Do responses vary with age regardless of time of testing and generation membership? Do responses vary among cohorts, i.e., do people who were aged 20 in 1940 make different responses than persons who were aged 20 in 1950 or 1960? Do responses vary as a function of time of testing, i.e., is there a tendency over all age groups to give answers in 1960 that differ from those given in 1940 or 1950?

Results

For economic responses to national problems, neither age, cohort or time had a significant effect, i.e., persons of all ages at all times of testing considered economic problems important. For foreign policy responses to national problems, time had a significant effect but age and cohort did not, i.e., the importance assigned to foreign policy varied from one time to another, but at a given time was considered equally important by all age and cohort groups. For economic responses to community problems, time had the sole significant effect; neither age, time nor cohort was significant for those expressing "no opinion." For economic responses to family problems, time had the primary effect and age had a secondary effect.

Only at the most immediate political level, the family level, did age enter at all as a significant determinant of political attitudes. These data support the hypothesis that the farther removed a political issue is from the individual (i.e., family versus community versus national) the less age will affect his attitude toward the issue. It would appear that time of testing and the political-economic-social climate of the time is a much more important determinant of political attitude than the age or generation membership of the individual.

Abstract 88

Age as a Political Issue

BARBARA F. TURNER, Ph.D. and ROBERT L. KAHN, Ph.D.

"Age as a Political Issue," *Journal of Gerontology*, 1974, *29*, 572-580.

This study investigated the relationship of chronological age, attitudes toward aging, and the role of age as a political issue in a primary election contest between two candidates of similar ideology but markedly different ages, a 40-year-old challenger versus an 84-year-old incumbent. Of importance was the extent to which common negative cultural stereotypes of aging and the aged might be mobilized effectively to influence political attitudes and behavior. Given the tendency for persons to be more negatively disposed toward groups that are increasingly dissimilar to themselves, it is of interest to determine whether voters might be inclined to "vote their age."

Political Setting: Both men were Democrats and very liberal; there were no real differences between them in their views on major political issues. The older man had served in Congress for the preceding 18 years, the younger man in the State Legislature for ten years, and the records of both for performance in these positions were considered very commendable. The younger man publicly minimized the importance of age in the competition, but the local newspapers and the older candidate emphasized it.

Method

SAMPLE: A quota sample of 256 white middle-class men and women, all of whom were Democrats and were politically well-informed, were interviewed during the six-week interval prior to the primary election. There were three age categories, 94 young (21-40), 107 middle-aged (41-60) and 45 older (65+) respondents.

PROCEDURE: Data collected included: (a) voting preference; (b) for each of 18 possible issues, the respondent designated the candidate to whom each issue was more favorable (e.g., age, political independence, may not be able to finish term of office, intellectual vigor, capacity for hard work, proven ability, conscientiousness, personality, civil rights, foreign policy); (c) descriptions of each candidate, including strongest and weakest point; (d) general attitudes toward old people and middle-aged people as measured by a semantic differential technique.

Results

The results indicated: (a) older respondents held significantly more positive general attitudes toward the aged; (b) the age of the respondent was only minimally related to measures pertaining directly to the primary contest between the two candidates, such as voting intention, perception of age as a salient issue in the campaign, and attitudes toward the age of the 84-year-old candidate; (c) candidate preference was unrelated to general attitudes toward the aged but was very strongly related to issues pertaining to the primary contest; (d) the most important age relationship was that old respondents were significantly less biased by candidate preference in evaluating specific campaign issues as favoring their candidate, i.e., young respondents tended to perceive their preferred candidate favorably on most issues, whereas the older respondents distributed favorable ratings between candidates with apparent objectivity.

These data suggest that in this primary election the age of the candidate was not a salient factor in determining voter preference.

Abstract **89**

Age and Sex-Role Identity

EVELYN A. PEPE, B.A. and MARY VIRGINIA WYLY, Ph.D.

"Age and Sex as Determinants of Sex-Role Identity." Presented at the Meeting of the American Psychological Association, Washington, D.C., 1976.

Research on sex roles in our culture have used a limited age population, usually adolescents and young adults. There is very little information regarding sex-role attitudes and self-perceptions of sex-role identity in middle-aged and older populations. This study examined the perception of sex roles of males and females in three different age groups.

Method

SUBJECTS: Subjects were 325 white, middle socio-economic class males and females divided into three age groups: 20-25; 40-49; and 60-69. Each age group contained approximately 110 subjects divided equally according to sex. The 1974 United States Census Bureau statistics for educational attainment by age, race, and sex were used as a guide for a representative sample.
PROCEDURE: A twenty-item questionnaire was administered to each subject. Each questionnaire statement was related to sex roles in family and professional life. Questions covered such topics as employment, marriage, child rearing and education. Subjects were asked to rate each statement in accordance with their own beliefs, values, and practices on a five-point scale. Questionnaires administered to males and females were the same except that references to the opposite sex were reversed. An example of one statement is as follows:

1   2   3   4   5

strongly agree   strongly disagree

I would put my children in a day care center so that my wife (I) could work.

Results

Males and females in the 20-25 year age group and females in the 60-69 age group were less traditional in their responses to the questionnaire items as compared to the other age groups. Their answers generally reflected an egalitarian view of masculine/feminine roles. Males in the 40-49 and 60-69 age groups reflected more traditional values, while females in the 40-49 age group were the most conservative in their view of sex-related behaviors.

Abstract **90**

Value Orientations by Age

IRVING WEBBER, Ph.D., DAVID W. COOMBS, Ph.D.
and J. SELWYN HOLLINGSWORTH, Ph.D.

"Variations in Value Orientations by Age in a Developing Society," *Journal of Gerontology*, 1974, 29, 676-683.

It is often assumed that as people become older, they tend to hold values characterized as conservative or traditional. This study tested the proposition that the value orientations of top leaders in Columbia, a developing society, tend to vary from modern to the more traditional as age increases.

Method

SUBJECTS: One hundred seventy-eight top leaders in industry, finance, church, education, etc., all but five being male, from three cities in Columbia. All were well educated and of at least upper-middle-class socio-economic status. The age range was from the 20's to over 65.

Materials: The Kluckhohn and Strodtbeck (1961) test of value orientations was given. The test consists of 22 items, each of which seeks to determine the respondent's orientation in one of four problem areas, as follows: Time (orientation toward past, present, or future); Activity (orientation toward being, being-in-becoming, or doing); Relational (orientation may be lineal, i.e., hierarchical, collateral or individualistic); Man-Nature (the relationship may be subjugation to nature, harmony with nature, or mastery over nature). Each item set forth a practical problem and offered three alternative solutions, each representing one of the three orientations. The S was asked to choose the best and second best solutions.

For data analysis, the respondents' choices were compared to the dominant value orientations of the U.S. middle class, which were taken as representative of a "modern" society. These are mastery over nature> harmony with nature> subjugation to nature; future> present> past; doing> being-in-becoming> being; and individualistic> collateral> lineal.

A rigorous method of scoring gave a score of one only for responses that agreed with the sequence of modern orientations. A less rigorous method gave a score of one if the first choice corresponded to the first item in the sequence of modern orientations.

Results and Conclusions

The rigorous method of scoring yielded a high inverse correlation between age and modernity in the Time area and for all items combined, a moderate inverse correlation between age and modernity for the Man-Nature area, and low inverse correlations between age and modernity for each of the Activity and Human Relational areas. For the less rigorous method of scoring there were high inverse correlations between age and modernity for all measures except Activity, for which the relationship was only moderately high.

The data support the hypothesis that being older tends to be strongly correlated with having more traditional as opposed to more modern value orientations. Whether this relationship exists because generational cohorts cling to orientations espoused early in life, or because aging individuals become more conservative or traditional, cannot be determined from these data.

Abstract **91**

Body Buffer Zones and Age

BRIAN L. MISHARA, Ph.D., PATRICIA BRAWLEY, MARY CHEEVERS, RHONDA M. KITOVER, ALICE M.KNOWLES, PATRICIA RAUTIALA and ARA SUVAJIAN

"Encroachments Upon the Body Buffer Zones of the Young and Old Woman: A Naturalistic Study,"*International Journal of Aging and Human Development*, 1974, 5, 3-5.

Are there generational differences in an individual's ability to tolerate the close physical presence of another person? This study adapted the methodology of body buffer zone research to naturalistically explore spatial proximity behavior in young and old women, whose body buffer zones were encroached upon by another young or old woman.

Method

SUBJECTS AND EXPERIMENTERS: The Ss were 30 young women judged on appearance to range in age from 18 to 25, and 30 older women judged to be 60 plus years of age. They were selected from midmorning commuters waiting alone in a Boston subway station. The experimenters were six undergraduate women and one 60-year-old woman. All were dressed similarly.

PROCEDURE: During each trial, a younger or older experimenter walked up to the S in a "natural" manner, as if she also had come to wait for the train. The experimenter stopped 12 inches to the left of the S and faced in the same direction (toward the tracks). Two observers independently recorded the elapsed time from the arrival of the experimenter to the time the S first picked up her left foot to move away.

Results

Movement away from the experimenter ranged from less than one second after the start of a trial to the longest duration of 114 seconds. Mean times to move away for all combinations of young and old experimenters and Ss are reported in Table 1. An analysis of variance revealed a significant interaction between the age of the experimenter and age of the S (p < .01). This interaction indicated that experimenters and Ss of similar age (either both old or both young) remained in close proximity for a longer period of time than experimenters and Ss of different ages. These results suggest that people tend to tolerate longer intrusions on their body buffer zones when the intruder is of the same rather than a different generation. Invasion of territory may provide valuable clues to the process by which intergenerational attitudes are formed and may suggest means for identifying changes in intergenerational attitudes.

Table 1
Mean Times to Move Away for All Combinations of Young and Old Experimenters and Ss

Age of Subject	Age of Experimenter	
	Young	Old
Young	26.1 sec.	15.4 sec.
Old	19.9 sec.	30.9 sec.

Abstract **92**

Age, Expectations, and Personal Space

JOHN A. FEROLETO, B.A. and BEVERLEY ROBERTS GOUNDARD, Ph.D.

"The Effects of Subject's Age and Expectations Regarding an Interviewer on Personal Space," *Experimental Aging Research*, 1975, 1, 57-61.

This study investigated whether how close individuals seat themselves to an interviewer is affected by the subject's age and by his expectations regarding the interviewer.

Method

SUBJECTS: Older Ss were six male and four female residents of an urban, county-operated home. The younger Ss were five male and five female college undergraduates. The older Ss ranged in age from 49 to 81 years, the younger Ss from 18 to 26 years.

PROCEDURE: Each S was individually escorted to the experimental room by a young man, ostensibly for the purpose of being interviewed by another individual concerning his views about restricted subject matter on television. En route to the experimental room, each S was given information about the interviewer designed to establish either a positive or negative expectation about the forthcoming interaction. The S entered the room alone and was invited by the interviewer, a middle-aged male dressed in casual attire, to have a seat. The S had to pick up a chair near the door and move it wherever he wished in the room. The distance between the right front leg of the interviewer's chair and the right front leg of the S's chair was measured and recorded.

Table 1
Mean Distance Assumed by Each Age Group as a Function of Negative and Positive Expectations

Age of Ss	Ss' Expectations	
	Negative	Positive
Older	58.8 in.	38.8 in.
Younger	36.0 in.	30.6 in.

Results

Those Ss who had been told to expect an unpleasant interaction seated themselves significantly farther from the interviewer than did those who expected a pleasant interaction (p < .005). Also, the older Ss seated themselves significantly farther from the interviewer than the younger Ss did (p < .001). As may be seen in Table 1, the difference between the age groups was minimal when the Ss' expectations were positive but was prononuced when the Ss' expectations were negative (p < .05). The results appear to reflect a greater susceptibility among older individuals to feeling threatened and ill-at-ease in an interpersonal situation. Since the older Ss did not differ markedly from the younger Ss when expectations were positive, it appears that older individuals can respond favorably when a third party presents them with information designed to reduce the amount of threat that a situation might pose for them.

Abstract 93

Middle-Aged Women in College

Carole E. Zatlin, M.A., Martha Storandt, Ph.D. and Jack Botwinick, Ph.D.

"Personality and Values of Women Continuing Their Education After Thirty-Five Years of Age," *Journal of Gerontology*, 1973, 28, 216-221.

This study investigated the hypothesis that women returning to college in their mid-years are a unique group in terms of personality characteristics, job values, interests and agreement with the feminist movement.

Method

SUBJECTS: Four groups of women were compared. The Late-College group included 29 women between 35 and 50 years (mean age = 41.2) who were college undergraduates at the time of data collection. The Young-College group included 27 women between 18 and 25 years (mean age = 20.4) who were undergraduates in the same college. The no-college group was composed of 25 women between 35 and 50 (mean age = 42.0) who had never been and were not in attendance in college. The Normal-College group included 26 women aged 35-50 (mean age = 38.5) who had attained a bachelor's degree before the age of 25 and were not attending college at the time of data collection. The Late-College group had a higher mean socio-economic status rating than the No-College group, and this factor required the use of analysis of covariance for comparisons between these two groups.

PROCEDURE: Each respondent completed eight separate questionnaires and tests, which were administered in the same order for all participants. The tests included the following: (1) Life values (theoretical, economic, aesthetic, social, political and religious) from the Allport, Vernon and Lindzey Study of Values; (2) Interpersonal relations (dominance/submission, hostility/love and abnormal/normal dimensions) from the Leary Interpersonal Checklist; (3) Ego strength, using Barron's Ego Strength Scale (high scores tend to be associated with resourcefulness, vitality and self-direction, whereas low scores appear to be made by people who are effeminate, inhibited and affected); (4) Occupational values using Center's Job Values and Desires questionnaire. Job values ranged from those that could be classed as managerial, emphasizing leadership, prestige, money and fame, to those that could be classed as personally fulfilling, including self-expression, service and security; (5) Occupational preference, using a modification of the Strong Vocational Interest Blank to obtain a preference for professional versus nonprofessional and traditionally male versus traditionally female occupations; (6) Preferences for Various Amusements, to determine whether Late-College group uniquely viewed college study as recreational in nature; (7) Agreement with Feminist Movement questionnaire; (8) Attitude Toward Others using items from the Strong Vocational Interest Blank to evaluate the possibility that Late-College women, being mildly deviant themselves, would be more tolerant of others at variance with cultural norms, especially in comparison to No-College women.

Results

The hypothesis was not supported. Women in the Late-College group were quite similar in terms of personality characteristics, job values, interests and agreement with the feminist movement to women of the same age who had received their college education at the normal age, and excluding differences that could be best accounted for by differences in socio-economic status, were also similar to women of the same age who had no college experience.

The Late-College women did, however, differ from the Young-College women in that they were less motivated by social values (i.e., less altruistic and philanthropic) and were more dominant (as opposed to submissive) in comparison to their younger college counterparts. They were also less in agreement with the feminist movement. Whether these differences were due to maturational (age) changes or to generational (cultural) effects cannot be determined from the data.

This study provided no evidence to support the hypothesis that women who enroll in college at mid-life have unique attributes of personality or unique occupational values and interests in comparison to like-aged women.

Abstract 94

Stability of Adult Personality Traits

K. WARNER SCHAIE, Ph.D. and IRIS A. PARHAM, Ph.D.

"Stability of Adult Personality Traits: Fact or Fable?" *Journal of Personality and Social Psychology*, 1976, 34, 146-158.

Most investigators have assumed that personality traits and attitudes remain stable over the adult life span, in contrast to the adoption by most investigators of an age decrement model for learning, intellectual functions and psychomotor behaviors. It has been demonstrated that much of the apparent age decrement in cognitive functioning is an artifact of the cross-sectional method of data collection. Perhaps the stability of adult personality traits might be equally artifactual, involving fortuitous combinations of generational differences in the expression of personality traits and attitudes, with secular trends and ontogenetic trends operating in opposing directions. This paper summarized the relevant theoretical and methodological issues and examined the results of a sequential analysis of 19 personality and attitudinal factors.

Method

The personality and attitudinal data were derived from a 75-item questionnaire administered in longitudinal studies designed primarily to investigate cognitive and related functioning. The present analyses were based on approximately 2,500 questionnaires completed by subjects ranging in age from 21 to 84 years, with approximately equal distribution by age and sex. Samples were first tested in 1963 and were retested in 1970. This yielded two cross-sectional samples of subjects arranged in eight 7-year intervals, and short-term longitudinal data for eight cohorts over the 7-year period. Factor analysis yielded 19 non-error factors, of which 13 could be described as personality traits (affectothymia, excitability, dominance, superego strength, threctia, premsia, coasthenia, protension, praxernia, untroubled adequacy, conservativism of temperament, group dependency, and low self-sentiment) and six could be described as attitudinal factors (honesty, interest in science, flexibility, financial support of society, humanitarian concern, and community involvement). Statistical analyses were used to assess age, sex, cohort and time-of-measurement effects for each of the 19 factors.

Results and Discussion

There were three major analyses as follows: (1) A cross-sequential repeated measurement analysis to test the stability model with respect to cohort differences, socio-cultural change (time-of-measurement) and sex differences (N = 410). Sex differences were found for eight of the 19 factors, cohort differences for 13 factors, and time trends from 1963 to 1970 were significant for five factors. Because in this method of analysis any ontogenetic trends would appear as spurious time-of-measurement effects, and the time-of-measurement effects that did occur were consistent with expectations for the historical epoch, these results support the stability model. The existence of personality and attitudinal differences among cohorts was also demonstrated. (2) A cross-sequential analysis with independent samples to test whether results obtained in the first analysis would be maintained when the effects of retesting are eliminated (N = 1556). The results of the repeated measurements analysis were replicated, and one or two additional factors were significantly different with respect to each of the main effects. (3) A time-sequential analysis with independent samples, conducted to test the assumption of the stability model and to differentiate ontogenetic changes from socio-cultural change (N = 1610). This analysis, in conjunction with the previous analyses, allowed for a clear differentiation of maturational effects and socio-cultural change; the time-of-measurement effects that were significant in the previous analyses and also in this analysis can be attributed unambiguously to socio-cultural change, whereas those that disappear must be attributed to maturational change.

The stability model was supported for all factors with the exception of excitability and humanitarian concern, both of which increased with age.

Examination of the characteristic profiles for each of the eight cohorts revealed a remarkable similarity and continuity between adjacent cohorts; however, a clear break was noted between the three oldest cohorts and the younger cohorts on protension, superego and coasthenia. The oldest cohort (mean birth year 1889) was highest on excitability, proxemia, responsibility for financial support of society and humanitarian concern, and lowest on self-sentiment and outgoingness. The youngest cohort (mean birth year 1938) was highest on conservativism of temperament, group dependency, flexibilty, interest in science and community involvement.

These results suggest that a simple trifold model based on biostable, acculturated and biocultural traits, does not allow for an adequate description of the adult life course of personality traits. The following model was suggested, with factors identified in the present study indicated in parentheses:

A. *Biostable traits*—traits that because of genetic or environmental influences show sex differences which are reliably maintained throughout adulthood.

1. Stable sex differences only—genetic determinants (perhaps premsia—tendermindedness).
2. Time-of-measurement differences only—genetic determinant, modified in expression by transient socio-cultural changes (untroubled adequacy decreased over the period studied).
3. Cohort differences only—based on early socialization (threat reactivity, coasthenia, expressed honesty, interest in science, community involvement).
4. Time-of-measurement and cohort differences—based on early socialization and transient social impact (praxernia and group dependency).

B. *Acculturated Traits*—no sex differences, but cross-sectional studies typically identify age differences for these traits. These may be culturally prescribed and age-related patterns, or longitudinal inquiry may identify suspected age differences as either cohort or secular trends.

5. Age changes only—such traits reflect social roles which might be determined by universals underlying a stage model of development which is impermeable to cohort differences and secular trends (humanitarian concern increased with age).
6. Age changes and cohort differences—traits would be mediated by stage changes in universally determined life role, modified by shifts in early socialization practices (perhaps affectothymia, protension and low self-esteem).
7. Age changes and time-of-measurement differences—traits would be mediated by universally determined life roles, impermeable to

early socialization, but subject to transient influence at all ages (none, and perhaps none exist).

8. Cohort differences only—traits mediated by early socialization and not subject to ontogenetic change (affectothymia, superego strength, protension, and low self-sentiment).

9. Time-of-measurement differences only—traits subject to transient modification by socio-cultural change at all ages (dominance and financial support of society).

10. Cohort differences and time-of-measurement differences—traits modified by early socialization and transient socio-cultural change affecting all ages (flexibility).

C. *Biocultural traits*–traits based on genetic differences (hence sex differences), modified in expression by universally experienced life stage expectancies, which may be affected by early socialization or socio-cultural change.

11. Age changes only—traits based on ontogenetic "programs" and impermeable to cohort or socio-cultural differences (excitability).

12. Age changes and cohort differences—(none, and perhaps none exist).

13. Age changes and time-of-measurement differences—this would require modification of the ontogenetic "program" for all ages, due to environmental interventions (perhaps premsia).

This study demonstrated the utility of applying cross-sequential methodology to personality trait development with age. Although the data supported the stability of personality model, much change was observed in the 19 traits studied. It was concluded that the observed change was a function of specific early socialization experiences, commonly shared generation-specific impact, and socio-cultural changes that affect individuals at all ages. For traits that are determined by biological constraints or early socialization, there appeared to be lifelong stability. Only one trait, excitability, suggested the existence of a definite ontogenetic "program" unaffected by cohort differences or socio-cultural change.

CHAPTER X

Environmental Impact

Abstract 95

The Impact of Environment on Old People

FRANCES M. CARP, Ph.D.

"The Impact of Environment on Old People," *Gerontologist*, 1967, 7, 106-8 and 135.

Can old people be changed by altering the environments in which they live, or have their responses become rigid with time? Are their dissatisfactions responsive to present reality or have they become intrinsic to individuals and therefore impervious to situational change? Specifically, do improved housing and social opportunities really matter?

Method

Data were collected on demographic, biographic, attitudinal and other psychological variables on 352 applicants for a new public housing facility. The median age of applicants was 72 years. Applicants lived in physically substandard housing and/or social isolation and stress. Decisions regarding admission were made by the Housing Authority staff. Inmovers and others did not vary significantly on variables relevant to this research.

Follow-up data were collected 12 to 15 months after the new residence was occupied. Data analysis dealt with changes over time which were different for the 204 persons who moved into the new residence and the 148 who did not.

Results

Evidence of the dramatic effect of improved life setting on this group of older people was overwhelming and was similar for men and women. Residents showed significant increments on each of the following measures: happiness, feelings about accomplishments in life, number of leisure activities, activities compared to those of age 55, present social activities, number of close friends, attitude to family, attitude to friends, attitude to health, and rating of health. They showed significant decrements in major health problems, neurotic problems, time on health care, time sleeping, and "lost" time. Consistently, the scores of the residents reflected improvements; those of the nonresidents showed no change or slight decrements.

On some variables, improvement was consistent among residents. On others it was related to the initial score, in some cases the "haves getting" and in others the originally most deprived showing the greatest change. The influence of improved physical and social environment appeared not only in the increased satisfaction of residents with their living situation but also in more favorable attitudes about themselves and toward others, in more active and sociable patterns of life, and in signs of improved physical and mental health.

The observed changes contra-indicate rigidity as an integral component of the aging personality. The findings suggest that more attention should be paid to the role of the setting in assessing the experience and behavior of people within it, including people who are old. The results also point to the necessity for more careful scrutiny of traits considered to be age-related. Some environmental alterations, including those which are restrictive, may so regularly accompany chronological age that their effects are mistaken for those of aging itself.

Abstract **96**

Effect of Environment on Morale

KERMIT K. SCHOOLER, Ph.D.

"Effect of Environment on Morale," *Gerontologist,* 1970, *10,* 194-197.

This study investigated the hypothesis that environmental characteristics affect successful adaptation to aging, but that the effect is mediated through the formation and maintenance of social relationships determined to some extent by various environmental characteristics.

Method

SUBJECTS: Approximately 4,000 persons, 65 years of age and older, were selected in an area-probability sample of all noninstitutionalized elderly living in the United States.

Procedure: In an interview of approximately two hours, each respondent was questioned about residential characteristics, formation and maintenance of social relationships, self-assessment of physical health, and emotional well-being and morale. A conventional list of demographic characteristics was also obtained.

The data were subjected to a number of statistical analyses, with data for male and female respondents treated separately. This paper reports results for males only, but the factor structure extracted for females was almost identical.

Results

Factor analysis yielded six environmental factors as follows: I. Distance to facilities—distance to bank, stores, barber, public transportation, etc.; II. Condition of dwelling unit—state of repair of unit, surrounding grounds, style, size, and condition of furniture, etc.; III. Convenience—respondent's judgment about the convenience of his location to facilities and to friends and relatives; IV. Features—safety and convenience features (adequate hallway illumination, maintenance, etc.), and opportunities for socializing (outdoor recreation and visiting areas, social room, and laundromat), etc.; V. Social and supportive services—the respondent's awareness of such services as personal counseling, overnight companionship, visiting nurse, etc.; VI. Size—number of rooms and room area of dwelling unit.

Six factors were also extracted for the social relations domain. These were: I. Neighboring—number of friends, frequency of visiting and being visited, etc; II. Organization—number of organizations, meetings attended, whether the organization maintains programs for the elderly, etc.; III and IV. Contact wtith children—both factors were based on frequency and recency of contact with children but differed as a function of family size. (The emergence of two separate factors may have resulted from an artifact of the coding system); V. Other social contacts—total social contacts, friendly visits, church, frequency of telephone use, etc.; VI. Original family size—number of siblings and frequency with which they are seen.

The six morale factors were as follows: I. Fears and worries—day-to-day fears, worries and upsets; II. Anomia; III. A combination factor—self-perceived agedness, alertness, and vitality; IV. Life-long accomplishments; V. Sustained happiness; VI. Financial situation and satisfaction.

After the identification of factors, factor scores were generated for each respondent on each factor. Stepwise multiple regression analysis indicated that the relation between morale and social relations was low but significant and was even lower when environmental factors were controlled.

The initial hypothesis had been based on the assumption that social relationships sustain morale, but the maintenance of those same relationships was made possible, mainly, by characteristics of the residential environment. The results suggest that social relations (social participation, social integration, etc.) are not as central to maintaining morale as the hypothesis suggested. At the same time, environmental characteristics took on more significance. A different hypothesis should be substituted, namely: environmental effects on morale are mediated directly through the senses and whatever perceptual and cognitive processes are brought into play.

Abstract **97**

Housing Characteristics and Well-Being

M. POWELL LAWTON, Ph.D., LUCILLE NAHEMOW, Ph.D.
and JOSEPH TEAFF, Ph.D.

"Housing Characteristics and the Well-Being of Elderly Tenants in Federally Assisted Housing," *Journal of Gerontology*, 1975, *30*, 601-607.

This research examined relationships between tenant well-being and four characteristics of housing environments about which there has been much debate among planners and designers—the type of sponsorship, the size of the community in which the housing is located, the number of people housed in a single project, and the height of the building.

Method

A national probability sample of 3,654 tenants was obtained. The tenants resided in either low-rent public housing projects which contained some units specially designed for the elderly, or in housing sponsored by private nonprofit organizations for the lower-middle income elderly. The probability sample included 154 projects located in 12 large geographic areas. Approximately 20 tenants from each site were interviewed. Data for this report were from the 2,457 tenants who gave complete responses to all questions.

Tenant well-being was assessed from responses to an interviewer-administered questionnaire. The six indices of well-being examined were friendship in housing (two items), housing satisfaction (three items), morale (two items), motility (two items), family contact (one item) and activity participation (the number of on-site activities named by the S as engaged in during the past year).

Environmental data gathered from the 154 sites included census information on each community, neighborhood characteristics, organizational characteristics of the housing, on-site services offered, administrator attitudes and preferences, and aggregate social characteristics of the tenants.

Results

The data were analyzed to determine the percentage of variance in well-being that could be accounted for by personal variables (age, sex, race, marital status, length of residence in the building, whether or not the person received welfare benefits, and self-reported health) and the percentage of variance that could be accounted for by each of the following environmental variables: (a) public housing versus housing sponsored by private nonprofit organizations; (b) size of community; (c) building size; (d) building height. The results of this analysis are summarized in Table 1.

Table 1.
Percentages of Variance in Well-Being
Accounted for by Personal and Environmental Variables

| | | Environmental Variables | | | | |
	Personal Variables	Sponsor	Community Size	Building Size	Building Height	All Environmental Variables	Total Variance
Friendship	3.2*	0.7*	3.4*	0.1	0.1	4.3*	7.5*
Housing satisfaction	2.0*	0.5	2.7*	0.1	1.2*	4.4*	6.4*
Morale	7.6*	0.2	0.0	0.0	0.0	0.2	7.8*
Motility	22.2*	0.0	0.0	0.2	0.7*	1.0*	23.2*
Family contact	3.0*	0.0	0.0	0.1	0.1	0.3	3.3*
Activity participation	10.3*	2.2*	0.6*	0.0	0.4	4.3*	14.6*

*$p < .01$ *and* variance increment $> 0.5\%$.

Personal characteristics accounted for more variance than environmental variables did on every index of well-being except *friendship* and *housing satisfaction.* When the effects of personal variables were controlled, friendship scores were higher in private nonprofit housing and in smaller communities, and *housing satisfaction* was greater in small communities and in lower buildings. No environmental characteristic was related either to *morale* or to amount of *family contact. Motility*, though primarily determined by personal variables, was greater in low buildings. With number of activities scheduled at the site as a control variable, *activity participation* was higher in private nonprofit housing and smaller communities but was not affected by building size or building height.

Thus, with personal variables controlled, private nonprofit housing was associated with higher friendship scores and greater activity participation. With personal variables and sponsorship controlled, small community size was associated with higher friendship scores, greater housing satisfaction and greater activity participation. With personal variables, sponsorship and community size controlled, building size was not associated with any index of well-being. With personal characteristics, sponsorship, community size and building size controlled, greater building height was associated with lower housing satisfaction and lower motility.

The finding that tenants in low buildings were more satisfied with their housing and more motile in their environment than tenants in high-rise buildings may reflect the low familiarity of this generation's elderly with the high-rise. The relationship was not strong enough to warrant recommendations against high-rise structures. Rather, recognition of a possible problem should lead to efforts to counteract possible negative effects of high-rise on some tenants.

Abstract **98**

Ego-Defense and Environmental Evaluation

FRANCES M. CARP, Ph.D.

"Ego-Defense or Cognitive Consistency Effects on Environmental Evaluation," *Journal of Gerontology*, 1975, *30*, 707-711.

It is common observation that older people in substandard or otherwise inadequate living environments tend to evaluate their situations more favorably than objective observers do. According to adaptation theory, if the living environment is inconsistent with an individual's self-concept, and he is unable to improve his situation, one way to reduce feelings of inadequacy (defend against anxiety) is to deny that the living situation is all that bad. If ego defense or dissonance reduction are involved in older people's evaluations of the conditions of their lives, these evaluations are invalid descriptors of their situations, underestimating the negative factors. A low rate of negative evaluations of an obviously poor situation may reflect strong ego threat or cognitive dissonance.

Although the evaluations by old people of current living arrangements tend not to be strongly negative, applications for new housing must reflect some dissatisfaction. During the time between notification that an application has been accepted and the actual move, the residential situation does not change; however, there need be no dissonance between a favorable self-image and a bad housing situation that one is leaving. If the housing situation has been resolved by direct action, there is no longer need for ego defense in this area.

In the present study it was predicted that among old people in substandard and undesirable housing, evaluations of present housing would become more negative among those who received notice that alternative and more desirable housing was to become available.

Method

SUBJECTS: Two samples of 352 and 371 elderly applicants for public housing. The samples included almost all (94 percent and 92 percent) of the applicants who were eligible for public housing. Mean age for both samples was 73. Four out of five were living in substandard and socially isolating housing, and the remainder were in living situations with physically adequate housing but difficult interpersonal relations.

PROCEDURE: All participants were interviewed twice. The first interview occurred after application but prior to the announcement of decisions. Immediately following the announcement, there was a second interview. Both interviews included evaluation of present housing.

Results

Table 1 shows evaluations of housing at the two points in time for applicants from the first sample offered apartments and those who were not. Because evaluations by the two samples were similar and justify the same conclusions, only data from the first sample are included.

Table 1
Percentage Distributions of Evaluations of Housing

Evaluations	Offered Apartments		Not Offered Apartments	
	Time 1	Time 2	Time 1	Time 2
Very good	0%	0%	0%	0%
Good	0%	0%	0%	0%
Fair, Okay	61%	18%	64%	67%
Poor	24%	49%	24%	24%
Very poor	15%	33%	12%	9%
N	204	204	148	148

Evaluations at Time 1 tend to be more negative than those generally reported by other investigators. These subjects knew that they *might* get into better living situations and, perhaps because of the potential option, were capable of more realistic assessment of their current situations. Although all of the respondents had indicated behaviorally by applying for new housing that the current situation was unsatisfactory, more than 60 percent of them rated their housing situation at Time 1 as fair or okay. Respondents who were not offered a new apartment showed little change in rating at Time 2. However, respondents who were offered apartments showed a statistically significant change in evaluation from Time 1 to Time 2.

The results support the suggestion that the verbal reports of an older person may grossly underestimate the negative valence of a situation that he cannot change. When an individual is locked into a demeaning living situation which is inconsistent with his view of himself as a worthwhile human being, one way he may reduce the dissonance is by changing his perception of the situation. This type of distortion may be a commonly used defense maneuver among the old.

Abstract 99

Context and Consequences of Fear of Crime

RICHARD A. SUNDEEN, Ph.D. and JAMES T. MATHIEU, Ph.D.

"Fear of Crime and Its Consequences Among Elderly in Three Urban Communities," *Gerontologist*, 1976, *16*, 211-219.

This paper reported an exploratory investigation into the social context and consequences of the fear of crime among the elderly.

Method

SUBJECTS: The subjects were recruited from three types of urban neighborhoods—central city ("Core"), an urban municipality ("Slurb") and a retirement community ("Retirement"). Ss were selected on an availability basis from members of senior citizens clubs for the Core (N = 26) and

Slurb (N = 28) areas and by random selection from the telephone directory for the Retirement area (N = 50). The three samples were all white, 70 percent female, with ages ranging from 52 to 90.

PROCEDURE: A structured interview was used to obtain information about behavioral and attitudinal reactions to crime. The attitudinal questions were asked in conjunction with an 11-inch thermometer-like scale, calibrated from 0 to 100, with high (70-100), medium (30-70) and low (0-30) side markings. The S indicated strength of feelings by touching the appropriate level on the thermometer.

Results

The Communities: Physical and Social Environments: The Core Ss lived in a downtown area of transition, with a mixed ethnic population, primarily in apartment houses, and the income level was low. The Slurb Ss lived in a middle-class, predominantly white, urban city area, half of them in single family residences, and had low incomes. The Retirement sample lived in condominiums within a walled and guarded retirement community and had high incomes.

Ownership or access to the use of a private car increased from Core to Slurb to Retirement, and of course, conversely, reliance on walking or public transportation decreased. Number of hours per day away from home decreased from Core to Slurb to Retirement, although Retirement Ss frequented more places per day than the other groups.

Response to a question about crime in the immediate neighborhood indicated that the Core Ss perceived more dangerous crimes going on around them than the Slurb Ss, who perceived more than the Retirement Ss.

Social Support: Using the number of persons living in the same residence, an estimate of the likelihood of neighbors calling the police if they saw the respondent being victimized, and the extent to which the person felt he was a part of the community as indicators of social support, Core members could be described as isolated individuals, with little apparent close social interaction, a low sense of dependence upon neighbors, and little solidarity with the community. In contrast, the Retirement group scored highest on all three social support indicators.

Perceived Safety: The perception of safety was measured by asking how safe the person felt from crime in his immediate neighborhood during the day and at night. For both day and night, perceived safety was highest for the Retirement group and lowest for the Core group. Both the Core and Slurb groups perceived themselves to be much less safe at night than during the day.

Fear of Crime: Ss were asked about their fear of being a victim of four specific crimes—homes burglarized, robbed on the street, car stolen and consumer fraud. For all four crimes, the Core Ss reported the most fear, the Retirement Ss the least. The Core Ss reported strong fear of being robbed on the street and having the car stolen (the N for car ownership was only ten) and somewhat less but nevertheless strong fear of home burglary and consumer fraud. For the Slurb Ss the greatest fear was being robbed on the street, with the other three crimes arousing equivalent and quite high amounts of fear. The fears of the Retirement Ss were low for all four crimes and highest for consumer fraud.

Security Precautions Taken: Table 1 summarizes the percentages from each sample that had taken specific precautions out of a concern for security and protection from victimization of crime. The Core group had the highest proportion who had obtained a weapon, obtained a whistle, locked doors during the day, used police property identification, and stayed at home. The Slurb group had the highest proportion who had installed locks and expressed more cautious attitudes. The Retirement group had the highest proportion who had property and theft insurance.

In summary, the Core or central city group members generally had fewer socio-economic resources, a perception of a more criminal environment, took more precautions for security, but of a rather piecemeal variety, and counted less on neighborhood support for security and protection, whereas the Retirement group, which had the greatest resources, was characterized by a perception of a noncriminal environment and the lowest fear of crime and took the fewest security measures and had the greatest sense of communal support.

Table 1
Percentage of Three Samples Indicating Safety Precautions Taken for Security from Crime

	Core (N = 26)	Slurb (N = 28)	Retirement (N = 50)
Safety precautions taken:			
Obtain a weapon, including a gun	15.4	3.7	4.0
Obtain a watch dog	0	3.6	0
Obtain a whistle	42.3	25.0	0
Install special locks	53.8	71.4	10.0
Lock door during the day	96.0	89.3	38.0
Obtain property theft insurance	16.0	33.3	47.9
Police property identification	15.4	7.1	10.0
Change behavior and activities:	87.5	60.7	22.0
Stay home	20.0	10.5	9.1
Stay home at night	65.0	47.4	54.5
More cautious	10.0	36.8	36.4
Hide things	5.0	5.3	0

Abstract **100**

Fear of Crime Among the Elderly

FRANK CLEMENTE, Ph.D. and MICHAEL B. KLEIMAN, M.A.

"Fear of Crime Among the Aged," *Gerontologist,* 1976, *16,* 207-210.

Despite popular assumptions, the victimization rates for crimes against the person are lower for the elderly than for any other age group over 12 years. For example, a 1974 survey by the U. S. Department of Justice indicated that victimization rate for crimes against the person was 4.4 per thousand for the age group 65 and over, in comparison to 10.9 in the 35 to 39 age group, and 31.3 in the 20 to 24 age group. These low victimization rates not withstanding, there is solid documentation that fear of crime among the aged is real and pervasive and has harsh behavioral consequences.

This paper reports an attempt to identify which segments in the aged population are most fearful. Fear of crime was examined in relation to sex, race, socio-economic status and size of community.

Method

The data were drawn from the 1973 and 1974 General Social Surveys conducted by the National Opinion Research Center. The sample included 461 individuals age 65 and over. Parallel data from 2,488 nonaged (i.e., younger than 65) respondents was available for comparison.

Fear of crime was ascertained via the question, "Is there any area right around here, that is, within a mile, where you would be afraid to walk alone at night?" Responses were dichotomized as "yes" or "no." This question was considered appropriate because it clearly gets at fear of crime rather than concern over crime rate, and because it addresses a behavioral consequence of fear.

Socio-economic status was categorized as family income less than $7,000 per year versus more than $7,000 per year. Education was coded as less than high school, high school and more than high school. Community size was coded on a five-category scale: large city (over 250,000), medium city (50,000 - 250,000), suburb of a large city, small town (25,000 - 50,000) and rural (under 2,500).

Results

Fifty-one percent of the over-65 group in comparison to 41 percent of the under-65 group said they were afraid, an indication that more elderly than younger people are afraid of crime.

The distribution of fear responses by age and sex was as follows:

	Males	Females
over-65	34 percent	69 percent
under 65	19 percent	60 percent

Clearly, more females than males and more older than younger people admitted fear.

Forty-seven percent of the white and 69 percent of the black aged reported fear.

The distribution of fear responses by age and socio-economic status was as follows:

	Income less than $7,000	Income more than $7,000
over-65	51%	43%
under 65	47%	36%

The frequencey of fear responses was appreciably higher in the low income category than in the higher income category for members of both age groups.

The following distribution of fear responses by age and education indicates that for the aged there is no apparent relationship between fear and educational level although for the nonaged there is a tendency for the more educated respondents to express less fear.

	Less than high school	High school	More than high school
over-65	49%	53%	49%
under 65	43%	44%	37%

Because poor persons are disproportionately concentrated in metropolitan areas, the distribution of fear responses in relation to community size was examined in relation to income level. For both aged and nonaged

Table 1
Fear Responses as a Function of Community Size and Income Level

	Large City	Medium City	Suburb	Town	Rural
Over 65, low income	71%	70%	56%	48%	24%
Under 65, low income	62%	54%	43%	38%	28%
Over 65, higher income	77%	75%	27%	26%	14%
Under 65, higher income	55%	46%	38%	38%	23%

residents, regardless of income level, the percentage of respondents report-ing fear decreased as the size of the community decreased. The aged residents of cities over 50,000 showed significantly greater fear than either their younger counterparts or older inhabitants of suburbs, small towns and rural areas.

These data indicate that fear of crime is especially high among the female, black and metropolitan aged. It may be assumed that it is primarily persons from these categories of the aged population who stay behind locked doors, subject to what has been termed "house arrest."

Abstract 101

Transportation and Life Satisfaction

Stephen J. Cutler, Ph.D.

"The Availability of Personal Transportation, Residential Location and Life Satisfaction Among the Aged," *Journal of Gerontology*, 1972, *27*, 383-389.

Carp has pointed out that lack of appropriate transportation constricts the life space of any person, limits his capacity for self-maintenance, restricts his activities and contacts with other people, and may contribute to his disengagement and alienation from society and his experience of anomie.

A number of studies have obtained, contrary to the predictions of disen-gagement theory, a positive relationship between life satisfaction and levels of social activity and interaction. However, the extent to which activity and life satisfaction are themselves dependent upon access differ-entials which tend to facilitate the social engagement of the aged and which are defined, in part, by the availability of transportation, has received only limited empirical attention.

The availability of transportation can increase the capacity for mobility among the aged and thereby expand the range of social interaction, engagement and activity; it can promote a sense of independence and reduce social isolation; it can lead older persons to feel that they have some control over their environment, and reduce the impact of "environmental docility." This study was designed to test two hypotheses. First, in the absence of public and commercial transportation, older persons who have personal transportation available will have higher life satisfaction than those who do not; second, in the absence of public and commerical transportation, there will be a stronger relationship between the availability of personal transportation and life satisfaction among the aged whose residences are farther from locations of social engagement than among those whose residences are more proximate.

Method

SUBJECTS: The respondents were a randomly selected sample of noninstitutionalized residents of Oberlin, Ohio, who were aged 65 and over. The sample included 121 females, 49 males, 137 whites and 33 non-whites. The median age for the respondents was 74 and the median family income (in 1970) was approximately $3,200.

Community: Neither public nor commercial transportation was available in the city of Oberlin with a population of approximately 9,000; therefore, vehicular mobility was for the most part a function of the availability of means of personal transportation. The community displayed a high degree of centralization of ecological structure; most facilities were located within a quarter-mile radius in the center of the city. Therefore, access to facilities was related in part to distance of residence from center of the city.

PROCEDURE: All Ss were interviewed for approximately 50 minutes, during which time the Neugarten, Havighurst and Tobin Life Satisfaction Index was administered. On the basis of the interview and objective information, it was possible to dichotomize the respondents as follows: without transportation (48 percent, including those who can drive but have no vehicle as well as those who cannot drive) and with transportation (52 percent); residence less or more than one-half mile from the center of the city (65 percent and 35 percent); high and low life-satisfaction (51 percent and 49 percent); higher and lower socio-economic status (50 percent and 50 percent); and better and poorer health (66 percent and 34 percent).

Results

More older persons having personal transportation available had high life satisfaction scores than older persons not having personal transportation (58 percent versus 35 percent high life satisfaction scores; p <.02). However, the consequences of transportation differentials were greater for the aged whose residences were more distant from the centralized resources, facilities and services of the community; for persons living more than one-half mile from the center of the city, 73 percent of those with transportation and only 22 percent of those without transportation earned high scores on the life satisfaction index (p <.01). For persons close to the center of the city, life satisfaction was not strongly related to transportation differentials (48 percent of those with transportation and 42 percent without transportation had high life satisfaction scores). Socio-economic status and subjective assessment of health were both related to life satisfaction and to availability of transportation. The lowest proportions of older persons with high life satisfaction were found among those who did not have personal transportation available to them, who lived more than one-half mile from the center of the city, and who were of lower socio-economic status (only 9 percent had high life satisfaction scores) or were in poorer health (only 11 percent had high life satisfaction scores).

Abstract 102

Accident Problems and the Aging Driver

THOMAS W. PLANEK, Ph.D. and RICHARD C. FOWLER, B.A.

"Traffic Accident Problems and Exposure Characteristics of the Aging Driver," *Journal of Gerontology*, 1971, 26, 224-230.

In 1967, drivers 55 and older represented 20.4 percent of the 103 million drivers in the United States. Different studies have yielded different conclusions with respect to accident rates and driving records of older in comparison to younger drivers. This study combined the use of questionnaire data and accident records in an attempt to relate variables such as speed, weather, and highway conditions to the older driver's experiences. It also attempted to profile the aging driver's perception of driving and associated accident problems.

Method

A questionnaire covering biographical, driving experience and opinion data was distibuted to 7,500 drivers aged 55 and older in California and Illinois and through the Association of Retired Persons to persons residing in various regions of the U.S. Of these, 3,633 (48.4 percent) were returned. From the 1967 records of the California Highway Patrol a sample of 9,500 urban and 9,570 rural accidents for at-fault drivers of all age groups was obtained. The 1967 annual statistics published by the state of Virginia covering 48,285 urban and 43,349 rural accidents involving a violation were also analyzed.

Results

Annual mileage driven by males dropped from approximately 11,000 at age 55 to 4,000 for males over 80, and approximately 4,000 for females at age 55 to less than 1,000 for females over 80. Responses to questions about frequency of motor vehicle usage and frequency of rush hour, dark and winter driving indicated that with respect to these variables older people can be categorized in three groups: (a) male drivers under 65—high frequency; (b) male drivers over 65 and female drivers under 65—moderate frequency; (c) female drivers 65 and over—low frequency.

The rank order of self-perceived driving faults from most to least frequent were as follows: failure to signal (1); following too close (2); speed too slow (3); improper turning (4); drove left of center (5); speed too fast (6); improper passing (7.5); ran stop sign (7.5); failure to yield (9); ran red light (10). The rank order for how frequently specific driving operations were troublesome to members of the sample groups, from most frequently to least frequently troublesome, were as follows: changing lanes (1); making left turns (2); parking (3); entering expressways (4); reading traffic signs (5); passing (6); keeping up with traffic (7); keeping following distance (8); backing (9); judging distances (10); keeping car in lane (11); making right turns (12); steering (13).

Analysis of the accident violation data indicated that failure to yield is a significant cause of accidents. Failure to signal, improper turning, changing lanes, running stop signs and red lights were also high violation categories among aging drivers. Average or low frequency violations occurred with respect to operations such as following too closely, speeding, keeping following distance, and keeping car in lane.

Abstract **103**

Perceived Latitude of Choice

IRENE M. HULICKA, Ph.D., JOHN B. MORGANTI, Ph.D.
and JERRY F. CATALDO, Ph.D.

"Perceived Latitude of Choice of Institutionalized and Noninstitutionalized Elderly Women," *Experimental Aging Research*, 1975, *1*, 27-39.

A number of authors have suggested that one of the consequences and hardships of becoming old is diminished personal autonomy. Do older people perceive themselves to have reduced freedom of choice with reference to matters of importance? Is perceived degree of autonomy related to psychological well-being? To answer such questions, a method for assessing self-perceived latitude of choice is needed. This study was designed to evaluate the validity and appropriateness of a newly developed latitude of choice scale. It seemed reasonable to assume that elderly persons living in an institution are subject to more restrictions than elderly persons living in private homes. Therefore, if the scale were valid, elderly institutionalized individuals should earn lower latitude of choice scores. A positive relationship between the latitude of choice score and life satisfaction and self-concept scores would provide additional, though tangential, evidence for the validity of the scale.

Method

SUBJECTS: The participants were 25 elderly women (mean age = 72.4 years; range = 69-75 years) who resided in church-related homes for the elderly and 25 elderly women (mean age = 71.3 years; range = 68-74 years) who resided in their own home or apartment. All respondents were ambulatory and reasonably healthy.

Materials: The perceived latitude of choice instrument was labeled The Importance, Locus and Range of Activities Checklist for subterfuge purposes. It consisted of 37 statements which pertained to the selection or timing of activities and the selection of associates or surroundings, e.g., what time to go to bed, what name to be called, where to shop, and whether to have a private room. Since it was assumed that free choice on an activity judged to be important would contribute more to perceived latitude of choice than free choice on an activity judged to be unimportant, and vice versa, the S was asked to rate each activity for its importance (very important, somewhat important, unimportant) as well as for degree of choice available (free choice, some choice, no choice). The latitude of choice score for each item was a derived measure based on the combined importance and choice ratings.

Self-concept was assessed by having the subject rate herself on a 29 bipolar adjective pairs, using a seven-point rating scale for each pair. A slightly modified version of the Neugarten, Havighurst and Tobin Life Satisfaction Scale was also used.

PROCEDURE: Each S was contacted individually. The scales were administered in the above order in the presence of the interviewer.

Table 1
Scores of Institutionalized and Noninstitutionalized
Elderly Women on Rating Scales

Group		Importance	Choice	Latitude of Choice	Self Concept	Life Satisfaction
Noninstitutionalized	M	2.15	2.03	4.66	5.52	2.52
	SD	0.31	0.50	1.45	0.69	0.34
Institutionalized	M	2.33	0.72	1.66	4.83	2.11
	SD	0.17	0.26	0.65	0.26	0.42

Results

Table 1 summarizes the mean scores for the two groups on each of the measures. Institutionalized Ss consistently rated as very important items related to privacy, personal possessions and the timing of activities, whereas the noninstitutionalized Ss rated as most important work, interpersonal association and money-related items. Overall, the institutionalized Ss perceived themselves to have much less choice than the noninstitutionalized Ss (p <0.01); on 31 of the 37 items the institutionalized Ss earned lower average choice scores. The derived mean latitude of choice score for the noninstitutionalized Ss was almost three times higher than for the institutionalized group (p <0.01). The institutionalized Ss earned particularly low latitude of choice scores for the following items: who to live with, when to take a bath, what is served at meals, personal privacy, when to go to bed and get up, whether to have a private room, and whether to live in the same place or go elsewhere.

The institutionalized Ss also earned significantly lower self-concept (p <0.01) and life satisfaction scores (p <0.01) than the noninstitutionalized group. Significant correlations between latitude of choice and self-concept scores (r = .62; p <0.01) and between latitude of choice and life satisfaction scores (r = .48; p<0.01) confirmed a relationship between perceived latitude of choice and measures of psychological well-being.

These data, along with other data from pilot studies, suggested that the approach to assessing perceived latitude of choice had validity. An improved version of the scale is being used to assess age differences and the effects of various living arrangements on perceived latitude of choice.

CHAPTER XI

Work, Retirement, Health and Widowhood

Abstract **104**

Work Versus Volunteer Activities

FRANCES M. CARP, Ph.D.

"Differences Among Older Workers, Volunteers, and Persons who are Neither," *Journal of Gerontology*, 1968, 23, 497-501.

Much has been said and written about the importance of work in the value system of today, and the loss which is suffered, as a consequence, upon retirement. However, work is not easily available to old persons. Can volunteer community service fill and structure the time, and provide basic satisfactions to safeguard self-concept and support interpersonal relationships? Insofar as volunteer service substitutes for work, similar levels of adjustment should be found in people past retirement age who continue to hold paid jobs and in those who perform community service for which they receive no payment. Both should be better adjusted than people of similar age who work neither for pay nor as volunteers. The basic question of the study is: in general, are volunteers, like persistent workers, happier and better adjusted than their peers?

Method

SUBJECTS: Data were collected from 352 applicants for public housing for the aged, in 1959-60. Fifty-four of the Ss were working, most of them part time and on lower job levels than previously; 53 reported volunteer activity on a regular basis; and 245 had neither jobs nor volunteer activities. The entire sample was fairly representative of the postretirement age group in general. Statistical analyses revealed no differences between the workers, volunteers and Ss who were neither employed nor volunteers for age, income, savings, sex distribution, education, job level during work years (of the man or the woman's husband), mental competence, number of health complaints, physical handicaps, and restriction of activity because of illness or disability. Moreover, work and volunteer activities accounted for approximately the same amount of time. The median number of hours of paid work per week was 15 hours; the median number for volunteer work was 14. Jobs and volunteer activities were regularly scheduled and involved interactions with other persons. Thus, the major distinction between the workers and the volunteers was payment or nonpayment for their activities.

Measures of adjustment and satisfaction. Comparisons were made in four general areas: happiness, self-concept, relationships and satisfaction with time scheduling. Happiness was measured by the Burgess, Cavan and Havighurst Attitude Scale (1948). Self-concept was indicated by self-identification as middle-aged rather than as old, elderly or aged, by score on a sentence completion test, and by the number of favorable adjectives selected for self-description from a checklist. Relationships with others was measured by the Burgess et al. (1948) scales on attitudes toward family and friends, by the number of "close friends" reported, and by the percentage of leisure pursuits that involved other people. Satisfaction with use of time was measured by the S's assessment of his "free time" as "too much," "about right" or "not enough" and by the amount of "lost time"—the number of hours during a one-week period for which the S could not account.

Results and Discussion

On each of the 12 measures, the workers scored significantly more positively than either the volunteers or the persons who had neither paid jobs nor volunteer activities. Volunteers were not different from Ss who were nonworkers.

The workers earned higher happiness scores than the volunteers and the nonactive group. The workers selected more favorable adjectives for self-description, more frequently identified themselves as middle-aged rather than old, and tended to perceive themselves as more useful and competent than did members of either comparison group. Moreover, the workers had more favorable attitudes toward their families and friends, reported a larger number of "best" friends, and engaged to a greater extent in leisure activities involving others than did the volunteers and nonworkers. The three groups did not differ for involvement in number of leisure activities, but workers tended to complain less than the other groups of having "too much free time."

The results of this study support the view that old people who work tend to be happier, to have more favorable views of themselves, to enjoy better relationships with others, and to be more satisfied with the way their days are filled than are old people who do not work. However, old people who volunteered regularly for unpaid community service were no happier, had no better self-concepts or social relationships, and were no less likely to complain about time hanging heavy on their hands than did people who neither worked nor served as volunteers.

These data suggest that work has far more favorable effects than does volunteer service on older persons, and that these effects are not due to the time-filling, time-scheduling, activity *per se*, or to social contact aspects of the job. Rather, the effects may stem from the payments that represent not only purchasing power but also a value placed by society on their contribution.

Supportive evidence for this interpretation was obtained subsequent to the main study. Ss known to have special skills were asked if they would like to make use of them. Almost unanimously they responded they would be glad to—if they were paid. Discussion revealed that unless others valued their work sufficiently to give it financial recognition, they viewed it as "busy work" invented to keep the old person happy. The respondents did not ask for a high fee; a token payment would assure them of the importance of their contributions of time and skill.

Abstract 105

Perceived Age Discrimination in Employment

PATRICIA L. KASSCHAU, Ph.D.

"Perceived Age Discrimination in a Sample of Aerospace Employees," *Gerontologist*, 1976, *16*, 166-173.

Age discrimination is receiving increasing attention as a social problem. Following a 1964 Department of Labor study which determined that there was very extensive and nonproductive age discrimination in employment situations, Congress in 1967 passed the Age Discrimination Employment Act (ADEA). Briefly, this law prohibits discrimination in employment on the basis of age in such matters as hiring, job retention, compensation and other privileges and conditions of employment. All employers with more than 20 employees, labor organizations with more than 25 members, employment agencies and, since 1974, federal, state and local governments are subject to the Act's provisions. All employees at least 40 years of age but under 65 in these employment establishments are protected under the Act. ADEA specifically sanctions mandatory retirement practices as bonafide applications of an age criterion by employers. Beyond the age of 65, ADEA offers the individual no protection whatsoever.

Violations of the Act are being disclosed and prosecuted with increasing frequency. Nevertheless, it was recently reported in Senate hearings that violations of ADEA are so widespread in the business world as almost to preclude vigorous enforcement; that there is nearly a universal acceptance of the tenet that young is better than old; and that firms blatantly practice age management policies in accordance with this principle.

No one really knows how pervasive age discrimination is in American society. This study was designed to obtain data about age discrimination on the job experienced or observed by a sample of currently employed workers.

Method

The population studied consisted of all employees 45 years of age and older in a division of an aerospace firm. Aerospace workers face unusual employment circumstances in that they are frequently laid off from one company when a government contract expires and hired by another firm which has been awarded a new contract. Hence, they may have had atypically frequent exposure to potential age discrimination experiences in seeking new employment.

Table 1
Description of Sample

Descriptive Category	Percentage of Total Sample	Percentage Rate of Return
Male	77.6	34
Female	22.4	22
Hourly employees	49	29
Salaried employees	50	30
Aged 45-49	37.4	29
Aged 50-54	35	33
Aged 55-59	13.6	24
Over 60	14.3	36

Questionnaires were distributed by mail to 905 employees. Only 298 completed questionnaires were returned. Description of the sample and rate of return is summarized in Table 1.

The 50-item self-administered questionnaire on attitudes toward work and retirement contained a section that asked respondents whether they had experienced age discrimination in employment since reaching middle age (specifically in holding a job, finding a job or advancing in a job), whether they considered their employer's mandatory retirement policy as a form of discrimination, and whether they had knowledge of age discrimination affecting the employment status of friends.

Results

As Table 2 indicates, on each of the employment-related items, approximately half of the sample or more reported that they had either personally experienced or witnessed age discrimination.

When responses were examined in relation to chronological age, in all cases, except forced retirement, it was the 55-to 59-year-old group that most frequently reported experiences with age discrimination. Perhaps the over-60 group represented extremely competent workers who had survived the culling process implicit in age management policies; in contrast, employees in their late 50's may have experienced the brunt of the firm's age management policies to get rid of the "dead wood."

Although respondents aged 45 to 54 were less likely than older respondents to report personal experience with discrimination, they were not necessarily working in an environment where there was less age discrimination; they reported observations of age discrimination against friends at least as frequently as the older respondents did. More than 69 percent of the entire sample indicated that they believed compulsory retirement was not fair to the employee, and the percentage increased with age.

Table 2
Percentage Reporting Age Discrimination

Age Discrimination	Self	Friends
Since reaching middle age	36%	Not asked
Finding a job	33%	45%
Job advancement	22%	22%
Job retention	10%	40%
Forced retirement discriminatory	20%	40%

In this sample, reported experiences with age discrimination did not differ substantially between male and female employees. Hourly workers tended to report somewhat more personal experience with age discrimination than salaried workers did. Probably, however, this difference was lower than would be found in most samples because these salaried employees had been, like the hourly workers, subject to frequent job changes.

Abstract **106**

Attitude Toward Retirement

GERDA G. FILLENBAUM, Ph.D.

"On the Relation Between Attitude to Work and Attitude to Retirement," *Journal of Gerontology*, 1971, 26, 244-248.

This study examined the hypothesis that those who are satisfied with their jobs will have a negative attitude toward retirement, whereas those who are dissatisfied with their jobs will have a positive attitude toward retirement.

Method

SUBJECTS: Approximately 100 persons within each of the age spans 25-34, 35-44, 45-54 and over 54, selected at random from a population of nearly 6,000 nonacademic employees at a medical and university center, were mailed a 95-item questionnaire. Fifty-six percent of the questionnaires were returned, and apart from a disproportionately larger number of females, the respondents were fairly representative of the contacted group with respect to age, sex, race, occupational status and length of employment.

Materials: A 95-item questionnaire on health, ease of getting to work, adequacy of expected retirement income; job satisfaction pertaining to achievement, recognition for achievement, work itself, responsibility, advancement, supervision, pay, interpersonal relations and working conditions; and two items on attitude to retirement (retirement is mostly good or mostly bad for a person, and I look forward to, dislike the idea or am undecided about retirement).

Results

Only one variable, achievement, bore any relationship to retirement attitude. Those who reported that they had less chance of increasing their skills were more likely to view retirement as a good thing. However, this relationship held only among the elderly, among whites and among males.

Abstract **107**

Life Adjustment of Retired Couples

DAVID M. DRESSLER, M. D.

"Life Adjustment of Retired Couples," *International Journal of Aging and Human Development*, 1973, 4, 335-349.

This study was designed to examine the retirement experiences of a sample of retired couples. The focus was on the marital relationship, but data regarding interfamilial relationships, leisure activities, health status, and attitudes toward death and aging were also explored. Specific questions pertained to characteristics of the intermarital relationship, changes in life pattern in comparison to age 50, satisfaction with current life and current level of social involvement.

Method

SUBJECTS: The sample consisted of 38 Caucasian, community resident, retired couples, which represented two-thirds of those contacted. The age range was 61 to over 80; more than half the respondents of both sexes were over 70 years of age. For more than three-quarters of the participants, this was the first marriage, and more than three-quarters of the couples had been married more than 30 years. The sample was primarily of "working class" background. In all couples, the husband had been the primary economic provider. Three-quarters of the husbands had been retired for more than five years, and only two had retired during the past year. None of the participants was employed at the time of the interview.

PROCEDURE: A structured interview was used for data collection. Spouses were interviewed jointly, except that questions reflecting attitudes or opinions such as those about marital adjustment and perception of retirement were asked in separate interviews.

Results

Sixty percent of the husbands and 40 percent of the wives had felt relatively unprepared for retirement; over half of them had had no special plans for retirement. Slightly over half of the sample reported the transition into retirement to be a difficult period, but their condition seemed to improve after several months.

Couples reported a high degree of satisfaction in almost all aspects of their marital relationship about which they were questioned, i.e., mutual support and understanding during transition into retirement life, amount of time spent together, amount of emotional support, effectiveness of communication and amount of household duties. Satisfaction with sexual relations was somewhat lower than in other areas, but more than one-half of the respondents were unwilling to answer this question. Husbands were less satisfied than wives with the way in which decisions were made.

Couples reported little change in the nature of their relationship as compared with preretirement, with age 50 being used as the preretirement reference point. No changes were reported with respect to amount of time together, communication effectiveness, emotional support, disagreement and the way in which decisions are made. Sexual activity was reported to be somewhat diminished, and wives spent less and husbands more time on household duties.

On the average, the respondents got together or talked with their children about once a week. Consistent with preretirement behavior, they tended neither to give nor receive much in the way of help, advice, or money, and most respondents were satisfied with the relationship.

The majority of respondents reported spending their present time on activities such as TV and radio, reading, household tasks, conversations with spouse and children, social activities and travel. Couples reported an average of three to four close friends whom they visited about once a month. They also reported attending religious services and organized group activities about once a month.

Approximately half of the sample reported some deterioration of health since retirement. In general, attitudes toward death indicated resignation or denial, with 44 percent appearing to accept its inevitability. Men appeared to be more concerned about death than women. Most respondents had adopted an attitude of taking things on a day-to-day basis; 80 percent reported no plans for the future. Most felt that involvement in living precluded worry about death. About one-third of the respondents were resigned to aging, one-half accepting, and a few were frightened or indifferent.

Almost all respondents (90 percent) felt they had made adequate adjustment to retirement, and looking back over their whole life, most of them (80 percent) expressed satisfaction with their accomplishments and little regret about important decisions they had made in the past.

There was a high degree of consistency between the interviewer's assessment of couples with their assessment of themselves. However, the interviewer sensed a higher degree of marital conflict and tension than the couples reported and also sensed that they were somewhat less close emotionally than reported. Nevertheless, the interviewer assessed the couples to be fairly realistic in their mutual appraisal and to have genuine fondness and respect for one another. It appeared that communication was generally effective and that there was a high degree of marital satisfaction.

Abstract 108

Perceived Need Fulfillment and Retirement

KENNETH N. WEXLEY, Ph.D., JANET L. McLAUGHLIN, Ph.D. and HARVEY L. STERNS, Ph.D.

"A Study of Perceived Need Fulfillment and Life Satisfaction Before and After Retirement," *Journal of Vocational Behavior*, 1975, 7, 81-87.

This study examined need satisfaction, need importance and overall life satisfaction as a function of four periods of proximity to the retirement date, with the goal of determining whether there are differences in an individual's gratification of psychological needs as he progresses from near retirement through postretirement. The study also attempted to determine whether retirement is troublesome and whether overall life satisfaction is related to specific areas of need fulfillment.

Method

SUBJECTS: Personnel directors of a large company identified 320 persons by four job levels and four proximity-to-retirement categories (greater than 48 months preretirement, 3-48 months preretirement, 3-48 months postretirement, and greater than 48 months retirement). Although questionnaires were sent to 20 persons in each job level-proximity-to-retirement combination, the relatively low rate of return made it necessary to discard the job level category. The number of Ss for the four proximity-to-retirement categories were as follows: far preretirement = 29, near preretirement = 52, near postretirement = 41 and far postretirement = 33. The median ages for the four groups were 58.6, 62.5, 65.7 and 70.8 years, respectively.

PROCEDURE: Respondents, contacted by mail, completed a modified version of Porter's (1961) need satisfaction questionnaire, a Life Satisfation Index (Neugarten, Havighurst and Tobin, 1961) and a general information blank pertaining to age, health, marital status, income and retirement status. The need satisfaction questionnaire, based upon a Maslow-type need hierarchy system, consisted of items measuring security, social, esteem, autonomy and self-actualization needs; two items were added to assess income and the feeling of "being-in-the-know." For each of the items pertaining to needs, respondents were asked to answer three questions: (a) How much of the characteristic is there now connected with your present life situation? (b) How much of this characteristic do you think should be connected with your present life situation? (c) How important is this characteristic to you? Each question was answered on a seven-point rating scale from minimum to maximum.

Results

The results for need satisfaction indicated that for most needs, there were no significant differences among proximity to retirement groups. However, the far preretirement individuals had significantly lower need satisfaction with respect to security and being-in-the-know than persons in some other groups. The different proximity to retirement groups ascribed similar importance to most of the needs, with the exception that the self-actualization and autonomy needs showed a pattern of decreasing importance from before to after retirement. Life Satisfaction scores did not vary as a function of proximity to retirement. Significant correlations were found between each of the need satisfaction category scores and the Life Satisfaction score, an indication that satisfaction in all of the need areas was related to overall life satisfaction.

These results suggest that approximately four to seven years prior to retirement, the worker may begin to worry about adjustment to retirement, that shortly before and subsequent to retirement self-actualization and autonomy needs might recede in importance, and that relatively advantaged retirees, such as were included in this sample, may be as satisfied with their life situation as comparable working individuals are.

Abstract 109

Values and Adjustment in the Aged

TONI ANTONUCCI, Ph.D.

"On the Relationship Between Values and Adjustment in Old Men," *International Journal of Aging and Human Development*, 1974, 5, 57-69.

This study explored relationships between values and adjustment in old age. It was hypothesized that adjusted people have different values than unadjusted people, and that because adjustment may be dependent on the acceptance of values that are appropriate to role and function in society, work-related values should be less important to well adjusted than to less well adjusted old men, since work should no longer be an important component of life in retirement.

Method

SUBJECTS: Forty white males between the ages of 60 and 80 years (mean = 70.6 years) were interviewed. All were volunteers recruited from a senior citizens center. All were retired, and in reasonably good health; none was institutionalized.

PROCEDURE: Each participant completed the Havighurst Life Satisfaction Scale and a Semantic Differential based on Rokeach's Value Survey, which included the ten value concepts listed in Table 1. (Other data were also collected but were not reported.)

Table 1
Means for Values as a Function of Adjustment Level

Values	Adjustment			Total
	High	Medium	Low	
Freedom	19.07	19.58	19.07	19.34
Comfortable life	19.28	19.58	19.28	19.44
Exciting life	17.92	18.50	18.56	18.92
Sense of accomplishment	18.50	18.58	19.42	18.67
National security	15.42	19.25	18.78	18.59
Ambitious	17.57	18.25	19.92	17.75
Capable	17.78	18.66	19.57	18.84
Obedient	18.35	18.41	19.92	18.34
Clean	19.14	19.33	19.85	19.37
Independent	19.14	19.25	19.64	19.22
Total	18.22	18.94	19.44	

Results

On the basis of scores on the Life Satisfaction Scale, the respondents were assigned to high, medium or low adjustment categories. Table 1 presents the mean scores of the adjustment groups on each of the value concepts as assessed by the Semantic Differential. For the group as a whole, the items that were not considered very important relative to the other values measured were ambitious, obedient, national security, sense of accomplishment and capable. All of these values, with the exception of national security, would seem to be related to work. The interacton between adjustment category and value was significant for the values of national security, ambitious, capable, sense of accomplishment and obedient. For each of these values the differences were in a consistent linear direction, with the high-adjustment group rating the value lower or less important than the medium- or low-adjusted groups. Thus, it would appear that well-adjusted old men considered work-related values to be much less important than less well-adjusted men did.

Abstract **110**

Social and Psychological Differences

ROBERT C. ATCHLEY, Ph.D.

"Selected Social and Psychological Differences Between Men and Women in Later Life," *Journal of Gerontology,* 1976, *31,* 204-211.

Although there has been a great deal of speculation and data collection concerning how older men and women differ with respect to social and psychological characteristics, many of the studies which included sex comparisons lumped together all respondents into a single age category, usually age 65 and over, or if more detailed age breakdowns were included, there may have been no control for sex differences in marital status, education or income. This study reports male-female comparisons that have been controlled for age, marital status, education and income adequacy.

Method

SUBJECTS: Data were collected via questionnaires mailed to a random sample of retired teachers and to the entire population of people retired from a telephone company. A total of 3,630 questionnaires were returned. The response rate varied from 50 percent for retired males to 81 percent for female retired teachers.

Measures: Appropriate measures were used to assess each of the variables listed in Table 1.

PROCEDURE: Test factor standardization was used to control for the effects of differences in age, marital status, education and income in the subgroups based on sex and occupation.

Results and Discussion

Table 1 summarizes the distribution of responses by sex and occupation for the major variables which were studied. There were no significant sex differences in the importance of work, though generally work was more important for former teachers than former phone employees. More than four-fifths of the respondents reported liking retirement, with more male than female phone employees liking it. In both work categories more men than women reported that they became accustomed to retirement quickly.

This finding is contrary to the popular assumption that whereas retirement may cause some important adjustment problems for men, it is of inconsequential importance for women.

Loneliness was significantly more prevalent among older women than older men. High anomie was not very prevalent among the respondents but was more prevalent among men than women. More older women than men reported high anxiety.

When actual age was controlled, a higher proportion of older men than older women identified themselves as old rather than middle-aged or just past middle-age; the gap was greated among former telephone employees.

The majority of respondents of both sexes reported high self-esteem and stable self-concepts, but women from both employee categories were more likely to report unstable self-concepts, and former women teachers to report low self-esteem, than their male counterparts. Older women were more

Table 1
Sex Differences Among Retired People by Industry for Selected Variables Standardized by Age, Marital Status, Education and Income Adequacy (In Percentages)

Variable	Total		Phone		Teacher	
	Male	Female	Male	Female	Male	Female
Work important	60.9	65.5	53.0	57.1	73.2	71.1
In labor force	27.4	24.2	22.3	25.2	36.4*	23.7
Like retirement	85.7	81.8	89.1*	84.1	79.4	80.7
Quickly used to retirement	54.9*	44.2	58.2*	53.5	46.7*	38.6
Often lonely	21.1*	28.9	20.9*	26.5	21.4*	31.5
High anomie	22.1*	17.3	22.1*	17.3	22.2*	17.3
High anxiety	31.3*	43.8	31.6*	48.4	31.0*	41.8
Identifies as old	85.6*	70.9	84.3*	59.6	87.9*	76.2
Low self-esteem	16.5	25.4	15.2	18.9	19.0*	28.5
Low stability of self-concept	8.4*	23.6	9.6*	17.9	6.7*	26.4
High sensitivity to criticism	27.1*	50.7	24.6*	40.5	31.5*	55.4
High depression	20.1*	29.6	17.0	25.4	25.9*	31.7
Poor health	11.7	12.6	10.6	9.4	13.9	14.6
Inadequate income	17.1*	28.1	13.9*	26.8	23.0*	28.7
Less contact with friends	26.7	19.7	35.5*	23.1	18.3	18.1
More contact with friends	35.6	34.5	31.4	29.5	42.7*	36.8
Less participation in organizations	21.6	25.0	23.0*	27.4	19.5*	23.9
More participation in organizations	29.6	30.0	30.1	27.0	28.7	31.4
N (3,620)	1,364	2,266	862	710	502	1,556

*Sex differences significant at the .05 level or below. Unless both phone and teacher categories showed significant sex differences, the total is not shown as significant, even though the percentage difference was technically significant.

likely to be sensitive to criticism and to be depressed than older men. Generally, older women showed a greater prevalence of "negative" psychological characteristics than older men did.

Most of the respondents reported themselves to be in good health. Older women were significantly more likely than men to describe their income as inadequate. Male telephone employees, compared to women, reported that they had less contact with friends; more male than female former teachers, on the other hand, reported increased contact with friends.

Abstract 111

Health and Retirement

ETHEL SHANAS, Ph.D.

"Health and Adjustment in Retirement," *Gerontologist*, 1970, *10*, 19-21.

One of the most widely held beliefs about the aged is that retirement from work has a deleterious effect on health. This study addressed three questions: What are the reasons men give for retiring from work? What are the satisfactions men report in retirement? How is adjustment in retirement related to health, if health is measured in terms of function rather than by extent of pathology?

Method

The data came from a national probability sample of persons 65 years of age and older living in the community. The four percent of all older persons in the United States who live in institutions were not represented in the sample. Respondents were interviewed about their living arrangements, families, work, income and degree of incapacity.

Results

About three of every ten men aged 65 and over in the United States were still working. Only a third of all retired men said they gave up working because they reached compulsory retirement age or because their jobs were eliminated. The remainder said they retired because, for various reasons, they wanted to stop working. Forty-one percent of recent retirees (three years or less) and 48 percent of long-term retirees (more than 3 years) gave poor health as the chief reason for retirement. Of these, some stated clearly that poor health was the reason, while others described the work as "too tiring" or "too exhausting." Twenty-five percent of the recent and 17 percent of the long-term retirees gave nonhealth reasons for wanting to retire, e.g., they preferred leisure to work, their income was adequate without work, etc. These data indicate, in contrast to popular belief, that most men who are now retired, retired voluntarily. Moreover, the health complaints of most retired men are not the results of their retirement. If any order of events can be inferred from these data, it is that poor health is a major cause rather than consequence of retirement.

About three out of every ten retired men said they enjoyed nothing about their retirement, while seven out of ten reported something about their retirement that they liked. Frequently reported advantages were resting, free time, and the opportunity to do what they wanted. Most men missed something about their work, with almost half of them reporting that what they missed most about their former jobs was the money. A few said they missed the work itself and the people at work, and a few said they missed nothing. In general, the findings indicated that most men with enough money to live on, and even some whose incomes were extremely low, were content in retirement.

Although many of the retired men said they stopped working because of poor health, most of them were functioning well. Two-thirds of the retirees reported no limitations in their capacity to carry on the ordinary activities of daily life. In general, the men who enjoyed nothing about their retirement were those with limitations in their day-to-day functioning. The men with limited physical capacity for carrying on a normal life were also more likely than the other retirees to say that they were often lonely and that time passed slowly for them.

Poor health may indeed create difficulties for the man who has retired, but there was no evidence that retirement had created poor health.

Abstract **112**

Home Health Needs of the Aged

ETHEL SHANAS, Ph.D.

"Measuring the Home Health Needs of the Aged in Five Countries," *Journal of Gerontology*, 1971, *26*, 37-40.

Although not all old people are ill, a substantial number of older people, particularly those aged 75 or more, are sick and/or enfeebled and require medical care and associated health services, including nursing services, health screening examinations, occupational and physical therapy, eye glasses and hearing aids, medication and home helps. To provide necessary health services, an estimate of the proportion of the population which requires a given service is required. This paper reports an attempt to measure in several countries the need by old people for community health services, i.e., services that should either be delivered to old people at home, or alternatively, available so that bedfast and totally or partially housebound old persons can have ready access to them.

Method

Data for institutions are taken from official publications. All other data came from surveys of probability samples of noninstitutionalized persons aged 65 and over. The data are based on reports of old persons themselves and, in the case of those old persons too sick to be interviewed, on the reports of persons taking care of them. The data were collected in 1962 in Denmark, Great Britain and the United States and in 1966-67 in Poland and Israel.

Table 1
Proportion of Population, Aged 65 and Over,
Bedfast, Housebound and Ambulatory only with Difficulty

Country	% Bedfast	% Housebound	% Ambulatory with Difficulty	Total %
Denmark	2	8	14	24
Britain	3	11	8	22
United States	2	6	6	14
Israel	2	13	NA	?
Poland	4	6	16	26

Results

The proportion of the population aged 65 and over resident in institutions was as follows: Denmark—5.3 percent; Britain—3.6 percent; United States—3.7 percent; Israel—5.5 percent; Poland—not available. Table 1 presents information on the proportion of older people, who, though not institutionalized, are sufficiently incapacitated to require a full program of community services. Table 2 presents the proportion of old people who reported they had been ill in bed at least one day during the preceding year, and of those, the proportion who were visited by a physician.

Table 2
Proportion of Population, Aged 65 and Over,
Ill in Bed During Year, and Proportion of Ill Visited by Physician

Country	% Ill in Bed	% Who Were Ill in Bed and Visited By Physician
Denmark	32	70
Britain	30	81
United States	26	50
Israel	53	81
Poland	46	66

The data demonstrate marked similarities among the various older populations. In each country from four to five percent of the population aged 65 and over is institutionalized, 14 to 26 percent, though not institutionalized, could benefit from a full spectrum of community services, and 26 to 53 percent were ill in bed at least one day during the preceding year. In Great Britain and Israel, four out of five old persons who were ill in bed were attended by a physician, in comparison to one out of two in the United States. Although the proportion of noninstitutionalized persons requiring a full complement of community services was low in the United States (16 percent) in comparison to the other countries (22-26 percent), this proportion represents approximately three million persons.

Abstract **113**

Age and the Perception of Common Ailments

FRED THUMIN, Ph.D. and EARL WIMS, Ph.D.

"The Perception of the Common Cold and Other Ailments and Discomforts as Related to Age," *International Journal of Aging and Human Development*, 1975, 6, 43-49.

How do people of different age groups perceive various forms of ailments and discomforts?

Method

SUBJECTS: The subjects were 256 Caucasian, ambulatory, noninstitutionalized persons who could be described as essentially self-sufficient normals. They were subdivided into four age categories as follows: 18 to 22 years (mean =20.7 years), 23 to 29 years (mean =25.3), 30 to 44 years (mean = 36.9) and 45 to 82 years (mean =58.6). The proportion of females in each group increased progressively with age.

Procedure: Questionnaires were administered, either individually or in groups. Ss were told the study was being conducted to learn more about the common cold and other familiar discomforts. They were asked about frequency and duration of colds, symptoms (a 15-item checklist), and treatments (a 15-item checklist). Then, they were presented with a list of 17 relatively common ailments, one at a time, and asked whether they would rather have that ailment or a "bad cold," if they had to have one or another.

Results

Older respondents, on the average, reported fewer colds per year than the younger respondents, 2.2 versus 3.1 (p<0.01), and the duration of colds was slightly less, 5.2 versus 5.5 days. There was no sex difference for either frequency or duration of colds. The only symptom that bothered the older Ss more frequently than the younger Ss was body aches, whereas the young reported a greated frequency of the following symptoms: inability to con-
.centrate, depression, inability to work effectively, nasal irritation or sneezing, head or nasal congestion, runny nose and sore throat. For two of these symptoms, runny nose and inability to concentrate, the apparent age dif-

ference was due in part to the greater tendency for males to complain about these symptoms.

With respect to treatment, Contac and Dristan were significantly more popular among the younger respondents, whereas the oldest group tended more often to use laxatives, seek medical advice and to stay home and rest. Aspirin, fluid and cough drops were the most frequently used treatments for all age groups.

The rank order of the severity of various ailments and discomforts for the youngest and oldest groups were as follows (rank for youngest group is given first): Sprained back (1,1); Two-day intestinal flu (2, 6); Bad case of hay fever(3, 3); Wisdom tooth pulled (4,8); Cut finger requiring two stitches (5, 7); Sprained ankle (6,2); Three-day measles (7,9); Earache (8, 4); Stub and sprain toe (9, 5); Bad case of indigestion (10, 10); Ingrown toe nail (11, 11); Tooth filled (12, 16); Burn finger on stove (13, 15); Bad headache (14, 13); Stiff neck (15, 13.5); Give pint of blood (16, 17); Hangover (17, 12). The oldest group equated the discomfort of a cold with a bad headache, stiff neck and hangover (ranks 12-14), whereas the young group equated a cold with a bad case of indigestion and an ingrown toe nail (ranks 10 and 11). The perceived severity of a number of ailments increased with age, namely, earache, indigestion, stiff neck, hangover and sprained toe. On the other hand, intestinal flu was viewed as much more severe by the younger than the older respondents (more than 90 percent of all younger respondents rated the flu as worse than a cold, in comparison to 76 percent of the oldest respondents).

In evaluating the severity of different ailments in comparison to the common cold, part of the observed differences between age groups would be due to the fact that the older people perceived the common cold as relatively less severe than the young people did, and part of the difference would be due to age differences in perception of the severity of other ailments.

Abstract **114**

Acute Drug Reactions Among the Elderly

DAVID M. PETERSEN, Ph.D. and CHARLES W. THOMAS, Ph.D.

"Acute Drug Reactions Among the Elderly," *Journal of Gerontology*, 1975, *30*, 552-556.

Drug use and misuse among the elderly has been a neglected area of research in the field of social gerontology. This paper described the social and demographic characteristics of elderly persons who were treated for acute but nonfatal drug reactions in a hospital emergency room, and compared the elderly cohort with all acute drug admissions.

Method

Data were gathered from the patient records of 1,128 persons treated during 1972 for acute drug reaction in a large hospital. Acute drug reaction was defined as those effects resulting from drug ingestion which either produced interference with adequate social functioning or were subjectively perceived to be so unpleasant that the user sought assistance from the hospital emergency room. Excluded from the analysis were 117 patients who were admitted for other drug-related reasons such as hepatitis, poisonings and addiction detoxification. Elderly was defined as age 50 and older.

Results

Of the 1,128 admissions, 60 individuals (5.4 percent) were aged 50 to 80 years (mean age = 59.6 years). The average age for all overdose admissions was 27.6 years. Table 1 summarizes comparisons between the older subsample and all overdose admittees. These data indicate that females outnumbered males for all overdose admissions (58.6 percent versus 41.4 percent) and the sex difference was particularly great in the older age category (68.4 percent versus 31.6 percent). The vast majority of these acute drug reactions involved whites (85 percent) and particularly white females (61.7 percent). In terms of age, sex and race characteristics of the general population served by the hospital, the aged were not overrepresented; however, white females and blacks of both sexes were overrepresented both for total admissions and admissions among the aged.

Table 1
Characteristics of 60 Aged Patients Compared to All Patients
Admitted for Emergency Treatment of Acute Drug Reactions

	Aged Admissions (N = 60)		Total Admissions (N = 1128)	
	N	%	N	%
Race-sex Distribution				
White male	14	23.3	322	28.6
White female	37	61.7	433	38.4
Black male	5	8.3	144	12.8
Black female	4	6.7	228	20.2
Number of drugs abused				
Single substance use	32	68.1	720	76.5
Multiple substance use	15	31.9	221	23.5
Alcohol-drug use in combination				
Present	5	8.3	123	10.9
Not present	55	91.7	1005	89.1
Suicide attempt				
Yes	14	35.0	272	33.7
No	26	65.0	535	66.3

Almost one-third of the aged patients (31.9 percent) had mixed two or more substances prior to their adverse drug reaction (contrasted to 23.5 percent among all admissions). About ten percent of all patients, including the aged, had used alcohol in combination with a drug. Although one-fifth (20.6 percent) of all acute drug admissions were the result of abuse of an illicit substance, no older patient was admitted for this reason. Slightly more than 80 percent of all acute drug reactions among the elderly involved use of a legally manufactured and distributed sedative or tranquilizer; another ten percent involved the use of nonnarcotic analgesics. The most frequently misused drugs among the aged were Valium, Tuinal, Phenobarbital, and Darvon. Approximately one-third of all persons admitted with overdose reactions, including the aged, reported that they had consciously been attempting to commit suicide.

Data for the prescription of drugs indicate that people over 65 years of age, though comprising only one-tenth of the population, received approximately one-quarter of all prescriptions. The availability of tranquilizers and sedatives increases the likelihood of an accidental overdose and their use in a suicide attempt. Acute drug problems seem to be more common among elderly women than elderly men.

Abstract **115**

Anticipatory Grief and the Aged Bereaved

IRWIN GERBER, Ph.D., ROSLYN RUSALEM, M. A.,NATALIE HANNON, B.A.,
DELIA BATTIN, M.S.W. and ARTHUR ARKIN, M.D.

"Anticipatory Grief and Aged Widows and Widowers,"
Journal of Gerontology, 1975, *30*, 225-229.

Although it has often been assumed that anticipatory grief has a positive effect on individual adjustment to the death of a significant person, there is reason to question both the validity and the generality of the assumption, particularly with reference to the aged bereaved. This study was designed to: (1) test the effect of anticipatory grief on the medical adjustment of the aged bereaved six months after the loss of a spouse; (2) explore whether length of anticipatory grief is a differentiating factor in medical adjustment; (3) investigate whether sex of survivor is significant in the analysis of the first two goals.

Method

SUBJECTS: This study involved 47 widows and 34 widowers. Of these, 16 had spouses who died of an acute illness without warning and prior knowledge of the condition, and 65 were bereaved because of chronic fatal illness. The 65 bereaved spouses of chronic illness death were subdivided into two categories of chronicity: chronic illness lasting "six months or less" and "more than six months." The mean age of the subjects was 63 years.
PROCEDURE: Three medical variables were selected as indicators of bereavement adjustment: (1) number of physician office visits; (2) number of times ill without contacting a physician, i.e., general malaise; (3) number of psychotropic medications used (e.g., antidepressants and tranquilizers). The source of data was an open-ended questionnaire completed by the surviving spouses.

Results

The small number of those bereaved by an acute fatal illness of spouse precluded definitive comparisons, but the data indicated that, in general, adjustment to a sudden death was neither better nor worse than to a chronic illness death. No male-female differences were noted for adjustment to an acute-illness death, but each of the three medical outcome variables revealed that male survivors adjusted less well than female survivors to a chronic-illness bereavement. A comparison of the "less than six months" and "more than six months" chronic illness categories revealed that those who were bereaved because of a chronic illness lasting more than six months showed poorer medical adjustment than those bereaved because of a chronic illness of shorter duration. The medical adjustment of widowers was more negatively affected than that of widows by the extended chronic illness of the spouse prior to death.

These findings therefore suggest that anticipatory grief does not necessarily facilitate the medical adjustment of the bereaved aged. Indeed, lengthy experience with anticipatory grief may contribute to poor medical adjustment to bereavement, particularly for elderly widowers. In general, anticipatory grief, if at all facilitative to the medical adjustment of the bereaved aged, is less facilitative to the adjustment of the aged widower than of the aged widow.

Abstract 116

Problems and Compensations of Widowhood

MARY VIRGINIA WYLY, Ph.D. and IRENE M. HULICKA, Ph.D.

"Problems and Compensations of Widowhood: A Comparison of Age Groups." Presented at the Meeting of the American Psychological Association, Chicago, 1975.

A woman's age when widowed may be an important factor in her ability to cope with the problems of widowhood. This study examined the differences in attitudes, problems and compensations of widows in three age groups.

Method

SUBJECTS: Widows in the age bracket of 30 to 40 years (n = 15), 41 to 59 years (n =29) and 60 years and older (n= 28) were interviewed. The sample was restricted to women in the middle socio-economic class who were widowed less than five years.

PROCEDURE: An interview, lasting from one to four hours, was structured into two sections. The first part was dsigned to obtain demographic and other factual information. During the second less structured section, the widow was asked to identify and describe the most serious problems associated with widowhood, the resolution of problems (extent and techniques), compensations (if any) of widowhood, changes in relationships with friends and relatives, and in social activities and social interests and ways in which various social institutions had or had not been helpful during widowhood. Following the interview, the respondents were given a nine-point scale and asked to rate themselves on a number of attributes as they perceived themselves to be now, and as they were two years prior to widowhood. Attributes listed on the scale included health, loneliness, freedom of choice, peace of mind and independence.

Results

The problem most frequently cited and deemed most important by widows in all three groups was loneliness. A second problem that was mentioned by many of the widows of all ages was that of home maintenance and car repair. Respondents in the two younger groups identified participation in social functions as a problem, since social activities in this culture are couple-oriented. Other problems cited frequently by widows in these two groups were as follows: decision-making, child-rearing, absence of sex life, and managing the family finances. For widows in the oldest group, the most frequently mentioned problems were as follows: learning basic finance, lack of transportation and fear of crime.

On the self-rating scales, the oldest subjects indicated less severe negative changes from two years prior to widowhood to the present than did subjects in the two younger groups. Some younger widows did, however, report as compensations of widowhood increased independence and freedom of choice. No widow in the oldest group indicated that widowhood had any advantage.

Across all age groups, respondents commented that there was a need to talk with friends or family members about their loss, but this was not allowed. Death and grief seemed to be uncomfortable topics even among close friends.

Abstract **117**

The Depression of Widowhood

PHILLIP E. BORNSTEIN, M.D., PAULA J. CLAYTON, M.D.,
JAMES A. HALIKAS, M.D., WILLIAM L. MAURICE, M.D. and ELI ROBBINS, M.D.

"The Depression of Widowhood after Thirteen Months,"
British Journal of Psychiatry, 1973, 122, 561-566.

This study examined the course of bereavement in widows and widowers during the year following the death of their spouses. All subjects were compared and categorized for degree of depression at one month and at thirteen months after the death.

Method

SUBJECTS: There were 109 randomly selected white widowers and widows in the subject group. The mean age of the group was 61 years; 39 percent were Catholic, 52 percent Protestant, three percent other Christian, two percent Jewish and three percent of no religion.

PROCEDURE: Each person was interviewed shortly after the death of the spouse and reinterviewed 12 months later. Questions included in the structured interview pertained to the subject's physical and mental health, family history of psychiatric illness, the social network of the survivor, and the medical and social actions taken since becoming widowed. An eight-point criteria for diagnosis of depression was part of the interview. Subjects were diagnosed as depressed if the depression cluster was present at the time of the interview.

Results

Thirty-five percent of the original 109 subjects (38) were diagnosed as either definitely or probably depressed one month after widowhood. A year later 17 percent were diagnosed as depressed. A large percentage of the depressed (67 percent) and nondepressed (93 percent) group became well or remained well during the follow-up year. Of the 16 subjects depressed at 13 months, 12 had been depressed one month after the death, and the remaining four became depressed subsequently. A subject depressed at one month after the death had a significantly higher risk of being depressed at one year (p<.01). Thus, depression at one month was a predictor of depression at one year.

Several factors were related to depression. Depressed subjects had significantly fewer children in the geographical area deemed close and able to render support and had less adequate financial and religious support. More of the nondepressed than depressed subjects had previous bereavements. This finding suggests that an individual's ability to cope with losses may be strengthened by prior losses.

Abstract **118**

Adaptation to Bereavement

DOROTHY K. HEYMANN, M.S.W. and DANIEL T. GIANTURCO, M.D.

"Long-Term Adaptation by the Elderly to Bereavement, "
Journal of Gerontology, 1973, *28*, 359-362.

This research examined the activities, attitudes, psychiatric and physical health of a group of older people before and after bereavement.

Method

SUBJECTS: The sample was drawn from a panel of participants in a longitudinal study. The criteria for inclusion in the present study were as follows: (1) The Ss were married and living with spouse at the time of initial data collection; (2) Comparable data were collected before and after widowhood. Data were available on 14 males and 27 females. The mean age of widowhood was 74.8 years for the men and 73.1 years for the women. Nine of the participants were black. Twenty-one of the women and 11 of the men owned their own homes.

Method: Four types of measurement were used prior to and after widowhood, as follows: (1) *Activities and attitudes*. These were obtained during social history interviews conducted by a social worker. The activity inventory consisted of 20 questions pertaining to health, leisure, security, family and friends and religious activities. The attitude inventory consisted of 56 agree-disagree statements about satisfaction with eight areas of life, including friends, family, work, religion, health, economic status, happiness, and feeling of usefulness. (2) *The Cavan Adjustment Rating Scale* was used by the social workers to independently evaluate the Ss on their activities and attitudes. (3) *Psychiatric Evaluations* were made by psychiatrists with respect to neurotic signs, including affect, anxiety and hypochondriasis. (4) *The Physical Function Rating* was based on extensive medical examinations. Ss were rated from 0 (no pathology or limitation) to 5 (severe limitation).

The mean lapse of time between the "before" and "after" examinations was 36 months. The mean interval between bereavement and the "after" interview was 21 months, with a range of three months to more than 36 months.

Results

There was no evidence of significant changes in health status from the first to the second examination. Likewise, there were no significant changes in activity levels; the Ss remained considerably involved with their friends, family, neighbors and church. Attitude scores changed only for work and usefulness. There was a trend for men to show a greater decline in work attitudes and for women in usefulness attitudes. A portion of such changes may have resulted from aging rather than from bereavement.

The social worker's ratings of happiness and adjustment showed no significant changes. The only noteworthy changes in ratings by psychiatrists were that four previously nondepressed women were rated as depressed, whereas two previously depressed men were rated as nondepressed.

These data point to a persistence of life style, indicating a relatively high and satisfactory level of interaction with the environment; widowhood did not appear to have altered patterns of living.

Abstract **119**

Late-Life Marriages

JUDITH TREAS, Ph.D. and ANKE VANHILST, B.A.

"Marriage and Remarriage Rates Among Older Americans," *Gerontologist*, 1976, *16*, 132-136.

Although there seems to have been a growing popular awareness of latelife romance, there have been few studies with demographic statistics on marriages by older people. In this study, United States Vital Statistics data for 1970 were used to assess the frequency of marriages in old age, document trends, and identify older people most likely to wed.

Method

The analysis was based on published data from marriage certificates sampled for 47 states and the District of Columbia in 1970.

Results

About 60,000 persons aged 65 and older married in 1970. Older people consitituted less than one percent of all brides and two percent of all grooms. The marriage rate for males was estimated to be only 17 grooms per 1,000 older single men, for women, fewer than three brides per 1,000 older single women. A comparison for marriage rates during the 1960s indicated that the marriage rate among the aged was essentially stable.

Marital prospects of both men and women decline after the mid-20's and continue to drop off in old age. An analysis of marriage rates for California in 1971 indicated that marriage chances plummet for every five-year interval beyond age 65; for example, a woman 65 to 69 is twice as likely to wed as one 70 to 74. Similar but less precipitous declines were found for men.

Older men have a substantial edge over women in the marriage market. They are more than six times likelier to wed than their female counterparts. Because of sex differences in mortality and widowhood, there are three times as many single women as single men in the population over 65. Approximately 20 percent of the grooms 65 and older marry women under 55, but less than three percent of the older brides marry such young spouses.

For men 65 and older, marriage rates per thousand are estimated to be 3.4

for bachelors, 19.4 for widowers and 23.6 for the divorced. Comparable rates for females are 1.1, 2.3 and 6.1 respectively. First marriages consititute only six percent of all marriages for older brides and grooms. The greater likelihood of marriage for the divorced than the widowed may be due in part to the fact that a larger proportion of the older divorcees than widows are between the ages of 65 and 70.

In the South and West, older men and women are about two times more likely to marry than in the Northeast and North Central states. Perhaps there are ethnic or religious regional subcultures which encourage or discourage late marriages.

Because the widowed numerically dominate the aged single population, widows and widowers are the most usual marital choices of older people, regardless of their own previous marital status. Fully 78 percent of the older brides and gooms marry widows. Nevertheless, there appeared to be a preference for spouses with like marital histories.

Data about the marriage ceremony suggested that older people attach the same symbolic importance to their nuptials as younger brides and grooms do. For example, older couples favored June weddings over any other month, were as inclined to honeymoon as other newlyweds, and a very high proportion solemnized their vows with a religious ceremony.

CHAPTER XII

Institutional Living

Abstract 120

Institutionalization and Self-Esteem

NANCY N. ANDERSON, Ph.D.

"Effects of Institutionalization on Self-Esteem," *Journal of Gerontology*, 1967, 22, 313-317.

It is sometimes assumed that institutionalization almost inevitably has a negative effect on the self-esteem of older persons. This study investigated the possibility that for those persons who choose to live in an institution, interaction will be more closely associated with self-esteem than will institutionalization.

Method

SUBJECTS: The Ss were drawn from 133 residents of a church-related retirement home and 115 persons on the waiting list of the same institution. One hundred one of the residents and 56 of the applicants completed the questionnaire. The two samples did not differ significantly for sex, education, nationality, place of residence (before institutionalization) or marital status. The mean age of the institutionalized sample was 82.0 years, while that of the applicants was 77.9 years. The institution provided an extensive program of activities.

PROCEDURE: A self-administered questionnaire was used. Interaction between Ss and others was measured by a variety of items designed to tap extent, kind, and alteration of social contacts as compared with the previous five years. Respondents were asked to report frequency of interaction with family, friends, neighbors, and other residents, participation in activities, and changes in interaction over the past five years. Scores of amount (life space), variety (role count), and change of interaction resulted. A ten-item self-esteem scale prepared by Mason (1954), utilizing statements such as "I am able to do things as well as most older people" provided the measure of self-esteem. Identification was estimated by asking residents how much they had in common with other residents of the retirement home.

Results

1. The institutionalized sample did not differ significantly from the noninstitutionalized sample in regard to self-esteem. Mean self-esteem scores were 7.24 and 7.22 for residents and nonresidents respectively.
2. Interaction and self-esteem were more closely related than institutionalization and self-esteem. The relationship between interaction and self-esteem was highly significant ($p<0.001$) but nonsignificant between institutionalization and self-esteem ($p>0.70$).
3. Institutionalized Ss who identified with the resident aged group had higher self-esteem than those who did not ($p<0.01$).

These results indicate that it is inappropriate to presuppose that going to live in a retirement or nursing home will have negative consequences on self-esteem. In interpreting the results, it should be noted that the retirement home could be generally described as a "good" one, which provided many opportunities for interaction. Movement from independent living arrangements to an institution could adversely affect interaction by interfering with previously established social patterns or could, especially for the isolated and/or physically impaired older person, provide new opportunities for interaction.

Abstract **121**

Social Status in a Home for the Aged

EDWARD P. FRIEDMAN, Ph.D.

"Age, Length of Institutionalization, and Social Status in a Home for the Aged," *Journal of Gerontology*, 1967, 22, 474-477.

This study examined the role of age and length of institutionalization as factors involved in the process of friendship formation among residents of a home for aged women. The hypothesis was that age and length of institutionalization would each function as a basis for homophyly or "a tendency for friendship to form between those who are alike in some designated respect."

Method

SUBJECTS: The participants were 58 of the 62 noninfirmary residents of a church-related home for aged women. All were ambulatory and none showed a noticeable degree of senile impairment. Their age ranged from 68 to 96 years (median = 81 years), and length of residence in the home ranged from less than one to 27 years (median = 5 years).

PROCEDURE: At the end of an interview dealing with other matters, participants were asked to name those persons living in the home with whom they were most friendly.

Results

The median number of names given was three, and only three participants claimed to have no friends in the home. A high degree of reciprocated choices provided support for the validity of the sociometric technique.

Both younger and older residents chose older residents, and both newer and veteran residents chose veteran residents more frequently than would be expected on a chance basis. Thus the older and longer-institutionalized residents received a proportionately high number of friendship choices from those both similar and dissimilar to themselves. The findings thus suggested that the value placed on extreme old age and long-term residence in an institution for aged, though perhaps generally low in American society, was high among these residents themselves.

Abstract **122**

Wish for Privacy by Young and Old

M. POWELL LAWTON, Ph.D. and JEANNE BADER, M.A.

"Wish for Privacy by Young and Old," *Journal of Gerontology*, 1970, *25*, 48-54.

With increased age, the likelihood of losses of all types—health, family, friends, or residence—increases. Institutionalization may compound the loss by depriving the older person of familiar surroundings, of freedom for self-determination, and of privacy. Massive building programs for older people have generated discussion regarding the comparative merits of building-care facilities with private and shared living arrangements. There has, however, been a lack of factual basis to support assertions and influence decisions. Decisions concerning the allocation of private and shared rooms have generally been made on either intuitive or purely economic grounds. This study investigated the wishes of people of a variety of ages and in a variety of conditions regarding their own present or hypothetical future institutional living.

Method

SUBJECTS: The 839 respondents included 345 community residents including college students, PTA members, a church group, members of a senior citizens club and professionals in applied gerontology; 56 applicants to a Jewish home for the aged; and 438 residents of homes for the aged including middle-class Protestants, some with no roommate, others with roommate, middle-class Jewish individuals, some with no roommate, others with roommate, and Protestant working-class individuals with roommate.

PROCEDURE: All institutionalized individuals were interviewed individually. Community residents answered the same questions on printed forms at group meetings. The seven questions pertained to age, sex, health, roommate status, preference for roommate vs. no roommate if single, in good health and institutionalized, preference for roommate vs. no roommate if sick enough to have to stay in bed for a couple of hours a day and institutionalized, and whether it is better for the average older person who lives in a home for the aged to be in a room by himself, with one other person, or more than one other person.

Results

Table 1 presents the percentages of older people preferring single rooms by subject group, age, and hypothetical condition. Within the restricted age range of 60 and older, there was no clear trend for preferences to vary as a function of age. Among the institutionalized groups, socio-economic status was related to room preference; for the self-well condition 71 percent of the middle-class Protestants with roommates, 44 percent of the Jewish respondents with roommates, and 38 percent of the lower socio-economic class Protestants would prefer singles. Institutional status was not a determinant of room preference; the community elderly did not differ significantly for room preference in the self-well condition from three groups of institutional residents (Protestant middle-class residents with and without roommates and Jewish residents without roommates). Community residents were, however, significantly more likely to wish for single accommodations than working-class Protestants, Jewish residents with roommates, and Jewish applicants.

Table 1
Percentages of Older People Preferring Single Rooms by Subject Group, Age and Hypothetical Condition

| | Condition | | | | | | | | |
| | Self-well | | | Self-sick | | | Other Person | | |
Subject Group	60	70	80+	60	70	80+	60	70	80+
Community residence	83	79	92	61	67	80	49	59	72
Institutional groups:									
Middle-class Protestant, no roommate	—	92	95	—	92	86	—	80	82
Jewish, no roommate	100	95	85	83	85	64	83	85	61
Middle-class Protestant, roommate	—	70	73	—	70	58	—	33	37
Jewish, roommate	50	42	44	30	39	34	40	34	26
Protestant, working-class	27	52	38	27	27	24	0	29	15
Applicants to Jewish institution	—	40	37	—	13	44	—	20	36

Among elderly institutionalized people, roommate status was the strongest determinant of preference. Of Jewish residents without and with roommates, 89 percent and 44 percent, respectively, wished for private rooms when well ($p < 0.01$); the corresponding figures for middle-class Protestants are 93 percent and 72 percent ($p < 0.05$).

For almost all groups and all ages there was a tendency for private rooms to be preferred more under the self-well than the self-sick condition. However, self-rated current health was not related to room choice under either the hypothetical self-well or self-sick condition.

There was a highly significant (p < 0.001) tendency for the more frequent choice of private room for self in comparison to the average older person. This trend held even among professional gerontologists; 84 percent expressed a preference for private rooms for themselves and 51 percent prescribed private rooms for the average older person.

The only significant sex difference was among community residents under 60; men chose shared accommodations as often as singles, but women were twice as likely to prefer single to shared rooms.

For the community residents there was a significant trend for choice of private room to increase with age. Only approximately 20 percent of the teenagers putting themselves in the place of the well institutionalized aged chose private rooms in comparison to more than 80 percent of community residents over 60 years of age. The percentage wishing a private room increased sharply from the teens to age 40 and increased only slightly thereafter. Generally, the trend with age was similar for the self-well, self-sick and average person living in a home for the aged conditions, except that percentage choices for private room were higher for the self-well condition than for the average person living in a home for the aged condition.

In summary, the major determinants of preference for a single versus a shared room appear to be age, socio-economic status, hypothetical condition of health, and among institutionalized people, present roommate status. Moreover, a private room tends to be selected by the individual for himself more frequently than it is prescribed for the average person living in a home for the aged.

Abstract **123**

Motivation of Aging Persons

RICHARD N. FILER, Ph.D. and DESMOND D. O'CONNELL, Ph.D.

"Motivation of Aging Persons," *Journal of Gerontology,* 1964, *19*, 15-22.

This study was conducted in a Veterans Administration domiciliary which provided shelter and medical care for about 1,300 male veterans aged 30 to

90 years (mean = 66 years). In accordance with the assumption that planned activities would promote health and general adjustment, the daily performance of some constructive work was planned for most residents. However, about 20 percent of the population was classified by physicians as having "no work capability"; this group was older (mean = 70 years), less active and more disabled than the general domiciliary population. In an initial study involving adapted sheltered workshop activities, it was demonstrated that many older, disabled persons could successfully participate in activities from which they were previously excluded if adaptive devices, task simplification and adequate feedback were used.

The present study tested the hypothesis that a greater percentage of aging, disabled residents would attain and maintain specific "desirable" standards of behavior if they were subjected to a stimulating, demanding environment with definite expectancies, translated into a system of consistent and discriminate rewards and restrictions. The standards of behavior, selected by the domiciliary staff were as follows: self-management of medication; dependability in keeping appointments; participation in constructive work; housekeeping maintenance of their own living area, responsibility for their own clothing; personal appearance and hygiene; management of their own finances; and not being a disciplinary problem. The five rewards selected were as follows: better ward environment (more space and privacy and better appearance); monetary pay for work in an adapted workshop; membership in club; increased privileges (e.g., excuses from weekly inspections or nightly bed checks); participation in ward governance.

Members of Group A received immediate, discriminate and consistent reinforcement related to performance in the eight behavior areas, whereas members of Group B did not receive differential reinforcement. It was predicted that more members in Group A than Group B would attain a satisfactory performance level, and that criterion level would be attained more quickly and maintained longer.

Method

SUBJECTS: Forty-four pairs of Ss were established with matching for degree of impairment (32 pairs with moderately severe and 12 pairs with modern impairment) and age (mean ages: 71.8 and 70.9 years). Members of pairs were assigned randomly to Group A and Group B. Pretreatment performance ratings were almost identical for the two groups (5.77 vs. 5.50 satisfactory ratings for Groups A and B, respectively, out of a possible eight). An additional seven pairs were dropped from the study because of the hospitalization, discharge or death of one member.

PROCEDURE: Members of Group A were asked to compare remodeled and redecorated wards to standard wards for space, privacy and appearance, and almost unanimously preferred the improved wards. Members of Group

A were moved to an improved ward, and members of Group B were moved to a standard ward physically remote from the improved wards.

At the beginning of the study a staff team met with the Ss to tell them specifically what was expected in each of the eight behavior categories. They were told their behavior would be evaluated regularly and every second week they would receive "report cards." The same expectancies were outlined for members of each group. Members of Group B were not told what would happen if they did or did not meet expectancies and were given no indication that they would be rewarded for satisfactory performance. Members of Group A were informed of the five rewards for which they would be eligible if they performed satisfactorily on all eight behavior categories for two successive rating periods and thus attained Level I status. If after attaining Level I there was an unsatisfactory rating on one of the behavior categories, the S was warned, and unless his performance was totally satisfactory on the next rating, he was transferred to a standard ward. On the standard ward he was allowed eight weeks to regain Level I, and if he did not do so, he was dropped form the program. Satisfactory performance on all eight behavior categories during the entire study was designated as attainment of Level II.

Formal ratings were made every two weeks, with different staff members rating different behaviors as appropriate. As soon as a Group A member reached Level I he was allowed to make his selection of rewards. "Hash marks" and "chevrons" were posted on the lockers of Group A members to publicize the maintenance of satisfactory ratings. If members of Group B asked about the rewards given to Group A, they were merely told that those residents were on a different program.

Table 1
Comparison of Groups A and B on Performance Dimensions

	Group A N = 44	Group B N = 44	P
Number attaining satisfactory ratings on all 8 behaviors prior to study	1	3	n.s.
Number attaining 8 satisfactory ratings on any one rating period	42	36	.05
Number attaining Level I sometime during the study	39	30	.02
Number attaining Level II	18	6	.01
Average number of weeks in program without reaching Level I	6.45	9.41	.01
Average number of weeks spent at Level I	22.18	16.45	.05
Number of earning consistent satisfactory for:			
Constructive assignment	31	14	.001
Personal appearance and hygiene	37	25	.01
Dependability for appointments	44	39	.05

Results

Table 1 summarizes comparisons between Groups A and B on various performance dimensions. Both groups improved in performance, an expected finding, since both were exposed to an increased expectancy climate and were given regular feedback and increased attention from the staff. Members of Group A attained satisfactory levels more often, more quickly and maintained them for a longer period of time than members of Group B. The two groups differed significantly for only three behavior categories as follows: constructive assignment, personal appearance and hygiene, and dependability in keeping appointments. Perhaps minimal reward conditions were sufficient to maintain satisfactory behavior in the other five categories, whereas additional rewards were needed with respect to work assignments, personal grooming and dependability.

Observations of the prestudy domiciliary climate revealed that in general policies established to control the behavior of residents focused on preventing "bad" behavior, such as excessive drinking, fighting, sloppiness or disregard of rules. These were handled by restrictions, weekly military type inspections, bed checks, and punishments such as taking away clothes, confinement and disciplinary discharge. If a resident maintained minimal standards of behavior, there was little incentive to improve; most rewards were distributed indiscriminately or inconsistently. Some of the deterioration of behavior observed in aging, institutionalized persons is probably fostered by the institutional climate and is not merely the result of the aging process. Elderly, disabled persons in such a setting may often function far below their capacity. When exposed to greater opportunity, increased expectancy, and increased attention and knowledge of approval or disapproval, functional levels rise.

Abstract **124**

Multiple Realities and Reality Orientation

Jaber F. Gubrium, Ph.D. and Margaret Ksander, B.A.

"On Multiple Realities And Reality Orientation," *Gerontologist*, 1975, *15*, 142-145.

This paper questioned the situational transferability of therapeutic programs for institutional elders and, in particular, addressed the nature and efficacy of reality training in reality orientation (RO) procedures. RO is a form of therapy which is purported to be a very effective tool to eliminate or control confusion in elderly people. The RO technique has two formats. The more structured one is a classroom-like session conducted daily, usually by an aide, with several patients serving as students. Instructional materials consist of an RO board which lists the name of the nursing home, its location, the date, the day of the week, the state of the weather, and the next holiday, and a cardboard instructional clock to teach time-keeping. The instructional materials are used to quiz patients about the day, state of the weather, etc. The less structured 24-hour RO requires that all staff consistently attempt to improve the patients' awareness of persons, time and place, by always addressing patients by name, reminding them of clock time for specific activities, and pointing out rooms and objects by name and, if appropriate, by owner.

Method

Intermittent observations were made at two large nursing homes of staff and patient behavior on the wards and in structured RO sessions.

Observations

Not all aides and patients assigned to RO programs were completely enthusiastic about their assignments. Aides may perceive the task as something that must be done as part of the job or to please a superior, a condition which may or may not result in positive outcomes. Negotiations may be required with patients to ensure their attendance and/or encourage their participation, e.g., a promise of special privileges or few questions during the session, or a plea that the aide may get into trouble if the attendance is low. Thus, it would appear that before therapy can begin, the therapist and the patients must establish the reality of their roles.

Once the structured RO begins allegedly objective reality may be super-seded by the reality of the RO board. For example:

Aide (pointing to weather on RO board which reads "raining"): What's the weather like today, Emma?

Emma looks out the window. Emma: Well, it looks like the sun is shining kinda bright.

The sun happens to be shining at the moment.

Aide: Are you sure? It says it's raining. Doesn't it? (Finger still pointing to the board.)

Emma: Well, it doesn't look like it from here.

Aide: What does it say here, Emma? (Directing Emma's attention to board.)

Emma: It says it's raining.

Aide (warmly): That's correct. Very good.

With respect to time, patients are tested for "realism" by whether or not they answer questions in proper clock-oriented terms. For example, after drilling patients in the time they are presumably put to bed, the aide questions Agnes.

Aide: Now, Agnes, what time do we go to sleep at night at Murray Manor?

Agnes: Oh, that depends. Sometimes, I go to bed at 6 and sometimes at 9. It depends on how busy I am and how tired.

Aide: But you usually go to bed at 8. Don't you, Agnes?

Agnes: Well, sometimes, but not always.

Aide: Yes, but we do go to bed at 8. Look here, Agnes. What does the clock say?

Agnes: It says 8 o'clock.

Aide: Yes, that's right (Aide turns to other patients). We go to bed at 8 at Murray Manor.

While pointing to the clock, the aide then asks each other patient what time he goes to bed at night.

The emphasis on clock-time in the structured RO sessions may be some-what out-of-line with the practical world of time on the floors. On the floors, keeping track of clock-time and place is treated as unimportant, and often annoying, by some patients, and by most members of the staff. Generally, activity schedules are affected as much by staff work demands as by clock time. Many patients do not keep track of time on the floor simply because it does not seem reasonable for them to do so rather than because they are unable to do so.

Conclusions

Various observations, similar to those summarized here, warrant a direct challenge to the implicit assumptions of RO. They suggest that behavior therapy in general is imperialistic in that it morally and officially imposes one group's definition of living on another in the name of allegedly "objec-tive" rehabilitation.

Abstract **125**

Age Bias in Referral

ARLENE B. GINSBURG, B.A. and STEVEN G. GOLDSTEIN, Ph.D.

"Age Bias in Referral for Psychological Consultation,"
Journal of Gerontology, 1974, *29*, 410-415.

This study investigated the hypothesis that older patients in a general medical hospital were less likely than younger patients to be referred for appropriate psychological consultation. The Minnesota Multiphasic Personality Inventory (MMPI) was used to assess psychological pathology.

Method

SUBJECTS: All subjects were patients of a large general hospital. There were two categories of Ss, the Referred Group and the Nonreferred Group. The Referred Group consisted of patients who had been referred by the Medical Service to the Psychology Service over a 17-month period. Of the 129 who had been referred, only those 88 for whom complete and valid MMPI profiles were on file were included. The Nonreferred Group consisted of 75 patients who were not referred to the Psychology Service, who were identified by their physicians as able to complete the MMPI, and who consented to do so. Of those nonreferred patients who were approached, 15 refused to participate and another 15 promised to do so but did not. Both groups included a wide range of physical illnesses, socio-economic classes and educational levels. The Ss were categorized into the following four age groups: less than 20, 20 to 39, 40 to 59, and over 60.

Results

The Ss were categorized as normal or abnormal according to standard procedures for interpreting the MMPI. Table 1 presents the mean ages of the referred and nonreferred patients classified as normal or abnormal. Within the group of patients whose profiles were judged to be abnormal, there was a significant tendency ($p < 0.05$) for the nonreferred patients to be older than the referred patients. However, within the referred group, those whose profiles were normal tended to be older than those whose profiles were abnormal. Analysis by sex indicated that the older male patients were particularly likely to be "psychologically neglected," in that physicians were likely to ignore their psychopathology.

Table 1
Mean Ages of Referred and Non-Referred Patients
Classified as Normal and Abnormal

Profile		Normal	Abnormal
Referred	N	20	68
	M	45.70	39.85
	SD	16.95	14.88
Non-Referred	N	25	40
	M	39.16	46.78
	SD	18.46	18.51

Abstract **126**

Reasons for Psychiatric Hospitalization

ROMUALDAS KRIAUCIUNAS, Ph.D.

"Age and Sex Differences in Reasons for Psychiatric Hospitalization," *Gerontologist*, 1969, 9, 221-222.

This study examined age and sex differences in reasons for psychiatric hospitalization.

Method

The data were obtained from clinical evaluation summaries which included identifying data, reason for admission and current findings. Records were selected from one section of a continuous treatment service within a state hospital. Reasons for admission were available for 226 females and 161 males between the ages of 20 and 89. Reason for admission was assigned to one of the following five categories: I.Patient's wish (self-initiated or induced by medical recommendation); II. Management difficulties (inability to manage by oneself or be managed by others); III. Outwardly-directed destruction (assaultiveness, destructiveness, family's fear of same); IV. Inwardly-directed destruction (suicidal threats or acts); V. Others (e.g., cessation of usual social role, irrational talk, alcoholism, etc.).

Results

Table 1 presents numerical and percentage frequencies by age, sex and reason for admission. There were no sex differences in age on admission. A significantly higher proportion of men than women in all age groups were admitted for Reason III—Outwardly-directed destruction. A higher proportion of the middle-aged group than the old group was admitted for Reason I—Patient's wish. With increased age, the proportion of admissions because of Reason II—Management difficulties—increased.

Table 1
Percentage Frequencies by Age, Sex
and Reason for Admission

Reason for Admission	20-24		45-64		65-89		Total %	Total Number
	M	F	M	F	M	F		
I	3.10	4.65	4.65	9.04	2.33	1.29	25.06	97
II	1.81	5.17	7.24	8.53	4.39	8.53	35.66	138
III	5.68	5.68	4.65	3.36	2.33	1.03	22.74	88
IV	1.29	1.81	1.29	1.81	.26	1.03	7.49	29
V	1.29	3.62	1.03	2.33	.26	.52	9.04	35
Number	51	81	73	97	37	48		387
% of Total	13.18	20.93	18.86	20.06	9.56	12.40		100

Abstract **127**

Decline in Institutionalized Aged

MORTON H. KLEBAN, Ph.D., M. POWELL LAWTON, Ph.D.,
ELAINE M. BRODY, MSSA and MIRIAM MOSS, M.A.

"Behavioral Observations of the Mentally Impaired Aged:
Those Who Decline and Those Who Do Not," *Journal of
Gerontology*, 1976, *31*, 333-339.

Is progressive decline characteristic in the behavior of the mentally-impaired aged, or can the behavior of some individuals stabilize? In this study it was hypothesized that group trends would support the notion of a continuation of deterioration, but that a significant percentage of individuals would manifest stability of behavioral functioning. It was further predicted that the stability-decline outcomes for the observed behavior of mentally-impaired survivors are in part predictable from antecedent functioning in a number of domains reflecting health, cognitive capacity, personality and social behavior.

Method

SUBJECTS: The Ss were all mentally-impaired aged Jewish women in the institution at the beginning of the project. At baseline, all had scores of six or less on the Kahn-Goldfarb MSQ, indicating possible moderate to severe organic mental impairment and a very low level of intellectual functioning. Sixty-seven Ss with an average age of 83 years (range 70-94) at the beginning of the project started the longitudinal study. Only the 43 survivors at the end of the two-year observational period are included in the present analysis.

Behavioral Observations: Eight categories of behavior, each defined in terms of specific behaviors, were selected for observation. These were as follows: (1) Passive nonfunctional, nonsocial, e.g., sitting, sleeping, staring; (2) Active nonfunctional, nonsocial, e.g., standing, talking to self; (3) Passive functional, nonsocial, e.g., waiting for physician, taking medication; (4) Active functional, nonsocial, e.g., self-locomotion, self-care, chores; (5) Involvement in group activities, e.g., listening to radio with others, planned activities; (6) Involvement in individual activities, e.g., reading, knitting; (7) Involvement in institutional activities, e.g., therapies, sewing; (8) Social functioning, e.g., talking, social interaction.

Each S was observed for a total of 40 min. per week over 104 consecutive weeks. Observations were made between 9 a.m. and 5 p.m. on week days. Each week four ten-min. observation periods were selected randomly from the 160 possible 15-min. time blocks. The random schedule selected for the first 13 weeks was repeated for each S in the seven remaining 13-week blocks. Ss were observed for two five-min. intervals separated by five min., which allowed observers to complete recordings and Ss to change behaviors. A score of three was given for a behavior exceeding 90 sec., a score of two for a behavior lasting from 60 to 89 sec., and a score of one for a behavior lasting less than 60 sec. In scoring, higher weights were given to behaviors that were active, functional and social than to behaviors that were passive, nonfunctional and nonsocial.

A weekly average level of functioning score was computed for each S for each of the 104 weeks of observation. This was based on the summed weekly rated observation score divided by a count of the total number of behaviors.

Results

Individual trend analyses for the 43 Ss based on behavioral scores over time indicated that 16 of the Ss showed behavioral decline, 19 remained stable and eight showed improvements. The shape of the group curve, which was quadratic, was produced by the dual effects of the downward linear pressure of the 16 Ss (37 percent) who showed decline, and by the interaction of many curvilinear trends at the level of the individual subject.

In an attempt to determine whether or not behavioral decline or stability had predictive baseline antecedents, Ss were assigned to two subgroups, those showing stable or improving trends (N = 16), and those with declining trends (N = 15). Sample size was reduced because of the lack of some of the nonbehavioral baseline measurements for some Ss. Five significant predictive factorial variables were identified. These were control of aggression and impulsivity; neurosis; comprehension of situations; sociability-responsiveness; and seriousness of medical condition. Control of aggression and impulsivity, neurosis, and seriousness of medical condition together absorbed most of the variance and produced equations which correctly assigned 28 of the 31 Ss to the "stable" or "decline" group. Control of aggression and impulsivity alone allowed for the correct assignment of 24 of the 31 Ss.

These findings suggest that behavioral decline and stability for senile patients is a highly predictable outcome. Moreover, more Ss showed stability or improvement than decline over the two-year period of observations. Perhaps for many individuals, after an initial decline, the decline reaches a plateau and functioning stabilizes.

Abstract **128**

Life Crises and Mental Deterioration

LESLIE ELLEN AMSTER, M.S. and HERBERT H. KRAUSS, Ph.D.

"The Relationship Between Life Crises and Mental Deterioration in Old Age," *International Journal of Aging and Human Development*, 1974, 5, 51-55.

This investigation was intended to be a beginning step in determining whether or not a relationship exists between life stress and mental deterioration in the aged.

Method

SUBJECTS: Twenty-five female patients constituted the "recently mentally-deteriorated" group. They had first shown signs of deterioration within the previous five years, and each correctly answered no more than one of ten items on the Mental Status Questionnaire (MSQ). Demographic characteristics for these women at date of decline were used in obtaining a matching sample of nondeteriorated controls. These 25 control Ss scored nine or ten on the MSQ. All subjects ranged in age from 65 to 95 years; approximately one-quarter were institutionalized (i.e., before decline), and educational level ranged from some elementary school to college graduation.

PROCEDURE: The Geriatric Social Readjustment Questionnaire (GSRQ) was developed by taking 35 items reflecting stressful life situations (see Table 1). Each item of the GSRQ was assigned a weight proportional to the importance attributed to its occurrence by a group of professionals familiar with the geriatric population (internists, social workers, psychiatrists, nurses, and clergymen). Close friends or relatives of the Ss were interviewed regarding occurrence of life stresses of the GSRQ over the preceding five years for nondeteriorated Ss, or over the five years preceding deterioration for the deteriorated Ss. Reliability was confirmed in interviews with two informants for a subsample of five control and five deteriorated Ss.

Results

The results indicated that mental deterioration in these elderly women was related to the frequency and intensity of the life crises to which they had been subjected. For the deteriorated women, the mean number of crisis events was 6.12, significantly greater than the mean of 3.40 for the control group (p<.01). Also, the mean magnitude of stress for the deteriorated group was 297.64, as compared to 176.72 for the control group (p<.01).

The results must be interpreted with caution, since it is possible that mental deterioration had already begun in the deteriorated patients before it was noticed by friends and relatives. Thus, these Ss may have been predisposed to a greater frequency of crises than the controls. Also, reporting bias may have facilitated the likelihood of reporting life crises when none occurred for the deteriorated group, or not reporting life crises that did indeed occur for the controls.

Future research is suggested on the use of the GSRQ in predicting the onset of mental deterioration in the aged and in identifying particular life crises associated with senility.

Table 1
The Geriatric Social Readjustment Rating Scale (GSRRS)

Rank	Life Event	Mean Value
1	Death of spouse	125
2	Institutionalization	82
3	Death of close family member	67
4	Major personal injury or illness	66
5	Being fired from work	64
6	Divorce	61
7	Major change in financial state	56
8	Retirement	55
9	Marital separation from mate	54
10	Eyesight failing	51
11	Marriage	50
12	Death of close friend	50
13	Major change in health or behavior of family member	47
14	Major change in gratifying activities	46
15	Hearing failing	46
16	Change in sexual behavior	45
17	Change in responsibilities at work	43
18	Change in residence other than institutionalization	43
19	Painful arthritis	42
20	Feeling of slowing down	41
21	Changing to different line of work	41
22	Spouse ceasing work outside home	40
23	Change in living conditions or environment	40
24	Marital reconciliation with mate	39
25	Change in social activities	38
26	Losing driver's license	34
27	Change in living composition	33
28	Reaching 65	32
29	Reaching 70	31
30	Major change in working hours or conditions	28

Abstract **129**

Social Environmental Effects on Cognitive Functioning

COMILDA WEINSTOCK, Ed.D. and RUTH BENNETT, Ph.D.

"From 'Waiting on the List' to Becoming a 'Newcomer' and an 'Old-Timer' in a Home for the Aged: Two Studies of Socialization and Its Impact upon Cognitive Functioning," *Aging and Human Development*, 1971, 2, 46-58.

These studies were conducted to determine if some types of social environments are related to the maintenance of a high level of cognitive functioning in the aged. In the first study, three groups of persons, "newcomers," "old-timers" residing in a home for the aged, and a "waiting list" group were compared. It was predicted that aged persons within a stimulating social environment, such as was provided by the home for the aged, would perform at relatively high levels on tests of cognitive ability as compared with their socially-deprived counterparts, i.e., the "waiting list" group. In the second study, survivors from the first study were retested one year later. It was predicted that members of the former "waiting list" group, having achieved "newcomer status" in a stimulating environment, would show improvement on tests of cognitive ability. It was thought that former newcomers might show signs of decline, because as familiarity with the environment increased, stimulation might have decreased. No prediction was made with respect to changes in the cognitive status of the former old-timers.

Method

SUBJECTS: For the initial study, 60 persons over 65 years of age, with comparable background characteristics such as age, sex, education, and religion, and differing only as to place and length of residence, were interviewed. The 20 waiting list Ss, residing in the community, had an average age of 79.3 years. The 20 newcomers, with an average age of 79.8, included consecutive new admittees to the Home who were English-speaking and could complete the interview. The 20 old-timers, with an average age of 83.7, had resided in the Home for more than one year. The waiting list and old-timer Ss were selected by the staff on the basis of fluency in English and psychological and social intactness.

One year later when the second study was conducted, the sample size had decreased as follows: waiting list group, 12 persons (six deaths and one medical condition which prohibited testing); newcomers, 14 persons (four deaths, and two were senile and not able to be interviewed); old timers, 14 persons (three deaths and three were senile and not able to be interviewed). PROCEDURE: During a structured interview of approximately one hour, the following indices were used: (1) The Adult Isolation Index, a measure of the extent of lifetime social contacts with family, friends, work and organizations; (2) Past Month Social Isolation Index, a measure of number of social contacts outside the institution in the month prior to the interview; (3) Three Wechsler Adult Intelligence Scale subtests: Information, Comprehension and Similarities; (4) Socialization Index, a measure of the amount of information learned about life in the Home, e.g., "What kinds of activities are available during the day?"; (5) A Mental Status Schedule, used to assess current pathology on the basis of observations made during the interview.

Results and Discussion

Table 1 presents the mean scores on the WAIS subtests and Socialization Index for the three groups at the first time of testing. These data support the

Table 1
Mean Scores on WAIS Subtests and Socialization
Index at First Time of Testing

Test	Waiting List	Newcomers	Old Timers
Information	13.10	15.00	13.55
Similarities	5.95	7.40	6.35
Comprehension	13.50	15.65	16.45
WAIS Total	32.55	38.05	36.35
Socialization Index	10.10	18.50	20.30

hypothesis that old people involved in a stimulating environment would perform best on tests of cognitive ability. Residents of the home for the aged obtained higher mean WAIS total and subtest scores than their waiting-list counterparts. In general, newcomers obtained higher scores than both old-timers and waiting-list persons on tests of cognitive ability.

Table 2 presents the percentage of subjects within each category whose total WAIS scores changed during the one-year interval from the first to the second study. Half of the members of the former waiting list group (which had by time of second testing been in newcomer status for a year), showed improvement in total WAIS score, in contrast to 36 percent of the former newcomer group and only 14 percent of the old-timer group. Improvement by such a large proportion of the new residents provided further support for the hypothesis that cognitive functioning may be improved by environmental stimulation.

Apparently the active involvement required by newcomers in the process of learning the role of membership in the Home, in combination with the opportunities provided within the Home for social and intellectual stimulation, had a beneficial effect on cognitive functioning in general. However, whereas newcomer status provides residents with daily stimulation and tangible goals, after a period of residence in the Home, the stimulation apparently decreases, and as routines become established, there may be less need for mental alertness with a consequent decline in cognitive competency, as evidenced by the high proportion of old-timers whose WAIS scores decreased from the first to the second test. Perhaps if meaningful learning experiences and positive milestones were provided throughout a resident's tenure in an institution, old-timers might then show fewer cognitive decrements.

Table 2
Percentage of Subjects Whose Total WAIS Scores Changed From Time 1 to Time 2

Change	Waiting List	Newcomers	Old Timers
% up	50%	36%	14%
% same	17%	28%	14%
% down	33%	36%	72%

CHAPTER XIII

Passage of Time and Death

Abstract 130

Personal Time Perspective in Adulthood

RAYMAN W. BORTNER, Ph.D. and DAVID F. HULTSCH, Ph.D.

"Personal Time Perspective in Adulthood," *Developmental Psychology*, 1972, 7, 98-103.

In this study personal time perspective was defined as self-assessment at present in comparison with five years backward (retrotension) and forward (protension) in time. A major purpose of the study was to examine age differences in retrotension and protension. The study had a number of additional goals which will not be summarized in this abstract.

Method

SUBJECTS: The 1,409 subjects were respondents in a survey based on a modified probability sample of the United States. There were 681 males and 728 females. The age distribution was as follows: 20 to 24 years (98), 25 to 29 years (138), 30 to 34 years (159), 35 to 39 years (166), 40 to 44 years (170), 45 to 49 years (151), 50 to 54 years (120), 55 to 59 years (100), 60 to 64 years (85), 65 to 69 years (93), 70 years and above (129).

PROCEDURE: The measuring device for time perspective was an 11-point zero to ten self-anchoring scale (a ladder rating scale), with zero below the bottom rung and ten above the top rung. Each S was asked to define in his own terms the worst and the best possible life he could imagine for himself and was told that these definitions would represent the zero point (worst) and tenth point (best) on the ladder. He was then asked to rate his present, past and future status with respect to these self-anchored extremes, as follows: present self—"Where on the ladder do you feel you personally stand at the present time?"; past self—"Where on the ladder would you say you stood five years ago?"; future self—"Where do you think you will be on the ladder five years from now?"

Retrotension was defined as the subject's past rating minus his present rating, and protension was defined as his future rating minus his present rating. A negative retrotension score indicated that the present was rated higher than the past, whereas a positive retrotension score indicated the present was rated lower than the past. A positive protension score indicated that the future was rated higher than the present, whereas a negative protension score indicated the future was rated lower than the present.

Results

Figure 1 presents mean retrotension and protension scores as a function of age and sex. Neither measure varied as a function of sex. Both the retrotension and protension measures showed an essentially linear function with age, and both measures began to cross the zeroline beyond the 50-to 59-year age level. Both measures showed significant differentiation among early, middle and late adulthood.

These data indicate that young adults viewed the present as much better than the past and expected the future to be much better than the present. This trend continued, with decreasing differences in perceptions of past, present and future by those through the age of 50. Responses of people in their 50's indicate that they thought they had made progress and would continue to make progress. For those in their 60's, the past, present and future were evaluated equally, and for respondents in the 70's the past seemed better than the present and the present seemed better than the future.

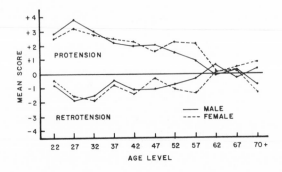

Abstract **131**

Correlates of Rate of Time Passage

RAYMOND G. KUHLEN, Ph.D. and ROLF H. MONGE, Ph.D.

"Correlates of Estimated Rate of Time Passage in the
Adult Years," *Journal of Gerontology*, 1968, 23, 427-433.

There is a long standing idea that the subjective rate of time passage increases with age. Explanations for the assumed rapid rate of time passage in old age have varied. One explanation is that a given span of time (e.g., a month) is smaller proportionally to the time that has already passed in the case of the older than of the younger adult. Similarly, it is assumed that the amount of time in the future, being more limited for the older person, is more valued. It has been argued that time seems to pass more rapidly in old age because it is unpunctuated by exciting events and, conversely, that time flies, regardless of age, both when one is happy and when one anticipates an unpostponable dreaded event.

On a Time Metaphor Test, which employs poetic phrases such as "a galloping horseman" and "a quiet, motionless ocean," which might be used to symbolize a sense of time, older people were found to prefer swift metaphors to a greater extent than young people did. In studies requiring people of different ages to reproduce short time-intervals (30 to 180 sec.), the results suggested that it is how time is filled, rather than age *per se*, that influences the rate at which it seems to pass.

This study checked on the above assumptions and findings and also compared two methods of measuring sense of time passage.

Method

SUBJECTS: There were two groups of subjects. The first group was composed of 144 male and 153 female graduate students ranging in age from 21 to 61 (mean age = 28.5 years). The second group of 96 males and 143 females, ranging in age from the 20s to the 80s (mean age = 49.4 years), was fairly representative of the general population.

Procedure: Two methods were used to measure sense of time passage, as follows: (a) The Time Metaphor Test, and (b) a specially devised questionnaire. The questionnaire contained two items which provided a fairly direct measure of an individual's subjective sense of the speed of time passage: "How rapidly does time seem to pass for you now?" and "How fast does time seem to be passing now compared to ten years ago?" Also included were items relating to the person's future orientation, his emphasis on career achievement, the degree to which he felt under time pressure, his preference for and ability to delay time gratification, his happiness and the degree to which he viewed his life as exciting. These items were all perfectly direct.

Results

Correlations were computed between the three-time measures (high rate of current time passage, higher rate now than 10 years ago, and preference for static metaphors) and between each of these time measures and each of the future orientation, achievement, time pressure, delay in gratification and life condition measures. Separate correlations were computed for males and females in each of the subject groups. The correlation between the Time Metaphor Test and the direct rating of current passage of time was significant only for males in the general sample, and even for that subsample, the correlation was low and not in the expected direction. Moreover, there was no evidence that the Time Metaphor Test measure was significantly related to any of the other variables which were measured. Only seven of the 64 correlations for *relative* speed of time passage (i.e., now versus ten years ago) were significant (and only at the .05 level). However, 24 of the 64 correlations were significant at the .05 level or better in the instance of direct rating of current speed of time passage. For males and females in both groups the direct measure of passage of time correlated with relative speed of time, not enough spare time, high degree of felt time pressure, past year of life more exciting and higher present happiness. Thus, sense of speed of time passage appeared to be related to the extent to which time is filled and to the degree to which events that fill it are viewed as having positive affect. Also, the direct question "How rapidly does time seem to pass for you now?" appeared to have more construct validity than either the Time Metaphor Test or the rating of relative speed of time.

Analyses of relationships between speed of time passage and age provided no evidence to support the frequently encountered contention that older people experience a sense of more rapid time passage than do younger adults.

For males, time pressure seemed to be greater in the 40's and 50's than in the younger or older decades, and degree of future orientation, subjective happiness, and excitement were inversely related to age. Females showed similar trends, but only the relationship involving age and degree of future orientation was significant.

Abstract **132**

Attitudes Toward the Future in Old Age

Ursula Lehr, Ph.D.

"Attitudes Toward the Future in Old Age," *Human Development*, 1967, *10*, 230-238.

Earlier research suggested that there is a great deal of variability among old people with respect to attitudes toward the future. This study examined the relationship between positiveness of attitude toward the future and a number of other variables.

Method

SUBJECTS: The sample consisted of 200 middle-class persons, 100 aged 60 to 65 and 100 aged 70 to 75, with an equal number of males and females in each age group. All respondents lived in their own household.

PROCEDURE: This study reports a cross-sectional segment of a longitudinal study which required intensive interviewing and testing of each particip-ant for five days per year. The interview included 20 questions on attitudes toward the future. On the basis of subject responses, raters categorized each S's attitude toward the future on a nine-point scale varying from completely negative attitude toward the future, complete absence of positive expectations, hopelessness (point one) to completely positive attitude to the future, no fears, expectation that the future will bring only pleasant experiences (point nine). Persons who were assigned scores of one to four were categorized as having a more negative attitude, those with scores of five to nine as having a more positive attitude toward the future.

Results

Seventy-six percent of the males and only 58 percent of the females were characterized by positive attitudes toward the future (p < 0.05). Women aged 70 to 75 had the lowest proportion of respondents expressing positive attitudes. For all categories of subjects above average intelligence, satisfaction with current life, high activity level, general responsiveness and positive mood or affect were related to a positive attitude to the future. For men and the younger women (60 to 65), but not for the older women, good health and high socio-economic status were predictive of a positive attitude toward the future. For males only, attitude toward the future correlated with general adjustment and ego control. No relationship was observed between feelings of security and attitude toward the future.

Abstract **133**

Age and Awareness of Finitude

VICTOR W. MARSHALL, Ph.D.

"Age and Awareness of Finitude in Developmental Psychology," *Omega*, 1975, *6*, 113-129.

Is the individual's awareness of the time left to him an inverse function of his age? Although some developmental theories are based on the assumption that awareness of finitude leads to various psychological processes such as disengagement and life-review, the question of the determinants of an awareness of finitude has not been examined. Rather, it has been assumed that awareness of finitude is uniformly related to age, and this assumption has led to the use of age as an independent variable when assessing various theoretical propositions concerning turning toward the self and "stock-taking" on one's life in relation to awareness of finitude. This study examined the possibility that age and awareness of finitude are not uniformly related, as has been assumed.

Method

SUBJECTS: Respondents were reasonably healthy middle-to upper-class white Americans residing in a retirement village. The age range was 64 to 96, with an average age of 80. Of the 68 persons questioned, 50 gave codable answers.

PROCEDURE: Following a series of questions about time perspective, the respondents were asked "Which of these would you say about your own future?"

1. I shall be around for some time yet, more than ten years.
2. I have a little while longer, oh, at least five to ten years.
3. Not too much longer, less than five years.
4. The end may be any time now.

In analyzing the data, responses to the last two items were combined.

Information was also gathered with respect to perceived health, age of death of parents, number of deceased siblings and death of close friends.

Results

Table 1 summarizes anticipated life-expectancy answers in relation to age. These data indicate that awareness of finitude is strongly related to age; older individuals estimate less time available before death than younger individuals do.

Table 2, which summarizes anticipated life expectancy as a function of whether the respondent is older or younger than his parents were at time of death, indicates that awareness of finitude is strongly associated with a relationship of the respondent's own age to age-at-death of both of his parents. A younger person who is now older than the age-at-death of both of his parents is more highly aware of finitude than an older person who has not yet surpassed the age of his parents' death. The comparison process to parents' age of death is more strongly related to awareness of finitude than is age itself.

Additional evidence for a social comparison process interpretation of the calculation of awareness of finitude was obtained from examination of anticipated life expectancy in relation to deaths of sibling and friends. For example, the individual who has outlived all or most of his siblings tends to predict death for himself sooner than the individual whose siblings are all alive, and this relationship holds more strongly if like-sexed, in comparison to opposite-sexed, siblings are deceased. Not surprisingly, individuals who report that their health is only fair or poor, as opposed to excellent or good, and those who report their health has changed for the worse, estimate fewer remaining years of life.

Because these ways in which awareness of finitude develop are only indirectly related to age itself, it would appear that research that substitutes measures of age for measures of awareness of finitude cannot provide adequate tests of theories incorporating awareness of finitude as a factor initiating developmental changes.

Table 1
Awareness of Finitude in Relation to Age

Anticipated life expectancy	Young (64-75)	Middle (76-84)	Old (85-96)
10 or more years	50%	28%	10%
5 to 10 years	43%	40%	40%
less than 5 years	7%	32%	50%
N	14	25	10

Table 2
Awareness of Finitude in Relation to Comparative Age at Death of Parents

Anticipated life expectancy	Respondent's Age:		
	Younger than both parents at death age	Younger than one parent at death age	Older than both parents at death age
10 or more years	46%	35%	7%
5 to 10 years	46%	52%	29%
less than 5 years	9%	13%	64%
N	11	23	14

Abstract **134**

Death Anxiety and Self-Concept

MILTON F. NEHRKE, Ph.D.

"Actual and Perceived Attitudes toward Death and Self Concept in Three-Generational Families." Presented at the 27th Annual Meeting of the Gerontological Society, Portland, Oregon, 1974.

The literature regarding actual and perceived levels of death anxiety and self-concept across generations is contradictory as to the extent and direction of misperceptions, if any. The present research was intended to assess actual and perceived self-concept and death anxiety within a three-generational family setting. In this way, the raters were familiar with the person being rated rather than being forced to rate a general age group where all combinations of attitudes are possible and probable.

Method

From a larger study, 25 female family groups were available with complete data for the college students, the mothers, and the grandmothers. The participants within each generation completed the Boyar Fear of Death Scale, and a 21-item semantic differential rating of self-concept, first with regard to their own attitudes (actual) and then with regard to the attitudes of the other two female members of the matrilineal line (perceived).

Results and Discussion

For the Boyar scale an interaction effect indicated that the rated level of death anxiety varied according to who was being rated and who was doing the rating. Members of each generation rated themselves lower in death anxiety than they rated the other two generations. However, the grandmothers accurately rated the anxiety levels of their children and grandchildren; the mothers accurately rated the college students but misperceived the grandmother generation. The college students viewed both older generations as significantly more anxious than the two groups actually rated themselves. The younger misperceived the older as being more anxious.

Regarding self-concept, the results are starkly different. The college students rated the older two generations accurately, whereas the parent generation accurately rated the grandparent generation but significantly over-rated the self-concept of their children. Likewise, the grandmother sample significantly overrated the parent generation and even more drastically overrated the college-age generation. The older generation misperceived the younger as more positive than was actually the case.

It was proposed that the older persons were able to draw on their own previous experiences in life as a mother and/or young adult and thus accurately rate the death anxiety being experienced by younger genera-tion(s). On the other hand, the younger generation, having not "been there" yet, could not, therefore, accurately determine how older persons feel about death, so they would be expected to respond in an egocentric manner.

In contrast, for self-concept, it may be postulated that the older genera-tion(s) have an emotional investment in their children and grandchildren. The investment leads them to overevaluate the positiveness of the self-concept of the younger generation(s). Thus, the younger persons are seen as significantly better than they actually are and significantly better than one's self, in spite of the fact that actual self-concept did not differ across the three generations.

It is evident from these data that misperceptions, a kind of generation gap, do exist within families, but that the occurrence, extent, and direction of the misperception is a function of the concept being assessed, the genera-tion being rated, and the generation doing the rating. Unfortunately, this study provides ample justification for the too frequently heard cry "You just don't understand me!"

Abstract 135

Death Anxiety and Ego Integrity

MILTON F. NEHRKE, Ph.D., GEORGETTE BELLUCCI, Ph.D. and SALLY JO GABRIEL, M.A.

"Death Anxiety, Locus of Control, and Life Satisfaction in the Elderly: Toward a Definition of Ego Integrity," *Omega*, in press.

Erikson has suggested that elderly persons who develop a sense of ego integrity will not fear death and will be satisfied with life, whereas the persons who fail to resolve the final psychosocial crisis, resulting in despair, will be characterized by fear of death, a feeling that life is too short, and a generalized sense of dissatisfaction with life and self. Thus, death anxiety may be posited as an index of ego integrity. The intent of this research was to examine the relationship between death anxiety and two more traditional measures of adjustment, life satisfaction and locus of control, in persons from varying environments.

Method

A total of 120 persons over 60 years of age were tested. Forty were from private nursing homes, 40 lived independently in the community, and 40 resided in public housing units. Half the respondents in each group were female. Each respondent completed Rotter's I-E Scale, (a measure of whether the locus or control is internal or external), the Neugarten, Havighurst and Tobin Life Satisfaction Index A, Boyar's Fear of Death Scale and Templer's Death Anxiety Scale.

Results and Discussion

For the life satisfaction, locus of control and Templer scales there were significant differences among the resident groups. On locus of control, the public housing sample was most internally controlled, whereas the nursing home group was most externally controlled, and the community sample was intermediate. The nursing home sample was significantly lower in life satisfaction than the community or public housing samples, which did not differ from each other. Finally, on the Templer scale, the community sample was significantly more anxious about death than the public housing or nursing home groups, who were not different from each other. There was also a significant correlation of life satisfacion with locus of control, but neither variable was significantly related to death anxiety.

Erikson's description of ego integrity was supported by the public housing sample, who evidenced the highest level of life satisfaction, internal control, and low death anxiety. The remaining data appear to be equivocal. The nursing home sample was least satisfied, most external but lowest in death anxiety, and the community residents were satisfied with life, more internally controlled but highest in death anxiety. Except for the death anxiety factor, the latter two samples characterize, respectively, the development of despair and ego integrity. It was proposed that the differences in death anxiety may be the result of group living. Illness and death are relatively common in age segregated settings and as such quickly become part of the conversation patterns which provide for the expression of anxiety and its neutralization. The community residents lack a sympathetic, continuous, and common reference group which could function as a desensitizing agent.

Although group living facilities may explain the differences in death anxiety between the samples, the significant differences in life satisfaction and locus of control between the nursing home and public housing groups, both low in death anxiety, must also be dealt with. It was speculated that such factors as independence, mobility, and relatively good health in the public housing and community samples were responsible for their higher levels of life satisfaction and internal control. In turn, the dependence, loss of mobility and poor health among the nursing home residents resulted in lower life satisfaction and external control. Thus, Erikson's description of the final psychosocial stage and his suggestion that death anxiety is a primary reflection of the resolution of the ego integrity-despair crisis must be modulated by other variables such as independence, mobility, health, and type of living arrangement.

Abstract 136

Relocation and Mortality Rates

GLORIA M. GUTMAN, Ph.D. and CAROL P. HERBERT, M.D.

"Mortality Rates among Relocated Extended-Care Patients," *Journal of Gerontology*, 1976, *31*, 352-357.

Several studies have demonstrated increased mortality rates for elderly persons following relocation, whether the relocation involves movement from the community to an institution, from one institution or ward to another, or from old to new facilities. The few studies that have shown no increase in mortality involved either transfer of relatively healthy people from one community facility to another or institutionalized individuals selected for transfer because of potential for rehabilitation. These findings suggest that, if possible, relocation should be avoided, especially for mentally impaired, physically ill or depressed older persons. However, it is a fact of life that relocation does and sometimes must take place. Therefore, transfer situations should be examined to identify significant variables that influence mortality rate. This study examined mortality rates before and after the transfer of all patients from the extended-care unit of an acute hospital to a new extended-care unit.

Method

SUBJECTS: On December 14-15, 1972 the entire population of the male extended-care ward of a general hospital was moved to a new extended-care unit two blocks away. The control population was defined as persons aged 60 and older who were patients in the initial unit on December 14 of each of the five preceding years. Of the 96 patients moved, 81 were aged 60 and older (mean = 78 years), 57 were nonambulatory, and 51 had some degree of confusion. There had been no change in admission policy during the period under study, and the experimental group was essentially comparable to each of the control groups.

PROCEDURE: An attempt was made to document the actual transfer procedure, staff efforts to alleviate relocation stress, and differences between the facilities. Data on the mortality of the relocated population were examined over a 21-month period.

Results

The move was organized and planned in detail to minimize confusion on the part of both patients and staff, and patients and their families were well informed in advance. New room assignments reflected friendship patterns and compatibilities. The transfer was accomplished by ambulance over a two-day period; personal possessions and most of the staff were transferred with the patients.

The new unit had better physical facilities than the old one, e.g., two- and four-bed rooms instead of wards, bright surroundings and storage for personal belonging. There were staff increases, including more ward aides and greater availability of therapists and attending physicians. Medications were reassessed and opportunities for activities were increased. Although staff morale was generally low because of problems associated with the move, staff attitudes toward patients were positive. Generally, the patients showed no negative emotional effects attributable to the transfer, and some showed more independence and motivation.

During the first three months after relocation, six percent of the patients (five persons) died in comparison to an average mortality rate of 17 percent during the corresponding three months for the preceding five years. After 12 months, the mortality rate was 33 percent in comparison to an average 12-month mortality rate of 41 percent for the preceding five years (yearly rates were 33 percent, 48 percent, 35 percent, 42 percent and 49 percent). After 21 months, almost half (48.14 percent) of the transferred patients were still alive. There were no significant differences between survivors and nonsurvivors with respect to age or length of hospitalization and mental status prior to transfer. The death rate was, however, somewhat higher for ambulatory than nonambulatory patients; perhaps the staff expended extra time and care on the more dependent patients.

These results suggest that the involuntary transfer of an elderly population with a high incidence of disability, physical illness, and mental confusion need not result in increased mortality. Relevant factors in the mortality consequences of relocation probably include the following: degree of environmental change, preparation of patients, efficient transfer procedures, limited disruption of everyday living and family visiting patterns, increased privacy, and improved treatment programs.

Abstract **137**

Control over Time of Death

SANFORD LABOVITZ, Ph.D.

"Control over Death: The Canadian Case," *Omega*, 1974, 5, 217-221.

A study of the relationship between birth dates and death dates of famous Americans (Phillips, 1969) indicated that death rates decreased during the month immediately preceding birth dates and increased significantly the month following birth dates. These data suggested the hypothesis that at least some people can exert control over their death dates and that such control is oriented toward important social dates, in this instance, their birth dates. Perhaps once an important date is reached, the individual "lets himself go," and death occurs within a short time. This study used two samples of Canadians to test the prediction that death rates decrease prior to birth dates and increase after them. Confirmation of the hypothesis would be rather remarkable considering that some deaths, for example those caused by assassination or accident, would appear to be beyond the control of the individual, and even if some people can exert control over their death dates they may "aim" toward a significant date other than their birth date.

Method

PROCEDURE: Students provided the birth and death dates of 50 elderly family members (the nonfamous Canadians sample). Birth and death dates were also obtained for 52 Canadians who had achieved fame in politics, religion, theater or sports. These data were examined to determine the percentage of persons who died during the one-and three-month periods preceding and following their birth dates. If there were no relationship between birth date and death date, it would be expected that approximately the same percentage of deaths (i.e., 8.3 percent) would occur during each of the 12 months following the birth date.

Results

Table 1 presents the percentage of deaths that occurred during the one-and three-month periods preceding and following the birth dates of the members of the nonfamous and famous Canadian samples, and for both samples combined. The sample of nonfamous Canadians conformed rather well to the hypothesis, in that death rates were markedly lower than would be expected on an equal distribution basis during the one-and three-month periods preceding the birth date, and were markedly higher during the one-and three-month periods following the birth date. For the sample of famous Canadians, death rates were markedly higher than would be predicted on an equal distribution basis during the one-and three-month periods following the birth date, but were also slightly elevated prior to the birth date. When the two samples were combined, there is fairly strong evidence for an increase in death rate following the birth date, but only a slight trend toward a reduction in death rate preceding the birth date.

Table 1
Percentage of Deaths by Number of
Months Before and After Birth Date

Time Span in Relation to Birth Date	Expected	Nonfamous Canadians	Famous Canadians	Combined Samples
3 months preceding	25 %	16%	26.9%	21.6%
1 month preceding	8.3%	2%	11.5%	6.9%
1 month following	8.3%	12%	17 %	14.7%
3 months following	25 %	34%	44 %	39.2%

Abstract 138

Suicide and Aging

H. L. P. RESNIK, M.D. and JOEL M. CANTOR, Ph.D.

"Suicide and Aging," *Journal of the American Geriatrics Society*, 1970, *18*, 152-158.

This paper reviewed suicide rate in relation to age and discussed indicators of suicidal potential. In the United States, suicide is listed as one of the ten leading causes of death, responsible for about one percent of the deaths reported each year. However, in most age groups, including the aged, many suicides are concealed in the data for accidents and natural deaths.

Table 1 presents data on suicides per 100,000 of the population by age and sex. For all age groups the suicide rate for males is considerably higher than for females. For males the suicide rate increases progressively with age, whereas for females the rate is highest for persons aged 35 to 64. Since 1900 the suicide rate for the entire population has been approximately 11 per 100,000. For males 55 to 74 the rate is approximately three times the national average, and for males over 75 the rate is more than four times the national average. Although persons aged 65 and over comprise only ten percent of the population, they commit about 25 percent of the reported suicides. The black suicide rate is comparable to the white rate until about age 35, when the white rate becomes two to three times higher than the black rate.

Table 1
Suicides per 100,000 Population by Age and Sex*

Age	Male	Female
5-14	0.5	0.1
15-24	10.5	3.5
25-34	17.2	7.6
35-44	22.9	10.7
45-54	27.5	12.1
55-64	34.4	11.5
65-74	32.9	9.4
75-84	41.3	6.6
85 plus	50.9	5.5
Total	15.7	6.1

*From "Vital Statistics of the United States," 1967, USPHS, p. 1-28.

Since 1950 there has been a noticeable decline in suicide for those over 65. The rate for white males aged 65 to 74 and for white females aged 75 to 84 has dropped by about 25 percent. A similar decline has been noted in England, Norway and Denmark. Part of the decline may be due to a reduction in economic distress as a result of the introduction of social security plans. However, with an increase in the absolute number of aged people, there is an increase in the number of suicides by aged people.

Several indicators of high suicidal potential may be applied to aged persons. The proportion of widows and widowers among the elderly is very high, and for all age groups, suicide rates are lower for the married and higher for persons living alone. For all age groups combined, one suicide victim out of three has a history of prior suicide attempts. An aged person with a suicidal history is a very high suicide risk. In comparison to younger groups, aged persons with suicidal inclinations are less likely to have a suicidal history and to "cry for help" and are more likely to use a sufficiently lethal technique. Suicide potential is heightened when there has been recent or recurrent bereavement, especially if combined with other losses (jobs, physical health and mobility, prestige, etc.). Suicidal behavior occurs more frequently when there is a history of organic brain disease, especially if accompanied by depressive affect. In one study of suicide victims over the age of 60 it was found that 85 percent had an active serious physical illness at time of death.

Abstract **139**

Death with Dignity

CLARA L. COLLETTE, M.S.

"Death with Dignity: Unsolicited Responses to a Gubernatorial Statement," *Gerontologist*, 1973, *13*, 327-331.

In 1971, the governor of Oregon publicly announced his concern that people of advanced years have the right to a death with dignity as opposed to death as a vegetable. Further, he stated that he intended to sponsor a symposium aimed at dealing with the issue in rational terms. His remarks were widely quoted in the press, and within two months he received 501 written responses from people all over the United States. This paper reports a content analysis of the letters.

Results

Of the 501 respondents, 59.9 percent agreed with the governor, 32.5 percent disagreed and 7.6 percent requested additional information. Of the 67 persons identifiable as aged 65 or older, 79 percent agreed and only 16.4 percent disagreed with the governor. The most frequently stated reason given by agreeing respondents was their personal experiences with prolonged death. For older respondents, the most frequently stated reason for agreement was a belief in the importance of the quality of life that one is living. Religious convictions were the most commonly named reason for disagreeing.

Although the results of this study are of limited generalizability, they do suggest the potential value of a carefully controlled study to obtain information about attitudes toward death with dignity.

Abstract 140

Attitudes Toward Euthanasia

CAROLINE E. PRESTON, M.A. and ROBERT H. WILLIAMS, M.D.

"Views of the Aged on the Timing of Death," *Gerontologist*, 1971, *11*, 300-304.

This study examined attitudes of two samples of aged institutionalized individuals toward euthanasia. Specifically, it questioned how people in homes for the aged view death in the face of terminal illness, accompanied by great distress and entailing heavy medical expenses, when dying would be the consequence of omitting life-sustaining or instituting life-shortening measures.

Method

SUBJECTS: The subjects were 35 women and 65 men, all Caucasian, with a mean age of 72 and an age range from 60 to 95 years. Eighty-two were residents in a Veterans Retirement Home, and of these, 19 were patients in the nursing care unit. Only veterans with low incomes were eligible for residence in the Home. Twenty-three respondents were patients in private convalescent centers. Thirty-four of the respondents had been institutionalized less than one year, 44 for one to five years and 33 more than five years. Participants were selected by the chaplain in the Veterans Home and by the head nurses in the convalescent centers. To serve as respondents, individuals had to be well enough oriented to respond meaningfully to the interview questions and sufficiently comfortable to tolerate the interview procedures. All who were approached accepted and completed the interview, and several expressed appreciation after the interview.

PROCEDURE: The structured interview included questions designed to assess current feelings of well-being, contentment, future orientation (optimism versus pessimism or apathy) and agedness. A question about the importance of religion was included because of religious proscriptions against euthanasia. The crucial questions about euthanasia were as follows:

"If you were fatally ill, in great distress, and under heavy medical expenses, would you want the doctors to do nothing to keep you alive?"

"If you were fatally ill, in great distress, and under heavy medical expenses, would you want the doctors to do something to shorten you life?"

Results

Less than one half (45 percent) of the respondents rejected both positive and negative euthanasia, one quarter (24 percent) accepted negative but not positive euthanasia, and one third (31 percent) accepted both positive and negative euthanasia. Of all the variables examined (age, length of institutionalization, sex, occupation, education, and subjective assessment of well-being, contentment, agedness, future orientation and religiosity), the only variable that related to euthanasia responses was importance of religion. More of the subjects who rejected positive or negative euthanasia claimed religious faith to be important ($p < 0.01$).

AUTHOR AFFILIATIONS

An attempt has been made to list the affiliation of one of the authors, usually the senior author, of each article abstracted in this book. The affiliation of the second author rather than the first is listed if authorization to abstract the article was given by the second author, usually because we were unable to contact the first author. For a few of the abstracted articles, we received no reply from the author, probably because the only address available to us was outdated. Most of the affiliations are those listed on the original publication, but if we were aware of a change, we have used the more recent affiliation. We apologize in advance for errors and the use of outdated affiliations. The numbers in parentheses following the author's name refer to the abstracts authored or coauthored by that person.

Note: Numbers following names refer to Abstract numbers in this work.

Acuff, G. (*64*)
Department of Sociology
Oklahoma State University
Stillwater, Oklahoma

Ahammer, I.M. (*56*)
Department of Psychology
Catholic University of Nijmegan
Nijmegan, the Netherlands

Allen, D. (*64*)
Department of Sociology
Oklahoma State University
Stillwater, Oklahoma

Anderson, N.N. (*120*)
Department of Sociology
University of Minnesota
Minneapolis, Minnesota

Antonucci, T. (*109*)
Department of Psychology
Syracuse University
Syracuse, New York

Arenberg, D (*36,46,47*)
National Institute of Health
Gerontology Research Center
Baltimore City Hospitals
Baltimore, Maryland

Arkin, A. *(115))*
Department of Psychiatry
Montefiore Hospital and
Medical Center
Bronx, New York

Atchley, R.C. *(110)*
Scripps Foundation Gerontology
    Center
Oxford, Ohio

Bader, J. *(122)*
Associate Research Psychologist
Philadelphia Geriatric Center
Philadelphia, Pennsylvania

Baltes, P.B *(9,56,57)*
College of Human Development
Pennsylvania State University
University Park, Pennsylvania

Battin, D. *(115)*
Senior Psychiatric Social Worker
Montefiore Hospital and
Medical Center
Bronx, New York

Beard, B.B. *(33)*
Social Science Research Institute
University of Georgia
Athens, Georgia

Birkhill, W.R. *(8)*
Department of Psychology
University of Michigan
Dearborn, Michigan

Birren, J.E. *(14)*
Andrus Gerontology Center
University of Southern
California
Los Angeles, California

Bortner, R.W. *(130)*
College of Human Development
Pennsylvania State University
University Park, Pennsylvania

Botwinick, J. *(10,14,26,82,93)*
Department of Psychology
Washington University
St. Louis, Missouri

Brown, I.D.R. *(58)*
Department of Psychology
University of Waterloo
Waterloo, Ontario, Canada

Bultena, G.L. *(69)*
Department of Rural Sociology
University of Wisconsin
Madison, Wisconsin

Busse, E.W. *(78)*
Center for Study of Aging
Duke University Medical Center
Durham, North Carolina

Cameron, P. *(50,81)*
Division of Human Development
St. Mary's College of Maryland
St. Mary's City, Maryland

Canestrari, R.E. *(18)*
1310 Todds Lane
Hampton, Virginia

Carp, F.M. *(76,95,98,104)*
Wright Institute
Berkeley, California

Chown, S.M. *(83)*
Bedford College
University of London
Regent's Park, London, England

Cicchetti, D.V. *(53)*
Veterans Administration Hospital
West Haven, Connecticut

Clark, W.C. *(41)*
NYS Psychiatric Institute
    and CCNY
New York, New York

Clayton, P.J. (117)
Department of Psychiatry
Washington University School of
  Medicine
St. Louis, Missouri

Cleveland, W.P. (87)
Duke University for the Study
  of Aging and Human Development
Durham, North Carolina

Clemente, F. (100)
Pennsylvania State University
University Park, Pennsylvania

Collette-Pratt, C. (52,139)
Oregon Center for Gerontology
Eugene, Oregon

Comalli, P.E. (11,12)
Department of Psychology
Temple University
Philadelphia, Pennsylvania

Coombs, D.W. (90)
Department of Sociology
University of Alabama
University, Alabama

Cutler, N.E. (1)
Andrus Gerontology Center
University of Southern California
Los Angeles, California

Cutler, S.J. (67,101)
Oberlin College
Oberlin, Ohio

DeCarlo, T.J. (70)
Department of Health, Physical
  Education and Recreation
Queens College of CUNY
Flushing, New York

Decker, T.N.. (15)
Child Development and Mental Re-
  tardation Center
University of Washington
Seattle, Washington

Dennis, W. (49)
Rt 1, Box 180
Doswell, Virginia

Doty, B.A. (29)
North Central College
Naperville, Illinois

Douglass, E.B. (77,87)
Center for the Study of Aging
Duke University
Durham, North Carolina

Dressler, D.M. (107)
New Britian General Hospital
New Britian, Connecticut

Drevenstedt, J. (51)
Department of Psychology
Ohio University
Athens, Ohio

Eber, J.T. (38)
Department of Psychology
Washington University
St. Louis, Missouri

Edwards, A.E. (85)
Veterans Administration Center
Wadsworth Division
Los Angeles, California

Edwards, J.N. (74)
Department of Sociology
Virginia Polytechnic Institute and
  State University
Blacksburg, Virginia

Ehrlich, I.F. (73)
Department of Social Welfare
College of Human Resources
Southern Illinois University
Carbondale, Illinois

Feroleto, J.A. (92)
323 Wellington Rd.
Buffalo, New York

Filer, R.N. (123)
Research Division
Mental Health and Behavioral
    Sciences Services
Veterans Administration
Department of Medicine and
    Surgery
Washington, D.C.

Fillenbaum, G.G. (106)
Center for the Study of Aging and
    Human Development
Duke University Medical Center
Durham, North Carolina

Fisher, J. (7)
San Francisco School of Medicine
University of California
San Francisco, California

Fletcher, C.R. (53)
Department of Psychiatry
University of New Mexico
Albuquerque, New Mexico

Fozard, J.L. (42,43)
Veterans Administration
Outpatient Clinic
Boston, Massachusetts

Friedman, A. (6)
Philadelphia Psychiatric
    Center   ,
Philadelphia, Pennsylvania

Friedman, E.P. (121)
Department of Sociology
University of Pennsylvania
Philadelphia, Pennsylvania

Furry, C.A. (9)
Department of Psychology
West Virginia University
Morgantown, West Virginia

Gerber, I. (115)
Department of Social Medicine
Montefiore Hospital
Bronx, New York

Gianturco, D.T. (118)
Department of Psychiatry
    and Community Health Service
Duke University Medical Center
Durham, North Carolina

Gilbert, J.G. (3,34)
Mount Carmel Guild
Newark, New Jersey

Ginsburg, A.B. (125)
Department of Psychology
University of Vermont
Burlington, Vermont

Glamser, F.D. (86)
Department of Sociology
Stetson University
De Land, Florida

Goldfarb, A.I. (45)
Departments of Psychiatry, Vascu-
    lar Surgery and Neurology
Mount Sinai Hospital
New York, New York

Goodrich, C.L. (27)
Gerontology Research Center
National Institute of Child Health
    and Human Development
Baltimore, Maryland

Gordon, S.K. (*41,65*)
Departments of Education and Psychology
University of Rochester
Rochester, New York

Granick, S. (*6,16*)
Philadelphia Psychiatric Center
Philadelphia, Pennsylvania

Gubrium, J.F. (*124*)
Department of Sociology and Anthropology
Marquette University
Milwaukee, Wisconsin

Gutman, G.M. (*136*)
Department of Psychology
University of British Columbia
Vancouver, British Columbia

Hannon, N. (*115*)
Research Sociologist
Department of Social Medicine
Montefiore Hospital and
    Medical Center
Bronx, New York

Harootyan, R.A. (*1*)
Andrus Gerontology Center
University of Southern California
Los Angeles, California

Havighurst, R.J. (*59*)
Department of Education
University of Chicago
Chicago, Illinois

Heymann, D.K. (*118*)
Center for Study of Aging
Duke University
Durham, North Carolina

Hochstadt, N.J. (*45*)
Department of Psychiatry
Mount Sinai Hospital
New York, New York

Hollingsworth, J.S. (*90*)
Department of Sociology
University of Alabama
University, Alabama

Hulicka, I.M. (*17,19,21,35,39,103*)
Department of Psychology
State University College at Buffalo
Buffalo, New York

Hultsch, D.F. (*20,24,130*)
Division of Individual and Family
    Studies
Pennsylvania State University
University Park, Pennsylvania

Jacobs, E.A. (*44*)
Veterans Administration Hospital
Buffalo, New York

Jacobson, J.H. (*45*)
Department of Vascular
    Surgery
Mt. Sinai School of
    Medicine and Hospital
New York, New York

Jakubczak, L.F. (*28*)
Jefferson Barracks Veteran Administration Hospital
St. Louis, Missouri

Kahn, R.L. (*88*)
Department of Psychiatry
    and Human Development
University of Chicago
Chicago, Illinois

Kasschau, P.L. (105)
Ethel Percy Andrus Gerontology
  Center
University of Southern California
Los Angeles, California

Kleban, M.H. (16,127)
Philadelphia Geriatric Center
Philadelphia, Pennsylvania

Klein, R.L. (84)
Department of Psychology
West Virginia University
Morgantown, West Virginia

Klemmack, D.L. (74)
Department of Sociology
University of Alabama
University, Alabama

Krauss, H.H. (128)
Department of Psychology
Hunter College
City University of New York
New York, New York

Kriauciunas, R. (126)
Kankakee State Hospital
Kankakee, Illinois

Kutner, B. (61)
Albert Einstein School
  of Medicine
New York, New York

Labouvie-Vief, G. (48,57)
Department of Educational
  Psychology
University of Wisconsin
Madison, Wisconsin

Labovitz, S. (137)
Department of Sociology
University of Calgary
Calgary, Alberta

Lawton, M.P. (75,97,122,127)
Philadelphia Geriatric Center
Philadelphia, Pennsylvania

Lehr, U. (132)
Psychologisches Institut
der Universitat Bonn
53 Bonn
An der Schlobkirche

Levee, R.F. (34)
Mount Carmel Guild
Newark, New Jersey

Lipman, A. (60)
Department of Sociology and An-
  thropology
University of Miami
Coral Gables, Florida

Maddox, G.L. (77,87)
Center for the Study of Aging
  and Human Development
Duke University
Durham, North Carolina

Marshall, V.W. (133)
Department of Sociology
McMaster University
Hamilton, Ontario

Mishara, B.L. (91)
Department of Psychology
University of Massachusetts
Boston, Massachusetts

Moenster, P.A. (40)
Nazareth College
Rochester, New York

Monge, R.H. (20,79,131)
Department of Psychology
Syracuse University
Syracuse, New York

Murrell, F.H. (25)
University of Wales
Institute of Science and Technology
Cordiff, Wales

Nahemow, L. (97)
Philadelphia Geriatric Center
Philadelphia, Pennsylvania

Nehrke, M.F. (65,134,135)
Veterans Administration Center
Bath, New York

Nicolay, R.C. (80)
Department of Psychology
Loyola University
Chicago, Illinois

O'Connell, D.D. (123)
VAC, Wood Psychological
    Service
Wood, Wisconsin

Owens, W.A. (2)
Institute for Behavioral Research
University of Georgia
Athens, Georgia

Palmore, E.B. (62)
Center for the Study of Aging and
    Human Development
Duke University
Durham, North Carolina

Pepe, E.A. (89)
Department of Psychology
State University College at Buffalo
Buffalo, New York

Petersen, D.M. (114)
Department of Sociology
Georgia State University
Atlanta, Georgia

Pfeiffer, E. (66,71,72)
Department of Health and
    Hospitals
Davis Institute
Denver, Colorado

Pierce, R.C. (7)
Department of Psychiatry
University of California
    School of Medicine
San Francisco, California

Planek, T.W. (102)
Research Department
National Safety Council
Chicago, Illinois

Preston, C.E. (55,140)
Department of Psychiatry
University of Wisconsin School
    of Medicine
Seattle, Washington

Rabbitt, P.M.A. (13)
Medical Research Council
Applied Psychology Research Unit
Cambridge, England

Resnik, H.L.P. (138)
School of Medicine
George Washington University
District of Columbia

Rowe, E.J. (22)
Memorial University
St. Johns, Newfoundland,
Canada

Rubin, K.H. (58)
Department of Psychology
University of Waterloo
Waterloo, Ontario

Rusalem, R. (115)
Research Sociologist
Department of Social
  Medicine
Montefiore Hospital
  and Medical Center
Bronx, New York

Schaie, K.W. (3,8,94)
Andrus Gerontology Center
University of Southern California
University Park, Los Angeles,
California

Schnore, M. M. (22)
Department of Psychology
University of Western Ontario
London, Ontario

Schonfield, D. (31,37,63)
University of Calgary
Calgary, Alberta, Canada

Schooler, K.K. (96)
Gerontology Center
Syracuse University
Syracuse, New York

Shanas, E. (111,112)
Department of Sociology
University of Illinois at Chicago
  Circle
Chicago, Illinois

Simmons, L.W. (68)
Department of Sociology
Case Western Reserve
  University
Cleveland, Ohio

Smith, K.J. (60)
Department of Sociology
  and Anthropology
University of Miami
Coral Gables, Florida

Smith, M.E. (32)
3221 Waialae Ave.
Honolulu, Hawaii

Sterns, H.L. (19, 108)
Department of Psychology
University of Akron
Akron, Ohio

Storandt, M. (93)
Department of Psychology
Washington University
St. Louis, Missouri

Strother, C.R. (4)
Department of Psychology
University of Washington
Seattle, Washington

Sundeen, R.A. (99)
School of Public Administration
University of Southern California
Los Angeles, California

Tallmer, M. (61)
Hunter College, CUNY
New York, New York

Thomas, C.W. (114)
Department of Sociology
Bowling Green State
  University
Bowling Green, Ohio

Thompson, C.I. (30)
Department of Behavioral Science
Hershey Medical Center of
  Pennsylvania
State University
Hershey, Pennsylvania

Thompson, L.W. (26)
Department of Psychiatry
Duke University
Durham, North Carolina

Thumin, F. (113)
Department of Psychology
University of Missouri
St. Louis, Missouri

Treas, J. (119)
Andrus Gerontology Center
University of Southern California
Los Angeles, California

Trela, J.E. (68)
Vocational Guidance and Rehabili-
tation Service
Cleveland, Ohio

Trembly,D. (5)
California State Polytechnic College
San Luis Obispo, California

Trimakas, K.A. (80)
Edward Hines Veterans Adminis-
tration Hospital
Hines, Illinois

Troll, L.E. (54)
Department of Psychology
Wayne State University
Detroit, Michigan

Turner, B.F. (88)
Department of Human Develop-
ment
School of Education
University of Massachusetts
Amherst, Massachusetts

Verwoerdt, A. (71,72)
Department of Psychiatry
Duke University
Durham, North Carolina

Webber, I. (90)
Department of Sociology
University of Alabama
University, Alabama

Weinstein, E.A. (45)
Department of Neurology
Mt. Sinai School of
  Medicine and Hospital
New York, New York

Weinstock, C. (129)
Program in Gerontology and Lei-
sure Education
Teachers College
Columbia University
New York, New York

Wexley, K.N. (108)
Department of Psychology
University of Akron
Akron, Ohio

Wittels, I. (23)
Department of Psychology
Washington University
St. Louis, Missouri

Wyly, M.V. (89,116)
Department of Psychology
State University College at Buffalo
Buffalo, New York

Zatlin, C.E. (93)
Department of Psychology
Washington University
St. Louis, Missouri

AUTHOR INDEX

SUBJECT INDEX

Note: All numbers refer to Abstract numbers.